AFRICAN RELIGION MEETS ISLAM

Religious Change in Northern Nigeria

Dean S. Gilliland, Ph.D.

UNIVERSITY
PRESS OF
AMERICA

LANHAM • NEW YORK • LONDON

University Press of America,® Inc.

4720 Boston Way
Lanham, MD 20706

3 Henrietta Street
London WC2E 8LU England

Library of Congress Cataloging in Publication Data

Gilliland, Dean S.
   African religion meets Islam.

   Bibliography: p.
   Includes index.
   1. Islam—Nigeria, Northern.   2. Nigeria, Northern—
Religion.   3. Hausas—Religion.   I. Title.
BP64.N5G55   1986   297'.1972'096995   86-18929
ISBN 0-8191-5634-5 (alk., paper)
ISBN 0-8191-5635-3 (pbk. : alk. paper)

Table of Contents

ACKNOWLEDGMENTS

Before mentioning others, this book is an expression of thanks and appreciation for my African friends. They have not only been generous in sharing their rich culture, but they have been gracious to me, personally, and to my family, for thirty years.

I also want to acknowledge the debt I owe to W.A. Bijlefeld of the Duncan Black Macdonald Center (Hartford). He helped me to see and organize what actually happens in religious practice. The information gathered for the last two chapters is largely the work of Selcan Miner, former Secretary to Military Government and Head of Service of Benue Plateau State (Nigeria). I thank him very much.

The actual production would not have been possible without the long hours that Betty Ann Klebe spent at the computer in typing and editing. Betty Sue Brewster provided the equipment and gave generous time in working out format and in printing. My thanks to both of these friends as well as to Pepper Grimes who was an optimistic supporter.

INTRODUCTION

Ijebu Ode is a dynamic town, situated to the northeast of the port city of Lagos. Ijebu Ode's is not much different from any other Yoruba town. Even though it is made up of both Christians and Muslims there is little about everyday life that gives the appearance of people following two religions. M. O. A. Abdul, a Yoruba Muslim, has observed about Ijebu Ode that neither "being a Muslim" nor "being Christian" is more important than "being a *Yoruba*.." Islamic and Christian practices have intermingled for a long time yet the worldview and lifestyle remain unmistakably "Yoruba." There is a quality about the way people practice religion here that fits into "being Yoruba." It is the *Yoruba* identity that really holds the community together.

> The very good relations (between Muslims and Christians) are due to the fact that Yoruba social institutions based on the traditional practices are stronger than the ties of the new religions. . . .Both Islam and Christianity tend to oppose this common factor even though they both condone its practice.1

Ijebu Ode is not in the area of Nigeria where this study will take place. Yet if what Abdul observed is true, something of first importance can be tested in other places. It would appear that when a secondary religion confronts a strong traditional system the new religion will conform to tribal institutions. Indigenous belief and practice form what is ultimate and real, both for individuals and the whole community.

In northern Nigeria traditional religion has changed in various ways due to the long influence of Islam. If the northern states of Nigeria were, in fact, categorically Muslim, the case would not be so complex. Islam in Nigeria forbids generalizations. The intensity of Islam varies from the almost completely Muslim states of the far North to the mixed states of what is still called the "middle belt." The major part of

---

[1]Musa O. Ajelogba Abdul, "Islam in Ijebu Ode" (unpublished M.A. thesis. Montreal: McGill University, 1967), p. 103.

our study deals with the long interaction between Islam and traditional religion. The third religion, Christianity, is much stronger now than it was twenty years ago, especially in this middle belt area, and has become a dynamic factor of change. Traditional religious practice and Islam have undergone changes since the sixteenth century but none so remarkable as the changes of the past thirty years.

Northern Nigeria provides the unusual opportunity to observe intricate patterns of response to Islam. This, is due, in part, to its long history. Islam was the first alien religion to have a major impact upon the ancient religions of Nigeria. In this area there is a wide variety of language groups and diverse tribal communities who live in close range. These groups have reacted to Islam in a variety of ways. The relatively steady norms of Islam interact in surprising ways with the fluid, irregular patterns of traditional religion. The result is a kaleidoscope of religious change ranging from rejection to quite orthodox reception as well as totally new forms. The task before us is to observe traditional factors that influence the changes effected by Islam and to observe the correspondence between traditional structures and the type of Islam these structures produce. The study will also have to account for the third option, Christianity, which has become increasingly important in the central states of Nigeria.

In approaching this kind of study certain handicaps have to be recognized. One is the risk of basing conclusions on data that is too limited. There is a danger in selecting a combination of ethnic groups for study and then making generalizations based on that data alone. Because of the diversity of well over two hundred tribes in the northern states of Nigeria, all with long exposure to Islam, the selection was not easy. I have given attention to twenty tribes, some more fully than others. These were chosen with various geographical, political, and historical factors in mind so as to illustrate the wide religious variations, so typical of West Africa. These tribes and their locations are shown on the map (see page 8). Even with these objectives, it is an arbitrary grouping. The point is that where observations are made on small units selected from a large field, and where wide variations exist within the field itself, conclusions cannot be absolutely final. Generalizations are always risky, especially in Africa.

Diversity of this kind brings with it a second problem. Norms are difficult to establish and definitions are not always clear. Starting from African religious phenomena as a base, certain themes of religious belief can be assumed, such as are common to animism. But no hard and fast definition of "African traditional religion" can be established which applies, in detail, to all groups. A normative view of traditional religion is quite impossible since all phenomena have primarily local significance. It follows that the influence which Islam has will apply to the particular tribal structure, rather than to some notion of "African religion" as a whole.

A third problem is that traditional religion provides practically nothing by way of written records. Granted, talking and listening is the African way of communicating, especially about the past, but oral traditions vary greatly even among groups living close to each other. I know the Hausa language well and it is the the most reliable tool for research all over this area. Yet the degree to which any *lingua franca* can give precise information is, at times, in question. My own knowledge of Hausa as well as of my African friends, is not an exact form of communication. Moreover, the variations within oral traditions result in a body of information that is fluid, and open to greater subjectivity than are the more rigid written sources. In this study we have gathered most of the information through interviews, and these oral traditions themselves have variations.

Further, the forces that change traditional religion are so complex that the singular influence of Islam is difficult to isolate. It is impossible to speak of the purely religious aspects of this interaction. Education, westernization, mechanization, and certainly politics, are powerful forces for change and have their impact on religion. No study such as this could do justice to all these dynamic forces around which, and within which, religion takes its shape. For example, when a son within a strong traditional family decides to become a Muslim, this is not due solely to the influence of Islam, but to the freedom he feels to differentiate from parents. This is one of the by-products resulting from Western-oriented education. We are aware of the fact that many of the forces changing traditional religious practice are not the strictly "religious" ones.

Since the peoples of northern Nigeria have been selected for study, the question is, *which* northern Nigeria. The far North is comprised almost exclusively of Muslim states while the central North is heavily Christian, as well as being animist and Muslim. These "Middle Belt" states (formerly Benue, Plateau, and large parts of Niger, and Adamawa Provinces) mark out the traditional, non-Muslim area. Historically, these areas also formed the more southern limits of the nineteenth century *jihad*. These traditional boundaries are still very real. Our investigation centers on ethnic (tribal) groups located in the central area of Nigeria. Here animism and Islam have had their most recent confrontation, and both systems are presently interacting with Christianity.

It will become obvious that we are dealing with two streams in the history of Islamic influence. The Hausa-Borno contacts with Arab-Muslim culture predate the middle belt contacts with Islam by some 200-400 years. Furthermore, the impact of Islam on the Hausa came from outside sources, while Muslim influence to the South in Nigeria is a secondary, internal development. This latter movement was led by the Fulani who waged the *jihad* as well as by Fulani clerics and Hausa merchants who took up residence in towns and villages.

The Islamization of the Hausa was not a quick or simple conversion of the masses by any measure. The process had profound sociological and political impact that carried consequences for both traditional religion and Islam. In attempting to document these changes, we do have historical data which identifies the change agents during the period when recombinations between Islam and primitive African society were taking place. The struggle of the two systems began in the eleventh century, and the integration which resulted is a matter of record. A valuable historical source is the *Kano Chronicle* . While the *Chronicle* is not an ancient document, it is held to be a relatively accurate account of a primitive oral tradition. It is a rich source for studying the tensions manifest between two fundamentally different systems of religion.[2]

---

[2]H. R. Palmer, "The Kano Chronicle," *Journal of the Royal Anthropological Institute of Great Britain and Ireland*, XXXVIII (1908), p. 62-98. Hereinafter referred to as K.C., the *Kano Chronicle* is a unique document for the purpose of understanding the interaction of Islam and traditional religion. Its translator, H. R. Palmer, feels that it represents a nineteenth century reconstruction of an earlier record which perished during the Fulani *jihad*. While not an ancient record, its written form has a consensus of support.

4

One of the most controversial figures early in this century was the anthropologist Leo Frobenius, famous for his massive collections of primitive art (1873-1938). His anthology of Hausa tales reflects the intense religious struggle which took place as Islam invaded animistic African religions. Only a genius could work with such scanty material and make conclusions seem so credible. In comparing the Songhai culture with that of the Hausa he said:

> The Hausa were forced to adapt themselves incontinently to the progressive advance of Mahommedanism, . . . they could only stem the Islamite wave which tore across the waste by conforming to the new nature of things in their views of religion; the laws which prevail on the surface of the earth primarily compelled them to assist the Mahommedan ideals and subordinate the indulgence of their own cult to the religion of the prophet Mahommed.[3]

Religious change is as much the by-product of cultural change as it is an agent of it. The socio-political factors of contemporary society which shape religion in northern Nigeria grow out of its past. While the modern situation presents a new set of response factors, the areas in which these responses are formed remain unchanged. Primitive African society showed its ability to resist alien forces only so long as the components of its ritual basis remained intact. It is essential, therefore, that we look carefully at the forces which are brought to bear when the contemporary traditional structures meet the Islam of today.

The culture and language in northern Nigeria show that Islamization is still going on. However, the dynamics of change within African religions are more complex than simply the changes involving Islam. African society is also experiencing secularization and urbanization. The shift to Christianity among middle belt peoples in the past two decades must be accounted for.

Yet the questions before us today are much the same as those of the past: What features peculiar to the African communities (tribes) govern their responses to Islam? Does the role of tribal practitioners

---

[3]Leo Frobenius, *The Voice of Africa*, Vol. II (London: Hutchinson & Co., 1913), p. 539. See also text, pp. 51-52. Frobenius drew his conclusions by attempting to reconstruct the original cultural situation. See discussion in Adolf E. Jensen, *Myth and Cult Among Primitive Peoples* (Chicago: University of Chicago Press, 1963), pp. 3,4.

and Muslim clerics continue as an influential force in the curve of religious change? What effect do politics and economics have as the modern African makes religious choices? Why do some tribal groups respond positively to Islam and others take a firm stand against it? Do the traditional chiefs and the administrative heads still shape religion into definite patterns? How are the ancestral beliefs recombined with Muslim practice to form a new folk religion?

I have had the privilege of a continuous relationship with Nigeria since 1956. The work on the first five chapters was completed in 1970, then revised for this publication. An update of developments is presented in Chapters Six and Seven as an evaluation of contemporary issues and a look, fifteen years later, at the same ethnic groups.

Comparatively little has been written on Nigeria since the Civil War that would give insight into the present redistribution of religious strength. For a number of reasons, Islam has quite a different role now than it did fifteen years ago. Christianity has shown significant gains in the same areas under study while traditional religions are in sharp decline as an official way of life.

The middle belt of Nigeria is an ideal place to observe changes in religious structures. These changes have taken place in a relatively short time. Ancestral religions of well over one hundred ethnic groups have governed the lives of thousands of people. The interaction of these local religions with contextual forms of Islam has been taking place for generations and continues today. As Islam confronted the modern state, Christianity simultaneously became a major factor in the transition.

The unusual part about Nigeria, especially the central or middle belt, is that an older person who is still living has experienced nearly all of these changes in one lifetime. So much has happened politically and socially in such a brief span of time that all the religious phenomena described in this book are still taking place at various levels. It takes only a short step in time to cross the bridge back to the nineteenth century *jihad*. Before the traditional forms died out we find ourselves in a post-colonial Nigeria with its new options, including Christianity and secularism. What follows is a description of this

6

exciting, complex drama of change and the deep issues of culture that bring about change.

Map of Nigeria

Showing the northern states and the twenty ethnic communities referred to in the book.

CHAPTER ONE

CHANGE AND RELIGIOUS STRUCTURE

CHAPTER ONE

CHANGE AND RELIGIOUS STRUCTURE

FEATURES OF TRADITIONAL AFRICAN RELIGION

African tribal religion is a mosaic of diverse cultures and localized idiosyncrasies. When describing African religion it is the particular case which must be emphasized. Generalities perpetrated on Africa have not only confused the search for truth but have misrepresented people to the world. The terms "traditional" and "tribal" are closely related. The term "tribal religion" emphasizes the distinct ethnicity of religion focusing on the local characteristics of a particular group. This is the best way to approach African religion. John Mbiti describes traditional religion as a system which, before everything else, is a "tribal religion."

> A traditional religion cannot be propagated in another tribal group. There is no conversion from one traditional religion to another. Each society has its own religious system, and the propagation of such a complete system would involve propagating the entire life of the people concerned. Therefore, a person has to be born in a particular society in order to assimilate the religious system of the society to which he belongs.[1]

In a rather abrupt way, William Howells feels inclined to refer to these traditional systems as "native cults." By this he means to convey that the religions are uniquely indigenous. In most instances they have developed among the very tribes they serve.[2]

---

[1]John S. Mbiti, *African Religions and Philosophy* (London: Heinemann, 1969), p. 4.

[2]William Howells, *The Heathens* (Garden City, NY: Anchor Books, Doubleday and Co., 1962), p. 5.

Our purpose is to observe the drama of religious interaction and religious change which is still going on in the northern states of Nigeria. The past and present of tribal religion is now cast into a dynamic modern setting. The historical analysis of Hausa religious history has shown that primitive tribal religion has a self-centered orientation which tends to resist any alien system. Songhai and Fulani Islam gradually decentralized the tribal cultus and introduced a supra-tribal basis for religion.

A study such as this must take into account the conflict of the primitive worldview with the philosophical system of Islam. On one hand we find the almost completely localized phenomena of tribal religions, and on the other, the more structured historical patterns of a supra-tribal religion. The traditional worship of the original Hausa took place in a grove called *Jakara*. It was the religion of a small, primitive society whose self-awareness was reinforced through ritual. The *Kano Chronicle* reveals that once the symbolic tree was cut down and a mosque was built, forces of religious conflict were set in motion which are still reverberating.

We can, perhaps, speak of an African ontology. It is speculative thought and an experiential intuition based on experience. The tensions and anxieties of this experience seek for order and coherence through ritual. Care needs to be taken when speaking of an African worldview or an African philosophy. It is not an academic, speculative thought system. Nevertheless, the attempt to analyze concepts of being in African thought are helpful if not pressed too far.[3] The worldview of traditional religion is not accidental nor is it an unorganized collection of stories and chance actions.

Granted, there are practices which have little solid religious meaning. The *dodo*, for example, is active in several tribes. He is a masquerader who parades through the village and across the farms

---

[3]Robin Horton, "The Kalabari World View: An Outline and Interpretation," *Africa*, XXXII, No. 3 (July, 1962), 199-201. Also see Mbiti's reference to Jahn's book, *Muntu*, for an outline of a Bantu "system" in *African Religions*, p. 1 and Mbiti's own "anthropocentric ontology" in five categories, *ibid.*, p. 16.

mainly to keep women and children in subjection.[4] Tribal priests, as we shall see, are not inconsistent when they deal in both magic and the sacred rituals. Still, traditional religion does exist in an observable and a significantly organized way. We must attempt to understand, as much as possible, the make-up of traditional religion.[5] How much this underlying structure contrasts to or is parallel with the structure of Islam determines the way in which the two religions interact with each other. The compatibility or incongruence of the worldview of the two systems is the key to understanding why indigenous tribes react to Islamic influence in various ways.

The changes which Islam brings to traditional religion are the consequence of systems which are in tension.[6] The material which follows illustrates that it is the particular data of a particular tribe set in the context of Islam which must be evaluated. This *particularity* accounts for the erratic and unpredictable directions which traditional African religions have taken in response to Islam.[7]

There are surprisingly few general features of African religion. Indeed, it is questionable if one should speak of *African religion* in this generic way. Perhaps at least three factors are common to the

---

[4]Much of the function of *tutelary genii* is something of a hoax perpetrated on the women by the men; e.g., among Mumuye and Kulung the masquerader threatens women who will not tell the truth to husbands. To look on him would result in sickness or barrenness. The men are sworn to keep the secret at the time of initiation. Gunn observes the same with respect to the Katab. He describes the *dodo* (*obwai*) as "used largely as a means of disciplining women and children." Harold Gunn, *Pagan Peoples of the Central Area of Northern Nigeria*, "Ethnographic Survey of Africa," Western Africa, D. Forde, ed., (London: International African Institute, 1956), Part XII, pp. 79, 80.

[5]The "understanding" of religion as distinct from "explaining" became important with Joachim Wach and especially with G. van der Leeuw, *Religion in Essence and Manifestation* (2 vols. New York: Harper and Row, 1963). Hereinafter referred to as *Religion and Manifestation*.

[6]The study of W. M. Watt, *Islam and the Integration of Society* (London: Routledge and Kegan Paul, 1961) is a creative analysis of economic and social factors which were in conflict in Mecca and Medina at the time of Muhammed. See pp. 4-42. This helpful source will be hereinafter referred to as *Islam and Society*.

[7]"African religions" is a functional term because it calls attention to the *particularity* of tribal practice and does not suggest a homogeneity which, in fact, does not exist. "Tribal religion" refers to the customs and rituals as well as the cosmology which are peculiar to a tribe and which describe the practice of the families attached to it.

worldview of contemporary African religions.[8] These are self-containment, naturalistic practices, and group orientation.

SELF-CONTAINMENT

African traditional religion explains man's own world and solves the problems which arise from it. That is, the anxiety with which a person lives and the needs he has are attributable to activity prescribed by his own world. He does not need to refer to another tribe for an explanation of his problems.[9] Ethnocentricity is the most obvious characteristic of traditional religion. The Tiv and the Longuda illustrate this self-containment.

The Tiv[10] will figure prominently in this study because they are a highly developed tribal culture with acute self awareness. What is more, they have fiercely resisted all the pressures of Islamization. I mention them here because of their hierarchy of spirits, both human and non-human, called *mbatsav*. The bad spirits negate the good works of the "high god"(*Aondo*) and control nature as they wish. These negative forces are sometimes manifest in human forms (e.g., witch), which are feared and must be placated. *Mbatsav* can make women barren, destroy crops, break up friendships, and even eat human flesh (in secret). These evil forces grow out of the tribal myth, and hence specific counteractive measures to handle the demons are structured into the religion. These measures are contained in an elaborate system of cultic gods, which the Tiv refer to as "idols" (*okombo*).

---

[8]These are descriptive categories. No attempt is made to systematize the more conceptual features of African religion. Mbiti's book *African Religions* does this kind of classification as he sees it. He writes, however, in a western theological format. Mbiti's book, *Concepts of God in Africa* (London: S.P.C.K., 1970) seems to "Christianize" the traditional African gods.

[9]Though certain features may be borrowed to assist local practice or to provide options, e.g., the Yendang adopted the Mumuye *dodo* and Kulung the Jukun *gabra* cult, but each retained its own cosmology.

[10]This highly ethnocentric society is located in northern Nigeria's extreme southeast and has been oriented more towards Ibo influence than towards the Muslim north. Refer to numerous studies by Paul and Laura Bohannan, especially *The Tiv of Central Nigeria* (London: International African Institute, 1953).

There is a series of ritualistic gradations through which a Tiv man passes. Each level is directed toward attaining ultimate power against the forces of evil. The highest rank available against *mbatsav* is that of *okombo or poor* [sic]. The possessor of *okombo or poor* acquires great spiritual and political rank in the tribe.[11] This illustrates the involute character of tribal cosmology both in the issuance of evil and in the means by which it is counteracted.

The Longuda of the northwest part of Gongola State have an interesting response to Islam. The traditional Longuda ritual includes an elaborate arrangement of earthen pots which are presided over by special persons, usually women. Meek refers to the use of these pots as the *kwandalowa* cults.[12] The pots are used in the treatment of specific diseases. Disease is a by-product of the Longuda cosmology. Unfulfilled ritual or harm brought by tribal spirits result in sicknesses which must be treated in the proper way. So disease-producing spirits are enshrined in the pots, and the human sickness must be transferred from the body to the pot. One pot, the *kwandol mwarwa*, is for general disease and is most commonly consulted. The priest of another group of pots, *kwandol thuwa*, must be approached for body aches and diseases of the joints. The ritual includes catching something alive near the patient, such as an insect. Whatever is caught is then put into the pot and covered. So the traditional world creates its own framework for religious practice. Specific needs are tribally oriented, and must, likewise, be resolved within the natural world. The point of *kwandalowa* rituals is to show how a wide range of needs can be cared for within the precincts of the tribe itself, without reference to another people or locale.

NATURAL WORLD AND DAILY LIFE

Traditional religion is expressed through cultic acts which are in rhythm with the whole natural world. Levy-Bruhl contends that the

---

[11]Timothy Anger at Bukuru on February 3, 1970.

[12]The practice which Meek described in 1931 is still substantially the same. My informant, Windibiziri, alluded to the more recent effect of modern medicine on the cults. See C. K. Meek, *Tribal Studies in North Nigeria* (2 vols.; London: Kegan Paul, Trench, Trubner and Co., 1931), II, 351-52. Hereinafter referred to as *Tribal Studies*.

primitive worldview is homogeneous in nature.[13] The natural world, created things, the earth, the air, all are continuous with the reality of man himself; he is contained in them. Winston King says accurately, "One might define primitive religion as an overwhelming, all-permeating consciousness of man's natural environment, in which sacredness always takes a naturalistic form."[14]

It would be very hard to find a more classic symbol of man's continuity with nature than the tribal personage of the Kutep known as *Kukwe*.[15] *Kukwe* is a mortal man, but he is also a representation of the very life of the tribe. Meanings attached to his person are directly related to the health of the tribe, as the people look to the land, the seed, and the rain for sustenance. He always leaves a little food in his bowl. This means there is food for all. The dirt on his unwashed body is a guarantee of fertile crops. He carries a blue cloth which will attract rain when he spreads it out on the ground. *Kukwe* is man, but he is Life, given and sustained for the tribe in nature.

Again, it is the custom among some of the Birom to consider the newborn as truly alive only after a clan priest finds a spider on the ritual hill, then brings it back to the child. Pressing the spider to the child's head, he says, "You have been brought spirit."[16]

Similarly, initiation rites for Rukuba boys on the Jos Plateau include the killing of a cock by the priest, one for each boy. If the cock jumps or runs about after it is beheaded, all can rest assured that the boy will live. Otherwise, a goat sacrifice has to be made and all the elders and initiates must eat the meat in order to guarantee life.[17] There is no real line of demarcation between man and his environment. Knowledge of the self is intimately associated with the natural world. Tribal religion

---

[13]"To the mind of the primitive there is existing and permeating on earth, in the air, and in the water, in all diverse forms assumed by persons and objects, one and the same essential reality, both one and multiple, both material and spiritual. It is continually passing from one to the other" (London: Geo. Allen and Unwin, 1928), p. 7.

[14]Winston L. King, *Introduction to Religion: A Phenomenological Approach*, (New York: Harper and Row, 1954), p. 54.

[15]Located in Benue State, intermingling with the Jukun at Takum and the Chamba on the eastern border. For further discussion on *Kukwe* see pages 169-70.

[16]Interview with Davou Dalyop; village of Ndu (Birom), February 21, 1970.

[17]Ishaya Ayok at Zagun (Rukuba), December 10, 1969. The initiation cycle is every seven years, but a boy cannot be over twelve years of age.

is one of the natural order, determining the individual and social life context.

COMMUNITY REALISM

The individual is related to his world by way of the group, and reality in religion is derived from identity with the tribe. The term "tribal religion" has specific merit at this point. Individual action outside the group usually brings negative results. Modern illustrations of the importance of tribal dynamics are widespread among the groups considered in this study. The recovery of myth by the whole clan or tribe is the most observable feature of the festivals. The Bachema of Gongola State have retained an ancient celebration held at a ritual place called *Fare*. This is a three-day commemoration of the Bachema god *Nzeanzo*.[18] While these ancient rituals have declined in importance, the shrine of *Nzeanzo* is still the scene of a community ritual which touches all levels of the tribe. In fact, many who are not active in the actual cult of *Nzeanzo* observe the rites and participate in the dancing. It is not uncommon for Christians to go to Fare, and Bachema-born Muslims feel free to attend as well.[19]

The Bachema revitalize their origins by celebrating the birth of the tribal god, *Nzeanzo,* while the Mumuye, who live to the south of the Bachema are bound together through strong initiation-ancestor rituals. This is a seven-year initiation cycle which includes most, if not all, of the main features of the Mumuye religious features: the elders as priests, the tribal masks and the clan masquerader, the sacrifice and communal meal.[20] Women are also included, through fearful taboo of the tribal ancestor figure (*dodo*) referred to above.

The Rukuba on the Jos Plateau used to join in a symbolic hunt each year to show their unity. All of the clans participate, since the corporateness of the tribe is the most meaningful frame of reference for religion. Following the hunt, each clan brings hair from the catch to a sacred pile of stones. After the hair is deposited on the tribal

---

[18]A full description of Nzeanzo and the festival at Fare is given in Meek, *Tribal Studies*, I, 33-42. Meek attended this rite, and it provides one of his best descriptions.

[19]Akila Todi in Jos (Bachema), June 14, 1970.

[20]From an interview with Malam Kani at Lankaviri, January 10, 1970.

shrine, the meat is cooked and eaten communally.[21] In other tribes the tribal symbol is a royal ancestor ritual, as in the case of the Gwari and the Jukun. A number of others have an agricultural motif, symbolizing both planting and harvesting.[22]

Therefore, while the point of reference may vary, whether celebration of the God, initiation or season rites, the religious exercise in nearly all the tribes studied shows the absolute centrality of the tribe. Tribal religion, therefore, seeks to resolve anxiety from within the structure of the tribe itself. It provides the way for a man to know himself through an intimate relationship to nature. Finally, African religion has validity through reference to and participation in the community.[23]

AREAS OF CONFLICT: TRADITIONAL AND ISLAMIC

Against this basic pattern came an alien or, at least, a conflicting system. Early Hausa religion showed that a linear (Islamic) worldview made its impact on the primitive cyclic Dalla society. Forces of change were set in motion as a weakened primitive society struggled against this massive new system. As one studies the impact of Islam on traditional religion, it is evident that conflicting systems are not only reacting to each other, but that each is being changed by the other.

---

[21]Ishaya Ayok at Zagun (Rukuba), December 10, 1969.

[22]The *mendeng* is considered as the principal festival of the Birom (Gyel clan). It is called by the chief, then after five days he calls again, this time each bringing his own seed. After the *sarkin mendeng* (chief of *mendeng*) ritually sows his seed, others follow. The *bidushe* is a harvest rite in which both the religious head and the legal head participate. The ritual is centered around the communal cutting of bamboo, which cuttings are taken to each farm before harvest. From an interview with Ndung Gyel, December 12, 1969.

[23]Compare Robin Horton's articles, "African Traditional Thought and Western Science," *Africa*, XXXVII, No. 1 (Jan. 1967), 50-71, and No. 2 (April 1967), 155-87. The value of Horton's approach is to establish factors of continuity between religious thinking of traditional Africa and theoretical thinking of the modern West. In this way some of the more puzzling features of African concepts in the religious context can be worked out on familiar Western models.

18

A reliable typology of the two systems would be helpful for a study of this kind. But this is complicated by certain factors. It is almost impossible to observe a "pure" model of any religion. There is always the particular coloration given by this or that tribe which is further complicated by the observer's own inexperience.[24] The mixtures and cross-fertilization of Islam with African religions makes typologies difficult.[25] Traditional religion is non-historical because it is undocumented, and because phenomena cannot be treated in a normative way. In contrast, Islam is a historical religion. Yet African Islam is so merged with the tribal religions that a historical view of Islam becomes unreliable.

A contrast between African traditional religion and African Islam may be seen as follows:

1. African traditional religion is based primarily on kinship, and its ritual is organized after this pattern beginning at the family level, then rising through the clan and tribe. African Islam, while still depending heavily on kinship groups, is more an inter-tribal — often political — religious unit, and inclusion is, in the first instance, on an individual basis.[26]

2. Viewed ritually, traditional religion has an oral basis with mediation by indigenous practitioners who make use of sacred places and sacred objects and have a high dependence on magic. While much of West African Islam is of the folk variety, Islam does present a written scripture, a prescribed ritual, a historical and systematized myth, and an intertribal clerical class.

---

[24]van der Leeuw, *Religion and Manifestation*, Vol. II, 593 says "in my own experience religion receives a special form which is, however, merely one specific form of the vast historic formation wherein I myself exist."

[25]In the plurality of the African forms there is so much differentiation that one must concern himself with the data as it "appears" specifically, without reference to a "standard" or an "ideal."

[26]As an *individual* type as distinguished from the *collective* type wherein the whole of "primitive religion" falls. See van der Leeuw, *Religion and Manifestation*, p. 594.

3. At a deeper worldview level, traditional religions appeal to nature, low and high spirits in the context of a loosely structured mythology, and vary in degrees of god-consciousness from monolatry to polytheism. Islam is monotheistic, and while admitting to a spirit world, it has a philosophical and theological tradition which gives it considerable systemization.[27]

The very nature of Islam does present a contrast to the non-historical primitive pattern, but Lewis contends it is not simply a matter of a so-called "revealed religion" in contrast to a "natural religion."[28] These are not meaningful categories in the dynamic African situation. It is important to apprehend what motivates the African as a religious *person.*. We shall see that where Islam has been able to fit into the traditional religious environment while bringing elements of its own, there Islam has been a specific factor of change.

There are two realities about African religion against which Islam comes into conflict: (1) Traditional religion is basically ethnocentric while Islam is supra-tribal; (2) Traditional religion has an "immediacy" about it while Islam has a more fatalistic acceptance of the circumstances of life.[29]

ETHNOCENTRIC AND SUPRA-ETHNIC RELIGION

The ethnocentric quality of African traditional religion refers to the tribal consciousness running through it and to the traditional ethos which surrounds it.

Religious practice is woven into the fabric of the myth and culture of the tribe, reflecting the worldview that undergirds reality for the whole society. Robin Horton has analyzed the Kalabari levels of "spirit," for example, to show the meaning of these spirits for the totality of Kalabari life. Ancestors are the forces underpinning the life

---

[27]King, *Introduction to Religion* includes an attempt to classify the phenomenological development of religion from the primitive to the universal types under three levels--the social, the ritual, and the ideational, pp. 52-53.

[28]I. M. Lewis. In his introduction to *Islam in Tropical Africa*; studies presented and discussed at the Fifth International African Seminar, January, 1964 (Oxford: International African Institute, 1966), pp. 58-67.

[29]*Ibid.*, p. 59.

and strength of the lineages. Heroes are forces which support the various institutions of the community and its skills, while "water spirits" appear as forces relating to all that lies beyond the confines of the established social order.[30] These phenomena are found in various forms among the northern tribes as well. Where institutions such as these are firmly maintained and the symbols which support the beliefs are intact, the influence of a new religion (Islam) will be limited.

The following examples come from a sampling of tribes which we shall describe as "open." By "open" we mean to say that the resistance to Islam is minimal and they have a high susceptibility to change. It will be illustrated, however, that even among these "open" societies, it is very important to maintain the tribal cultus as it has been handed down.

The Maguzawa

The Maguzawa are one of the few modern tribal groups which can be studied from data recorded in the *Kano Chronicle*. They are generally referred to as the "pagan Hausa," because they are direct descendants of the people in the Dalla-Hausa tradition. From the beginning they resisted Islam, and it did not matter whether pressure was brought to bear by high Muslim chiefs or by war. Today they live in scattered villages between Kano and Katsina.[31]

During a visit to the village of Madaurare, fifty miles west of Kano, one fact became clear: for all their resistance to Islam, the Maguzawa appear, on the surface, to be Muslim. Their long identity with the great Islamic North and the common Hausa language has obliterated much of the animism they once practiced and which is so evident among the tribes to the south. The lines of demarcation between the Maguzawa and Muslim Hausa are barely noticeable at first. The casual observer will see that the times of prayer are not kept, yet the appearance and conduct of daily life are not recognizably "pagan."

---

[30]Horton, "African Traditional Thought," p. 155.

[31]Reference is to the relationship of the Maguzawa to the Muslim culture around the city of Kano, treated by Joseph Greenberg in *The Influence of Islam.* Also refer to an anthropological summary, valuable for its description of religion, by P. Krusius, "Die Maguzawa," *Archiv fur Anthropologie*, Vol. XLII (1915), pp. 288-315.

My visit to Madaurare was, specifically, to observe Islamic influence on a Maguzawa wedding.[32] The two days offered opportunity to study other customs as well. The tribal ethos was very strong. This village shared a common heritage with other Maguzawa clans scattered about, but local practices and beliefs were the most significant. The chief, Gelo, our host, showed us the sacred burial plot of his father who was chief before him. The grave was but five steps from the door of his house. Across the compound, less than forty feet away, a granary was built over the grave of his grandfather. Gelo himself had been practicing the Muslim prayers for a number of years, but his real basis for leadership was symbolized by these two graves.

The marriage was performed by a Muslim cleric (*liman*) from the nearby town of Tsanyawa. There were careful pre-wedding rituals. This included a two-day preparation and communal drinking of beer, first at the groom's compound and later at the bride's. This was the only group activity, as the ceremony itself was private. I was taken to a carefully guarded corner of one house where the clanic beer pot is kept. It is an immense clay vessel about three feet high and, as Gelo explained, it is the symbolic marriage pot. Only this pot can insure a happy marriage, and it has been in the clan for over 120 years. Every feature of the wedding was traditional Maguzawa. Judging from the marriage ritual, the conclusion is that Islam has had only a superficial influence.

The Pabir

The Pabir are located in southern Borno State.[33] The effect of their history was an Islamization of the royal class which has had a steady

---

[32]There is no recognized marriage among the Maguzawa except that which is solemnized by the Muslim *liman*. Yet the customs of the Maguzawa are non-Muslim in every respect of the wedding apart from the actual ceremony. This assent to Muslim legal sanction of the *rites de passage*, while persisting in traditional rites, is unique with the Maguzawa.

[33]The Pabir lie mainly to the north of the main road, east and west of Biu. They have intermingled with the Bura, the names being derivations of the same root, *bir* or *bur*, meaning" the male organ, and generalized to stand for "man" or "people." There are more Bura than Pabir. Both have Islamized to a considerable degree in the towns.

influence on the people around the town of Biu.[34] As in most cases, the influence of Islam lessens as one goes from the towns into the villages. Meek did considerable reporting on the Pabir in 1922, but the changes which have taken place since then have now made his observations unreliable.[35]

Even with continued change, the tribal orientation of the religious practice continues. The Emir of Biu has been the central figure of Islamic influence[36] since the conversion of the twentieth chief, Ali Pasikur, reckoned to be about 120 years ago. The conflict, which is not yet fully resolved, is whether the chief should submit to Pabir initiation ceremonies while being the titular head of Pabir Islam. This highly symbolic Pabir ritual requires that he be washed in the river. The ritual washing includes throwing rice and benniseed into the water, after which beer is also poured into the water. This act is in harmony with the family rituals of the Pabir performed at sacred family trees. The fact that this ritual persisted up to the time of the chief who was installed in 1967[37] indicates that even in a highly developed Muslim group, major tribal institutions do not submit easily to the "pure" Muslim practice.

Granted, much that is traditionally Pabir has faded in recent years, but the texture of Pabir culture still lies beneath the surface of this royal Muslim town. When I asked how the inconsistency might be accounted for, Tashkalma, an alert elder of about 75 years, assured me that I should not confuse custom (*al' ada*) with religion (*addini*). There was no inconsistency in his mind. Loyalty to the tribal custom could

---

[34]Tashkalma Biu told of Kanuri traders who came from Borno and took Pabir natives back with him as what he called "free slaves." The Kanuri advised Ali Pasikur (1840) that if he wanted to be an enlightened king, he should recognize God and do Muslim prayers. He had sixty wives but prayed faithfully. Interview at Biu, January 7, 1970.

[35]Meek, *Tribal Studies*, Vol. I, pp. 137-180.

[36]The Pabir, while the smaller of the two tribes, had a connection with Borno. One result was domination by a Kanuri clan known by the name of "Woviri." This became the royal Pabir clan and resulted in the establishment of a central authority among the Pabir which also controls the Bura.

[37]When Tashkalma Biu was pressed as to why the induction ritual was abandoned, he replied that the present emir has enough money to give away instead of his doing the traditional rites. The assumption would be that the principal figures were helped with funds so that he was granted reprieve from the ritual and could, thereby, affirm himself to be an orthodox Muslim, which by all external standards he is.

not be looked upon as contradictory to the practice of religion (Islam).[38]

The tribal cultus is always the last factor to be surrendered to a new system, and where this is unusually strong the Islamic influence will be greatly reduced. One of the important conclusions reached by Nadel is that among the Nupe, Islam must be understood mainly in terms of a reorganized Nupe religion. "Integration between Nupe religion and Islam is complete only where it bears the ethos of Nupe religion."[39] His observation comes out of an area in northern Nigeria where Islam has had a long history. Among the Nupe, time is the most significant factor in change.[40] Our studies show it is the indigenous pattern that dominates. In practice, this dominance is overlaid by an Islamic veneer. Yet indigenous practice is strong enough to insulate the tribe from no more than peripheral penetration by Islam.[41]

In contrast to the ethnocentrism of traditional religion, the Islamic community, generally, is formed across tribal lines by individual choice. In villages as well as towns, those who perform the *salat* are from various tribes. But now they have joined a new community, adopted Hausa dress, and are using the Hausa language exclusively.[42] For instance, a large group of Muslims live in the village of Usmanu, near the river town of Lau. Their original tribal homes could have been any one of the surrounding groups, mainly Kulung, Kwanchi, Piya, or Jen. These communities do not provide a congenial environment for one who is converted to Islam, so the converts now

---

[38]Though Tashkalma claimed to be a practicing Muslim, yet he proudly pointed to the spears and artifacts from three generations of fathers which hung on his wall. "These are my past and my present," he said.

[39]S. F. Nadel, *Nupe Religion* (London: Routledge and Kegan Paul, Ltd., 1954), pp. 257-58.

[40]Reference also to P. J. A. Rigby in his paper to the Fifth International Seminar (I.A.I.), "Sociological Factors in the Contact of the Gogo of Central Tanzania with Islam," *Islam in Tropical Africa*, p. 272. He makes the point that "studies from West Africa have shown that time is *not* the major factor in the Islamization of an African society." Our studies bear this out. In contrast, the "stages" advocated by J. S. Trimingham leave the impression that little is needed but time for a society to move methodically to Islamization. See *Islam in West Africa* (Oxford: O.U.P., 1959), pp. 33-40.

[41]The society which has progressed the farthest to what might be called "Islamization" is the Nupe, yet Nadel's conclusion is that Islam has become, to a large extent, an overlay on the traditional base.

[42]Joining Islam as a move outside the tribe and in this way forming a new non-tribal community will be dealt with in Chapter Two.

live in what might be called a supra-tribal relationship. They have played down their indigenous features and look very much like they belong together as Muslims. Usmanu village illustrates the problem which Islam has in accommodating to strong tribal elements, while at the same time it shows the inter-tribal character of Islam, especially among rural groups.

IMMEDIACY AS A FACTOR IN TRADITIONAL RELIGION

Immediacy in African religion means that the rituals are performed carefully so as to produce the desired results quickly and concretely. The well-worn paths of tradition are the most pragmatic. In contrast to the here-and-now quality of indigenous religion, Islam presents itself more as a belief system and can seem irrelevant, even powerless.

I have kept an interesting diary of different responses that were given to the question, *Why do the people of your tribe not accept the Muslim way?* In most cases the answers reflect the ethnocentricity of the tribe and the need for results within the shortest time possible. A sampling of responses is as follows:

> Only my fathers know the reason for my sickness.[43]
> God is not in the ground (where the Muslims pray).[44]
> I will use the best medicine, and it doesn't matter to me who dispenses it.[45]
> I don't want my reward in Lahira; having good fortune now is better.[46]
> When the children are sick in the village, only the ancestors can tell us why.[47]

This utilitarian aspect of traditional religion is one of its most positive features. Lewis observed this to be the special character of indigenous religion:

> Traditional religious powers are normally believed to sustain a moral order in which the just prosper and the good are rewarded, not so much in some nebulous after-life as within society itself.[48]

---

[43] Audu Shellam (Bachema), at Numan, January 18, 1970.

[44] Iliya Madaki (Kutep), at Bukuru, March 2, 1970.

[45] Tom Gyeng (Birom), at Jos, April 15, 1970.

[46] Nyala Pai (Jukun), at Ibi, April 22, 1970.

[47] John Kwambila (Kilba), at Mubi, February 21, 1970.

[48] Lewis, "Islam and Traditional Belief," *Islam in Tropical Africa*, pp. 58-9.

This, Lewis feels, is an earthly security which is antithetical to the "universalistic spirit of Islam and its concern with eternity rather than with today."[49] In the theology of indigenous religions, there is little which rises above the level of nature spirits; hence traditional religion does not see religious activity as approaching an all-powerful divinity.[50] Reality and power are as close as a magic formula, the trees, or a ready sacrifice. Islam has had to demonstrate that it can meet needs and provide answers without delay.

The Mshelia people developed a local folk Islam, because they needed tangible, secure forms which would keep the community intact. Islam was introduced to a pagan Mshelia village by an unmarried Fulani man, who, it is said, had to leave his Muslim relatives because he had been disinherited. His children, in turn, drastically modified their Islamic ritual to accommodate the pagan bias of the village.[51] The motivating factor for the change was that the Muslim men could not get wives unless they adopted forms which were closer to Mshelia religion. The indigenous Mshelia cared nothing for Muslim prayers until they developed a new Islamized ritual designed to placate their own local gods. The Fulani males had no success in marrying pagan women until one of the Muslim sons became a kind of doctor, who was known to have powerful cures for sickness. Once this was known and the pagans began to seek his help, he could demand daughters and even other men's wives for his services. This was service rendered on behalf of immediate needs, and this immediacy did give the Muslim religion new credibility.

Nadel observed among the Nupe[52] that even where there has been a long period of Islamic influence and a higher type of Islamic practice, Allah, the God of Islam, is as remote and abstract as the people's own traditional god (Soko). Hence, nothing is gained by the introduction of Allah into Nupe cosmology. Allah and Soko are mostly regarded as the same being.[53] I asked an old Muslim man in the town of Bida what

---

[49]*Ibid.*

[50]Rigby, "Contact of the Gogo with Islam," *Islam in Tropical Africa*, p. 287.

[51]This unique example of direct Islamic influence on a primitive tribe was observed on April 3, 1970. It was two miles from the Bura town of Shafa and the informant was the clan's oldest living head, aided by a teacher who is himself Mshelia.

[52]Refer specifically to the chapter, "Islam in Nupe," *Nupe Religion*, pp. 232-58.

[53]See *ibid.*, p. 235.

he believed to be the most powerful part of his religion. He replied that after Muslim prayers he had most faith in the *walamia*.[54] This, as it turns out, is a communal meal which consumes a sacrificed cock. The *imam* attends and says a brief prayer for the occasion, remembering to mention whatever the trouble may have been.[55] This "powerful ritual," as he called it, is an indigenous practice which has been reset into a Muslim context. The *walamia* reflects the variety of adaptations possible when immediacy is a demand. To this Islam must conform.

There is a law of selectivity which works in the society when the option of Islam is open to it. This calls for a filtering-out of the non-utilitarian elements of Islam, that is, those practices which serve no useful purpose for the traditional man in his immediate needs. When a Hausa practitioner (*malam*) is known for his ability to dispense "strong medicine" (*laya*), he is useful. To the extent that his services produce the desired results, Islam is a friendly ally of the tribe. This flexibility of Islam is an advantage, because it poses no threat to the indigenous religion. Strict Islam is not a requirement when an "unbeliever" is in need. Watt speaks of this when he discusses the ways in which Arabic Islam interacted with Arabic animism. Many of the pragmatic features of Arabic religion were placed in the new Islamic setting. But, he says,

> There was always the danger, of course, with the retention of numerous animistic forms, that something of the essential spirit of animism might remain and might more and more flourish if the vitality of Islam decreased.[56]

In the African setting, however, the traditional world has a power gain if indigenous practice can be enhanced by Islam. This is not "corrupted animism," for there is no orthodoxy, as such, in animism. Islam, on the other hand, does have more generally established norms which limit the amount of distortion that can be allowed.[57]

---

[54]From a conversation in Bida with Doko, January 22, 1970.

[55]Nadel refers to the *walamia* in *Nupe Religion*, p. 238.

[56]W. M. Watt, *Islam and Society*, p. 189. The expectation is, however, expressed that "these traces (animism) would eventually, after some centuries, be expunged or transmuted."

[57]The widespread use of Muslim *laya* (leather-covered packets which contain a verse of the Qur'an) is considered normal traditional practice (see Chapter Four). *Laya*, a Hausa word, is from the Arabic *al-aya*, meaning a "sign" or a "verse" of the Qur'an.

FACTORS IN ACCEPTANCE AND
REJECTION OF ISLAM

Particularity is, without doubt, part of the essence in traditional African religion. It is almost impossible to view the religions of different tribes with generalities. Obviously, many particularities end up in diversity. For this reason the term "African tribal religions" may be preferred to that of "traditional religion."[58] The influence of Islam, therefore, must be described in the context of this diversity.It is out of the genius of this or that particular tribal society that the response to Islam must be measured. Anyone who falls into the error of generalities with respect to African religion(s) will also fail to understand why the pattern of response to Islam has so little uniformity. This is because the strength or weakness of the tradition of the tribe will determine its response to Islam.

In studying the Pabir and the Longuda, the question unavoidably arises as to why the Pabir have a high degree of accommodation with Islam while the Longuda have forcibly resisted Islamic culture and politics.[59] The ethnocentric Mumuye tribe has responded in two ways to Islam. The Zing Mumuye, while animistic (with many Christians), have had a Muslim chief for many years, whereas the Lankaviri Mumuye have stubbornly refused any kind of Muslim authority.[60] These examples show the irregularity which makes the of study of African religion so lively and unpredictable. One has to work within the frustrations of this particularity. No two groups are alike. However, the intense local quality of African religion brings the

---

[58]This can be illustrated in many ways, but the diversity in concepts of the "supreme gods" was striking. Granted, many common elements were present ("father," "creator," "sky," etc.), but out of twenty-one tribes only three (Kilba, Bura, and Pabir) shared a god by the same name. Two tribes had the notion of their god once being close but subsequently removed (Gwari and Tiv). But the more striking impressions are the distinct local differences.

[59]See also the discussion on the Longuda in Chapters Two, p. 64, and Five, pp. 137 ff *et passim.*

[60]The Zing Mumuye chief has built a strong local government by his prestige within the Muslim hierarchy. (See Chapter Five, p. 153.) But the Lankaviri Mumuye all keep their local indigenous chiefs and refer to the Fulani at the district headquarters only when absolutely necessary.

observer into close range with religious *persons* and it is this personal quality of African religion that has been most tragically neglected.[61]

LEVELS OF TRIBAL RESPONSE TO ISLAMIC INFLUENCE

Any classification of the twenty tribes studied will be done with certain reservations, due to the high particularity factor. Ideally, each tribe is a case on its own merits. But this attempt to classify will give guidance when seeking factors of acceptance or rejection of Islam. The danger is to suggest that any three categories are final. The differentiation within each group is not sharp, and the overlapping of features and ranges of strength or weakness among the groups is considerable.

Active-resistant

Of the twenty tribes studied the majority show a weak to strong resistance to Muslim influence. I use the term "active resistant" to describe the more conservative groups, because these tribes have been aware of Islam over a long period and have shown a negative pattern of response. Incidences of conversion are few, and the texture of the religion remains traditional with negligible Muslim influence. The basis for this resistance is usually found within the ethos of the tribal society itself. However, it may also be a sociological or political image which the Muslim community has projected. In most cases, it is an intermingling of these phenomena, depending on the tribe. The major factors appear to be as follows:

1. Active-resistant tribes have a high degree of self-consciousness combined with a strong central cultus. They live in the environment of a well developed ritual which they have been able to transmit, to a great degree, to the young people. The central cultus which dominates is of a particular motif, for example, divine king or *rites de passage.*

---

[61]On "person centered" African religious studies as an area which needs to be cultivated, see M. J. Greschat's article "Understanding African Religion," *Orita*, II/2 (December, 1968), p. 59-68.

29

2. The rituals of these tribes are intact in spite of secularizing influences and are, correspondingly, supported by a well defined cosmology.

3. There is a negative historic bias, in varying degrees of strength, against the "Hausa image," which is sociological and political and which directly affects the level of religious influence.

4. In the case of some tribes, these factors have been further complicated by an isolationism resulting from ethnocentricity, geographical location, and only recently by education.[62]

In this active-resistant group we place, for this study, the Jukun, the Tiv, the Mumuye, the Birom, the Longuda, the Kutep, the Taroh (Yergam), the Jen, and the Rukuba.

Open-traditional

This is possibly the most difficult category to describe since these groups show a freedom to opt for Muslim practices without serious repercussions, but at the same time their primary tribal identity is retained. For various reasons, Muslim influence and a Muslim ethos are prominent in religious practice, but the structure is clearly that of the traditional religion. The following are important aspects of this group:

1. The open-traditional are not considered as Islamized except very superficially, for the traditional core still governs religious life.[63]

---

[62]Cf. the discussion by Evans-Pritchard in his *Witchcraft, Oracles and Magic Among the Azande*, (Oxford, 1965). "They reason excellently in the idiom of their beliefs, but they cannot reason outside or against their beliefs because they have no other idiom in which to express their thoughts." Horton observes that the "absence of any awareness of alternatives makes for an absolute acceptance of the established theoretical tenets, and removes any possibility of questioning them." "African Traditional Thought," p. 156.

[63]These statements are made while being aware of the large groups of people in these tribes who are Christians as well as those who say they do not subscribe to any particular religion. (See Chapter Six) In the groups who actively resist Islam are those who show a high response to Christianity, for instance, the Birom and the Jen. Until 1960 the Mumuye were as resistant to Christianity as they were to Islam, but they are now open to the Christian religion.

2. The negative bias against Islam is not strong; rather, a high level of interaction exists, especially between native and Muslim practitioners.

3. The political influence of Islam has had an *entree* at the local level, but the diffusion of the Muslim way of life takes place mostly at the social level. Generally, Hausa Muslims and the indigenous Muslim converts live in community, and the attitude toward Muslims is usually non-critical.

The tribes which best fit into this open-traditional group are the Bachema, the Eggon, the Gwari, the Kilba, the Kulung, the Mwaghavul (Sura), and the Yendang.

Open

This group describes those tribes which show the greatest degree of Islamization. In most cases the historical pattern has shown a special relationship to Muslim peoples. These were in early contact with Islam, resulting in a relationship that has been sustained over a long period. It does not mean that these tribes are fully Islamized. This may appear to be so on first observation, especially in the towns. Nupe is, unquestionably, the society most changed by Islamic influences. Yet Nadel says:

> The Islamization of the country is far from complete—both in that it reached only a portion of the population and in that it often remained superficial. Thus Islam, far from superceding the indigenous ceremonials often merely furnished new, additional ones.[64]

The open group is characterized as follows:

1. They show the highest degree of Muslim conversion, with large segments of the society, especially in the towns, having adopted Islamic mores. They have modified traditional practice, giving it the cultural appearance of Islam.

---

[64]Nadel, *Nupe Religion*, p. 234. Trimingham, writing in 1959, places the number of Nupe who have Islamized at two-thirds of the total (350,000). The model of Islam, however, is qualified by the Nadel statement above.

2. Hence, a more marked systemization of the Islamic way of life prevails, including Qur'anic schools, prayer circles in the towns and villages, a widespread observance of Muslim festivals, and a more conspicuous sense of Muslim community (*umma*).

3. The open pattern is a phenomenon of the larger villages and towns and, consequently, does not follow into the more isolated compounds and deeply rural areas.

Suggestive of this group are the Maguzawa, the Pabir, the Bura, and the Nupe.

We have attempted this classification in order to have some line of differentiation in the extremely fluid pattern of Muslim influence. Our concern is to see which combination of factors is the most conducive or resistant to Islamization, and how traditional features have reacted, both negatively and positively, to the Muslim environment.

THE PRINCIPLE OF COMPATIBILITY

When the African worldview is being observed with respect to change, it is always the primary culture which has the greatest amount of influence upon the emergence of the new. Hence, when we speak of acceptance or rejection of Islam, the terms "compatibility" and "incompatibility" are relevant. That is to ask, To what extent does Islam "fit" the traditional structure? The *Kano Chronicle* shows that an ancient animistic culture (Dalla) was predominant over an immigrant religion (Bagoda) which brought some traces of Islam. Subsequently, the "pagan" Hausa religion which developed from these two streams, distorted the Islam which came from Mali, casting it into a synthesis with traditional Hausa practice. The strength was always on the side of traditional animism until the *jihad* of 1804. In Rigby's study with the Gogo, an East African tribe, he makes a strong point of cultural correlates between basic Islam and African religions.[65]

---

[65]". . . superficial correlations between broad 'structural' generalizations and the absorption of Islam are misleading and unfruitful. What must be demonstrated is the compatibility (or incompatibility) of specific structural relations and the accompanying religious and cosmological ideas within a society, with the basic elements of Islamic religion and its cultural correlates." Rigby, "Contact of the Gogo with Islam," *Islam in Tropical Africa*, p. 274.

When there is a marked "fitting together" of the two systems, the change comes more quickly and completely. But more frequently the Gogo religion was incompatible both in values and form.[66]

In a similar study among the Boran of northern Kenya, Baxter does not see Islam as a "coherent belief system" presenting itself to the tribe, but as elements of Islam which are perceived by the Boran as being "congenial or antithetic to traditional culture." Bascom and Herskovitz's study, *Stability and Change in African Culture*, establishes the principle that the kind of Islam which will emerge in African cultures is unpredictable. This is because the degree to which innovations are accepted or rejected is determined by the primary culture and not by the alien factors forced upon it.[67]

An example of this unpredictable effect on the traditional pattern is seen when contrasting ancestor practice among the Pabir and the Mumuye. The pantheon of the Mumuye is indirectly related to the ancestors, as also are the initiation rites and rituals of harvest and hunting. But the oldest of the Pabir ancestor ceremonials shows a less active, almost casual, reference to the ancestors.

To illustrate, in the case of the Mumuye,[68] there is a very strong dependency on the ancestors. The *dodo*, a figure clothed in long grasses and wearing a bird mask, is an active feature of the tribal religion. The *dodo* almost always appears as a symbol of the ancestors. At the initiation rite the *dodo* is prostrate on the ground in his masquerade, representing the dead. It is over the prone *dodo* that the initiates are told that all traditional ritual is done in the name of the fathers. The blood of a cock is sprinkled on the *dodo*'s head, and the

---

[66]Watt shows how slowly it dawned on Muhammed that his system did not fit the old Arabian animism. "In time, however, he came to see that, as things were working out in practice, worship at these (pagan) shrines was in conflict with the monotheism that he was preaching." *Islam and Society*, p. 188.

[67]W. R. Bascom and M. Herskovits point out that even the variety of African reaction to European contact cannot be explained in terms of colonial policy. Neither can it be laid to intensity of contact. "Equally, if not more important, are the preestablished patterns of African culture. *Continuity and Change in African Culture* (Chicago: University of Chicago Press, 1959), p. 5. Watt adds that "the borrowed elements conduce to the expanding vitality of the borrowing culture only insofar as they draw their nourishment from the activities which led to their borrowing in the first place." *Islam and Society*, p. 184.

[68]Reference to description by Malam Kani Lankaviri on January 14, 1970.

chicken itself is eaten communally.[69]   The annual hunting rites are
still important to the Mumuye, and here again the ancestor motif
predominates. The skulls of the important dead are prepared three
months after burial. They are kept together in sacred pots at the foot
of the clan's ritual tree. Very strong prohibitions are associated with
the tree. When the hunt is ready, the skulls are washed and placed in
rows upon a new mat, and words are spoken such as, "The hunt is
ready, here is our beer. We request that you remember us in the
hunt." Having done this, the priest places a small amount of beer mash
on each skull, then washes them and returns them to their pots.[70]

In contrast to this, the Pabir celebrate a feast of ancestor
remembrance even though there has been a rather general Islamization
of the tribe. From the very first it did not seem to conflict with Islamic
practice, and it has been retained with Islamic innovations.   The
ancestors are remembered in connection with the harvest. The "first
fruits" of the corn are used in making ritual food for the living and the
dead. Four lumps of corn mush (*tuwo*)[71] are eaten by the father, after
which four are eaten by the mother. With this, the ancestors have
"finished the food." At this point the ancestors are asked to help in the
problems which may arise, and a prayer is offered.

At Biu I talked with the oldest man who could give the information
clearly. He was a practicing Muslim with strong traditional ties. He
pointed out, however, that this was a practice of the Pabir, "since
before they had Islamized." They saw no need of giving up the
practice because (1) it was done in each family with the head of the
house acting as priest, and (2) the prayer offered was one taught them

---

[69]The communal meal is an event which occurs frequently, being carried out as a
symbol of the living tribe with the dead. This motif recalls W. Robertson Smith's classic
interpretation of the "sacred meal" communally received, whereby religion is manifest in
relationships of men with each other as kindred, and included in this is the god or gods who
are in continuity with nature. W. R. Smith, *Lectures on the Religion of the Semites* (New
York: Appelton, 1889), pp. 117-19.

[70]That the priest is the oldest man of the village is important, for in the continuity
between the living and the dead he has become the vital link. When the above rite is over,
the "old man" converses with the dead, telling them they have been returned to their "pots"
and that they should return to their "rest."

[71]*Tuwo* is the dough-like food usually prepared from guinea corn or yam.

by the Muslim *imam*.[72] The role of the ancestors among the Mumuye is normative and has never been compromised even when the political forces of Islam surrounding the tribe were strong. The Pabir custom, however, was not incompatible with the Borno model of Islam received by the Pabir clans and could be incorporated into the new cultus.

However, the conflict which arises within the Islamic belief system as it interacts with the ideas of indigenous religion is important. The unity of Allah and divine authority is a factor of relevance or irrelevance, depending on the tribe itself. With the Jukun, the cosmology is centered not around the "high god" (*Chidon*) but rather around the *Aku Uka*, the divine king of the Wapan.[73] The supremacy of God is not primary, and therefore the idea of a powerful one-God is an unacceptable idea. The difference is irreconcilable, in spite of the Jukun who have Islamized for various reasons.[74]

In contrast to this, there is a heavy Muslim influence in the Bura towns, where, as a tribe, there is no conflicting idea centering around the "divine king." The chief of the Pabir people also has authority over the Bura. Since there is no chief of the Bura, this kind of problem does not arise. Among the Bura there is no active idea of a "high god."[75] Even so, the Bura god, *Hyel*, belongs to a type which fits admirably into a concept of the unity and self-existence of Allah.[76]

---

[72]Lewis shows that nature and fertility spirits are not congenial to African Islam, hence their veneration is usually condemned. But the "lineage ancestors" are not considered as gods, so the veneration given them is not in conflict with Muslim teaching. They are, therefore, usually tolerated. "Islam and Traditional Belief," *Islam in Tropical Africa*, p. 62.

[73]Wapan is the indigenous name preferred by the Jukun. Jukun has colonial associations. The *Aku Uka* will be taken up in Chapter Five.

[74]The passing of the chief of Wukari (February, 1970) revitalized interest in the meaning of the *Aku* symbol for a kind of totality of life. Jukun Muslims, however, have an ambivalent relationship to the *Aku*. See the discussion in Chapter Five, pp. 138ff.

[75]The Bachema references to *Nzeanzo* reveal a concept of the divine which is unusual. While, generally, notions of the supreme being are quite undefinitive, the Bachema maintain a variety of epithets which reveal some depth; e.g., *dembu*, "as the hollow of the tree"; he is *nzo teko vene*, "as a house lizard who sees all"; he is the *fafelo*, "the black ant" who can scent food--so god knows man's thoughts. These strong indigenous ideas have not transferred easily to the notion of Allah. (From a conversation with Binoutu {Bachema} at Numan, January 10, 1970.)

[76]Meek suggests that *Hyel* of the Bura may have connection with the Semitic EL, and was introduced from North Africa. The unity of *Hyel* is a dominant theme and fits well into the openness of the Bura, Pabir, and Kilba to Islam, all of whom share possession of *Hyel* in their traditional religion.

But it is important to note that the belief in *Hyel*, while quite systematized, has never been an exclusive notion with the Bura. *Hyel* is a "high god" shared by at least three tribes—the Kilba, the Bura, and the Pabir. *Hyel* as a theological symbol does not have a tribal myth surrounding it, as does the god of the Bachema, *Nzeanzo*. Rather, *Hyel* is a model which does not conflict with Islamic ideation and has the further advantage to Islam of being relatively peripheral in Bura cosmology. In contrast, *Nzeanzo*, the Bachema god, is a particularistic tribal god and represents a highly developed traditional concept.[77]

Islamic beliefs, therefore, can be appropriated by the Bura from the standpoint of Bura theology and because the traditional mode "fits" with Islam. With the Bachema, however, the tribal god is the very essence of tribal ritual and for this reason is not easily accommodated to Islam. We have also shown that where the divine king motif predominates, the tribal concept of a high god and "Allah idea" is minimal, if not rejected altogether.

BREAKUP OF THE THE ARCHAIC CYCLE

The *Kano Chronicle* also demonstrated that as long as the archaic cycle of the primary religion was intact, it could successfully resist the forces of change. There was constant return to the original sacred place through acts of ritual which reinforced the tribe at its center. This assured strength to the indigenous forms. The archaic pattern, in contrast to the Islamic forces which were thrown against it, had no concept of progress or change. The strength of the traditional system lay in its essentially non-linear view of life. When religion was decentralized and the mythical observances were broken up, change began to take place.

The correlation between this and what actually happens in contemporary society is striking. The African concept of time has been observed by John Mbiti in *African Religions and Philosophy*. He sees the time factor of African religion as bound to the past and the immediate present. He says there is no real notion of future time. The

---

[77]See note 75.

more linear concept of time with an "indefinite past and an infinite future," he claims, is alien to African conceptualization.

> Beyond a few months from now . . . African concept of time is silent and indifferent. This means that the future is virtually non-existent or *actual* time, apart from the relatively short projection of the present up to two years hence.[78]

The inevitable result of this notion is a backward rather than a forward orientation in religion. Subjects "set their minds not on future things but chiefly on what has taken place."[79] Mbiti's observation is helpful for seeing the tension between the cyclic religions of Africa and the more universal religions of the linear type. The time observation is, however, not peculiar to African religions. In the religions of the ancient Near East, time was not something grasped as having uniform duration or as a "succession of qualitative moments." Henri Frankfort's observation is that this archaic concept of time is so intimately connected with life crises and with nature that it could be viewed as "biological time."[80]

Where the tribe has retained a strong traditional center, changes taking place will be minimal. This is the major feature of the tribes which we have called active-resistant. Two Hausa tribes, the Maguzawa, and to a lesser extent, the Kutumbawa, are groups that actively resisted Islam for generations. The Kutumbawa[81] have remained close to Kano city while the Maguzawa are distributed over a wide area, intermingling with other tribal groups. In the case of the Maguzawa, their history of resistance to Islam and their continued belief in *iskoki* (spirits, good and bad) are facts which support each other. Even though the Maguzawa show many signs of Muslim enculturation, their distinction from Islam is still unmistakable. Hausa

---

[78]Mbiti, *African Religions*, p. 22.

[79]*Ibid.*, p. 17.

[80]H. and H. A. Frankfort, J. A. Wilson, and T. Jacobsen, *Before Philosophy*, Penguin Books (Baltimore: 1964), p. 32. In contrast, Mbiti's use of the word "philosophy" in connection with "African Religions" seems to assume too much.

[81]The Kutumbawa are considered to be the actual descendants of Bagoda, the conqueror of Dalla. It would be the Kutumbawa, therefore, who were the ruling kings of the *Kano Chronicle* up to the time of the Fulani conquest. Greenberg notes, "The Kutumbawa themselves show that while they prayed in the Muslim fashion and performed other canonical duties, they still retained pagan practices to a marked degree. This can be taken incidentally of further proof of how gradual was the spread of Mohammedanism at Kano." *Influence of Islam*, pp. 12-13.

Muslims see the religion of the Maguzawa as *maguzanci*, a cognate term deriving from their name, which means "the pagan way." The non-Muslim Hausa religion recognizes Allah as a category of belief, but it is a casual, meaningless belief which is admitted only upon direct questioning.[82]

Maguzawa ritual is based on the manipulation of "wind spirits" (*iskoki*) by practitioners and sacrifices. Except for the practice of a special cult (Bori),[83] there are no complex rituals which reenact the past or hold the tribe together by one sacred event. In the village of Madaurare I attempted to find a single predominating ritual from the past, but it appears there is none. There is the recognition of spirits by clans, and each has ways to cope with these spirits. As for ancestors, there is an annual alms-giving (*sadaka*) and graves of dead leaders are respected. But any archaic festival of beginnings has long been lost. Even the Maguzawa spirits (*iskoki*) have intermingled with the Muslim *jinn* (*aljanu*). This has happened because the Maguzawa do not have a strong form of cyclic religion.

On the other hand, a tribe which has had only superficial influence from the Hausa-Fulani group is the Kulung, a sub group of the Wurkum.[84] Bambur, which is the center of the Kulung people, has felt the usual forces of secularization and Westernization. Islam has not made much headway among the Kulung, though it is acclaimed by many who have left the environs of the tribe. The Bambur Kulung are traditionally linked to a center of religious ritual, vested in one family and located at one place (Banbanala). The ancestor cult for the whole tribe is called the Basali, which rites are carried out by a special priest each year in July.

---

[82]"He (Allah) does not occupy the central role in their beliefs and practices that is so characteristic of the Muslim Hausa. Among the Maguzawa there are no rites connected with the belief in Allah, and all supernatural response to worship, whether good or bad, is attributed to spirits called *iskoki*." Ibid., p. 27.

[83]The widespread Hausa cult of possession which is subsumed under the *iskoki* spirits of "pagan" Hausa and who began as part of the regrouping of indigenous Dalla forces in their resistance to Islam (*Tchibiri*).

[84]The term *Wurkum* is misleading since it describes a grouping of tribes who live in a general area between the hills in northwest Muri (Gongola State). *Wurkum* is a Jukun word and recalls the past days of the Jukun kingdom which included this area. The word means "people of the hills" and embraces seven distinct groups of various origins. There is little homogeneity among the Wurkum tribes especially linguistically.

Basali is the principal cult, but there are less important institutions as well. Gila, Uku, and Zuki, each perform special religious functions. Basali has always been controlled by one family, the priest of which passes on his rights to the eldest son. The whole life cycle of the Kulung has traditionally been under the authority of Basali. For example, crops are not harvested until the Banbanala priest declares the time. While Basali does not have the control it once did, it was still being practiced to some extent by the Kulung in 1970. Family shrines in the name of Basali were still kept sacred, and some of the newborn were being initiated into these to ensure health and good fortune.[85] However, in contrast to the Maguzawa, the Kulung have taken over very few cultural traits of the Muslim religion, and, up until recently, no one would perform Muslim prayers in public.

The basis for Mumuye religion is the initiation rites, which occur every four or seven years depending on the district. These rites are typical of primitive cyclic religion. The rites are attended by former initiates. The initiates are introduced to the traditional practices, including the *dodo*, the sacrificial killing and eating of meat, and ancestor myth. Following this is a swearing in, symbolic beatings, and a revealing of the sacred god-mask. Up to 1970 the Mumuye maintained authority over all segments of their society, including religion, in spite of being open to main roads and having access to markets, transport, and schools. The initiation rites are supported by fertility rituals occurring at regular intervals during the year. This gives a continuity and rhythm to all of life, touching at some point all members of the group. The Mumuye have stubbornly resisted Islam, and the strength of the tribal religion is seen almost everywhere.

Accommodation to Islam is directly related to the degree to which the traditional system can maintain its archaic structure in the stress of change. P. T. W. Baxter states categorically that "Islam has not spread where pagan theological beliefs are supported by the repetitive cycle of ceremonies."[86] Where there are no active rituals of the primitive cyclic type, Islamic influence will be more marked. The ability of

---

[85]The local shrines are dominant, but a father may ask permission of a clan priest and give the prescribed ritual at a cultic shrine borrowed from neighboring tribes which have the reputation of being effective (Samuila Bako at Bambur, April 18, 1970).

[86]P. T. W. Baxter, in his paper to the Fifth International African Seminar, "Islam Among the Boran," *Islam in Tropical Africa*, p. 244. See also his discussion on factors of incompatibility. *Ibid.*, pp. 244-47.

Islam to affect religious patterns will be in direct relation to the strength or weakness of the tribe at its center.

CHAPTER TWO

COMMUNITY PSYCHE AND RELIGIOUS ADJUSTMENT

CHAPTER TWO

COMMUNITY PSYCHE AND RELIGIOUS ADJUSTMENT

We have been observing some of the fundamental elements that come into conflict when an alien religious system is juxtaposed with the indigenous system. The traditional African worldview needs to be brought into still sharper focus by examining specific areas where change takes place. Our concern is primarily with human persons struggling in their environment for fulfillment and stability. Change touches the world closest to them. It connects their own personalities to the tribal community. Modifications are beyond human power to control, as social, political, and economic factors combine to put a strain upon traditional religion. As the totality of life is being restructured, the religious person selects, adapts, and manipulates to find resolutions to needs. The curve of change has no absolute predictability. It is slowed or speeded up by an array of individual and social factors. Our concern here is in three areas. First we want to see how conflict and anxiety will result in altered practice. Second, we must account for the important non-religious factors which bring about change and, finally, see how these changes result in new patterns.

RESPONSES TO CONFLICT AND ANXIETY

Motivation for religious acts arises from the urgency of human need. These religious acts are not prompted by awe or reverence for their own sake. The *mysterium tremendum*[1] of Otto is quite other-

---

[1]Reference is to Rudolf Otto's classic, *The Idea of the Holy* , translated by John W. Harvey, originally published 1923 (New York: Galaxy Books, Oxford University Press 1958).

worldly but it is tied to a humanistic base. Traditional religion traces the struggle of man trying to live with the uncertainties of his physical and economic environment. His *needs* are foremost, while the awe and reverence which run through his rituals are by-products of his sense of dependence. This is of such importance to Radin that he reckons it to be a factor of origin in religion.

> Merged and interpenetrated with what is always primary, the implications of living and the economic struggle for existence in an inimical environment, they give us primitive religion.[2]

THE INDIVIDUAL AND EXISTENTIAL NEEDS

Traditional religion, as any other religion, is made up of the full range of adherents, from the intensely religious to those who care little about the rituals. These individual variations need to be taken into account. Religion among African peoples cannot be viewed as something in which all participate equally at every stage. However, there is some justification for setting up two levels of the "religious thinker."[3]

Within the communities studied there are, obviously, different levels of individual awareness. Compared to those set apart for special religious functions, the participation of the ordinary man in ritual practice is noticeably less. There are actually many people today who disclaim any religious preference, especially among the young men. They have rejected the "pagan way" because it is associated with the past, but they have not aligned themselves with either Islam or Christianity. John Mbiti says categorically, "African peoples do not know how to exist without religion." In the final analysis this is true.[4]

Dangemu is a Kilba man who said his parentage was animist but that most of his brothers, like him, just follow "the things which we see as best." But this does not mean he has no religion. Dangemu went on to

---

[2]Paul Radin, *Primitive Religion* (New York: Dover Publications, Inc., 1957), p. 9.

[3]*Ibid.*, pp. 8-14: "the one (layman) only secondarily identified with action, the other (thinker) primarily so; the one interested in the analysis of the religious phenomena, the other in their effect," p. 14.

[4]Mbiti, *African Religions*, p. 2.

describe his basic needs in this order: (1) how to find a wife, (2) where to get sufficient money, (3) how to protect himself from harmful magic, and (4) how to secure good health. He felt certain practices which his father taught him would be helpful for one of these (protection from bad magic). But he was quite sure that Muslim "doctors" could prescribe more effective "medicine" for the other three, especially for his health.

When asked why he felt that Islam could provide for most of his personal needs, Dangemu described the way in which the Fulani Muslims were recognized as dispensers of power. They brought the *luguji* to the Kilba people. The *luguji* is a special personal prophecy written out for the client on a long sheet of paper and then rolled up. The client who asked for the *luguji* test must give seven gowns as payment. The client then chooses what he desires most, whether health, money, children, or power. Two requirements, however, are expected of the client: he must begin to do Muslim prayers, and he must accept the prophetic message of the ritual concerning the means of his death.[5]

This last is the most unusual part of the *luguji*. The client is given four possibilities as to how he might die—by fire, by water, by snake, or by knife. When the contract is completed and the money paid, the client appears before the *malam* with a witness. The *luguji* scroll is rolled up and tied to a chicken's neck. Four symbols of death are arranged in close proximity: fire, water, a knife, and a snake. The direction in which the released chicken runs will tell, without question, how the man will die. The testimonies of the power of the *luguji* to give the man his wish are many, as well as the very interesting tales of death which confirm the death-prophecy.[6]

I have illustrated the utilitarian approach to religious practice to show that even among the less religious the meeting of personal need is the most important function of religion. The Kilba people, mentioned above, retain initiation rites and have a complex belief in nature spirits

---

[5]The Hausa use of *kadara* has a strongly fatalistic connotation which is not present in the Qur'anic use of this term.

[6]A Kilba man, Ishaku Kwambila, told of one man who had become rich through the *luguji*. But he had been destined to die by water, by the *luguji* prophecy. One day a flash flood came up in the river, and as the client tried nobly to save a woman, he was drowned.

of many kinds. It does not appear that Islam has developed into an institutional system such as that of the neighboring Pabir. Among the Kilba there is an openness to intermarriage and, in general, a Kilba feels his lot has been improved by "taking on the habit of Muslim prayers." The impact of the *luguji*, cited above, was reported by quite a few to be the reason why they became Muslims.[7]

A high school student confessed that even though his background is Christian, he felt that the Muslims have better "medicine" for attracting girl friends. Among his peers it is felt that young men should have a large number of Hausa friends, for this greatly enhances their chances for marriage.[8]

This same attitude prevails, to some extent, among the Mwaghavul (Sura) who show an openness to intermarriage and have, in the last decade, allowed Muslim marriages to be performed in compounds of the traditional Mwaghavul people.[9] Beyond marriage, the ever-present problem of childbearing can be solved by either Muslim or traditional practice. The inability to bear children was pointed out as the major cause of anxiety in marriage (cited in seventeen out of twenty tribes studied) and stands out, next to ill health, as the most important personal problem of women. Health is the leading problem in all tribes.

Nearly all the tribes have prescribed methods for barrenness. The Kilba, for example, must consult the *yaku*, who will divine whether the problem is a black spirit or a white spirit. A black goat is sacrificed by the husband, and the *yaku* will touch the woman with the blood. After the ceremony she must not speak until she reaches home. On her way home some of the meat is left at the ritual tree for the black spirit.[10] The variations on this ceremony differ with each group, but the pattern is the same in that the practitioner is consulted, prescriptions are made, and usually sacrifice is included.

---

[7]Ibrahim Mambuka (Mubi, April 12, 1970) said his father was the owner of a *luguji* which brought him three wives and twelve sons. The *luguji* meant he would have to become a Muslim.

[8]Sara Kwara, at Jos, December 12, 1969.

[9]Also reported as the situation with the Kilba and the Bura; tribes which border each other share a common "high god" (*Hyel*) and have a common history.

[10]Peter Mambaka, at Bukuru, March 4, 1970.

Muslim clerics, however, become very useful to the community as the traditional rites begin to lose their power. The ambivalence created by the inefficacy of customary ritual is, of itself, a common source of anxiety. When someone is desperate with pressing needs, it is easy to turn to a Muslim friend for help. George Homans makes an observation which shows how the right performance of tradition is related to anxiety.

> When the primitive or peasant has done his practical work as well as he knows how and has fulfilled the 'religious and magical' which the tradition requires—he displays little overt anxiety. But he does feel anxiety if the ceremonies have not been properly performed.[11]

The result is that when the desired results are not obtained in the indigenous way, he may turn to other methods (Muslim). This, in turn, tends to undermine his confidence in the traditional prescriptions and, if the Muslim scheme produces good results, he will be favorably conditioned toward the new system. It is in this way that a great many conversions take place. This is certainly not the turning of the whole tribe or even a segment of the tribe to Islamic forms. It is usually the individual acting on his own. Skinner, in his study among the Mossi, showed that the desire to have children has been instrumental in leading many into at least a primitive practice of Islam.

> When a Nobere woman was found barren or her young children died . . . she was told that she should consult a 'marabout' or that her Muslim children (children who wished to become Muslims) had become angry and had died because they had been given pagan names . . . . She was advised to give a gift to a Muslim—any Muslim, outside his hut so that when the children 'returned' (were born again) they would see it.[12]

This sort of occurrence can be illustrated in a number of ways among traditional tribes in our study. A Mwaghavul man showed me "medicine" that was prepared especially for him in order to render him invisible to certain "devils" (*aljanu*) which an enemy had put upon him. A magic verse had been written by a Hausa *malam*. It was kept in a leather packet made by his own brother. *Aljanu* (*jinn*) are Islamic spirits, and therefore he felt that his tribal medicine could not protect

---

[11]George Homans, "Anxiety and Ritual: The Theories of Malinowski and Radcliffe Brown"; *Reader in Comparative Religion*, W. A. Lessa and E. Z. Vogt, editors (2nd ed., New York: Harper and Row, 1965), p. 127.

[12]Elliot P. Skinner, a paper delivered to the Fifth International African Seminar, "Islam in Mossi Society," *Islam in Tropical Africa*, pp. 360-61.

him. An Eggon man living at Lafia[13] told me that he was giving religious payment (*sadaka*) to a certain man by the name of Jibir, who lives in a village near Lafia. This was in order to keep "*aljanu* out of the east" from molesting his wife, who was a Muslim. Malam Jibir had warned the wife that the marriage would be handicapped by powers which the "pagan medicine" could not affect.[14]

The conflicts arising with respect to one's own dignity and social status cause much more tension than now.The younger as well as the older are looking for tangible ways to enhance their status and to be regarded as "respectable" people. The idea is widespread that to be attached to traditional religion is backwardness. A Kilba man reported that he had improved his social situation by becoming a Muslim. When we discuss the role of the chief, we shall see that association with the Islamic royal court is a definite improvement in social standing for some tribes.

Hausa terms which distinguish modern society from the traditional society are numerous. The more common are *wayewa* (seeing the light) and *zamani* (the modern age). Often these words are used in conversation when the question of Islamic benefits is being discussed. To be accused of *duhun kai* (darkness in the head) or *rashin wayewa* (lack of seeing the light) usually means stubbornness and ignorance.[15] At the Maguzawa village of Madaurare I met the chief's brother who, it was pointed out, "does *salla*." This means he is a practicing Muslim. This kind of break with the Maguzawa past is common, though the Muslim prayers are usually done in secret. Such secret prayers do not keep the person from participating in Maguzawa festivals. When I asked this man why he kept the Muslim prayers, his reply was, "Paganism is a shameful thing. No one wants to be accused of not recognizing or knowing God."[16] Furthermore, if he will do Muslim prayers at least two or three times a day, a *malam* will bury him when

---

[13]Since the threat was from Islamic spirits (*aljanu*), he would feel that his own traditional charms could not give protection.

[14]Ayok Shella, at Lafia, February 15, 1970.

[15]There are other terms of this kind, such as *jahilci*, "ignorance" (from Arabic *jahil*); *mutumin jiya*, "man of yesterday"--i.e., old fashioned; *bakauye*, "one from a little village"--i.e., a "country bumpkin."

[16]This was the brother of the village head of Madaurare, who does his prayers in the open, in contrast to Gelo, the village head who prays in secret. He also said that prayers and the fast are the main observances which he keeps. He does *sadaka* on special occasions.

he dies. Such a proper burial is looked upon by all as suitable for a progressive man.[17]

MAGICO-RELIGIOUS SOLUTIONS FOR PROBLEMS AFFECTING THE COMMUNITY

One of the most complex of phenomena is the interaction of religion with magic. Any kind of arbitrary separation of the two is almost impossible. Building on the evolutionary model, Frazer contended that magic was prior in time to religion, and, in contrast to religion, was dependent on man alone without any reference to a higher power. In fact, however, this is an unreliable guide.[18]

Any definition of magic will show that its distinction from religion is difficult. Howells says that magic "properly means all the formulas for doing things which are beyond one's personal power."[19] Peter Lloyd says even more simply that "magic is any non-scientific means to attain ends."[20] The Western mind, which wants to know the scientific reasons for phenomena, tends to feel uncomfortable with the idea of magic. The African who wants "something to happen" will use whatever means are available to him, not questioning the science involved.

A distinction between religion and magic is that the theological rituals centered in a priest (religion) differ from the methodology of the diviner who works in a self-sufficient way (magic). The diviner may refer his client to a traditional priest. Certain cases will fall between the parameters of the diviner and the priest, since there is an obvious overlap between magic and religion.[21]

---

[17]Yawai, the present chief of Bambur (Muri), turned to Islam because Muslims offered to give his only son a good burial, provided he were a Muslim.

[18]James B. Frazer, *The Golden Bough*, Pt. I, "Magic Art" (London: Macmillan and Co., 1920), pp. 234-37. Also the discussion by E. O. James, *Comparative Religion* (London: Methuen and Co., Ltd., 1961), p. 62.

[19]Howells, *The Heathens*, p. 46,47.

[20]Peter C. Lloyd, *Africa in Social Change* (Harmondsworth: Penguin Books, 1967), p. 77.

[21]The Mwaghavul diviner discovers that a woman has committed a theft, so he does not proceed with his diagnosis. Instead she is told by the practitioner exactly which religious priest she should see (Linus Bulus, Bukuru, March 2, 1970).

Contrary to what might be generally assumed, Peter Lloyd notes that magic and "anti-witchcraft" are an increasingly important part of city life. One would assume that there would be a higher level of sophistication in urban areas. What he calls "anti-witchcraft shrines" operate in the cities almost entirely within the context of traditional beliefs, especially where Christianity is strong. He suggests that such special practices are less common in the Islamic areas, because "the Muslim religion as taught and understood in West Africa is far more accommodating to traditional beliefs about witchcraft and magic."[22] Indeed, the participation of both animists and Muslims in traditional institutions of this kind is of the highest importance.

Animist Spirits vs. Muslim *Jinn*

Before illustrating the fusion of Islamic and traditional practices about evil spirits, something must be said with respect to the sources of evil. The German anthropologist Leo Frobenius called attention to two categories of spirit in his collection of religious legends of the Hausa.[23] The interesting fact is that they were collected among people whom he calls "pagan Hausa," who lived at Wukari and Ibi. This is important since what Frobenius calls "pagan Hausa" are, in fact, the modern Jukun-Muslims (*amgbakpariga*).[24] These Jukun who have a Hausa-Muslim background are very knowledgeable about their past, and I found them an exciting source for studying both traditional and Muslim practices.

It was somewhat disappointing that neither in Wukari or the highly Islamized town of Ibi could I find authentication for Frobenius'

---

[22]Lloyd, *Africa in Social Change*, p. 255.

[23]Leo Frobenius, *The Voice of Africa* (2 vols. London: Hutchinson & Co., 1913), pp. 537-39. Frobenius makes the point, ill founded, that *Bori* is a pre-Bagoda religion, as well as the observation that "The Hausas were forced to adapt themselves incontinently to the progressive advance of Mohammedanism because, living in unprotected towns on the level steppes, they could only stem the Islamite wave which tore across the waste by conforming to the new nature of things in their views of religion," p. 539. The stories follow through page 572.

[24]Frobenius received the account of Kundare the "alledjenu" from a pagan Hausa at Ibi, whom he called the "Abagua-Riga" (*amgbakpariga*). For information on this syncretistic group see Chapter Three, p. 88f.

legends.[25] The legends do read with an authentic use of the Hausa idiom, even though they have gone through at least two translations before the English.[26] The value of these stories is that they show a definite bifurcation of the spirit world owing to the difference between the Muslim and traditional structures. The tales are built around *Sarkin Aljanu* (King of the Jinn) and *Sarkin Bori* (King of the Bori spirits). These figures are the personifications of the Muslim *jinn* and the *iskoki* (traditional spirits). The stories show how two categories of spirit variously affect the land and its people. The two systems are in conflict, and the legends play on various themes of the tension and anxiety which arise in the community.[27]

In the story of Pati (traditional) and his friend Kundare (Muslim) a companionship develops which results in a sickness for Pati's child, appearing to be leprosy. This sickness broke out each Friday, Islam's holy day. When the rest of the people saw it, they said to Pati, "The thing thou hast brought into the land is not good. It is not good at all." To which Pati replied, "What shall I do? It is my friend Kundare. When my friend comes to me, I cannot prevent him."[28]

What we have here is a symbolic interaction between members of the spirit world. Practically all the tribes who have adopted Hausa religious terminology have developed also a syncretistic notion of the spirit world. Consequently, the distinction between *iskoki* and *aljanu* has been lost for the majority of the tribes. The basic question is whether harm or evil caused by indigenous spirits (*iskoki*) require the same ritual as the ills brought on by Muslim *jinn* (*aljanu*)? I have already mentioned that the Jukun-Muslims agree that these are different categories of spirit. Consequently, the Jukun-Muslim practitioners deal with problems associated with *aljanu*, exclusively. In asking the same questions some 450 miles from Wukari among the

---

[25]At Ibi I could not find anyone who was old enough to remember Frobenius' visit of 1920. As for the stories, the Hausa men gave accounts which were partially those of Frobenius, but most of the time they agreed to give assent to my own information without appearing to be knowledgeable themselves.

[26]That is, the English translation is such that one can fill it with appropriate Hausa idioms even in a casual reading.

[27]The temptation to attempt a hermeneutic of these stories was diminished by not finding authentication for the tales. This section on the Hausa and Islam (*Voice of Africa*) leaves the unmistakable feeling that Frobenius was a genius who made overdrawn generalizations.

[28]Frobenius, *Voice of Africa*, p. 555.

Maguzawa at Tsanyawa, the same distinction was made. It will be remembered that the Maguzawa are Hausa people who resisted Islam. The village head, Gelo, said that the Muslims do not have power over ills caused by *iskoki*, but these problems are always referred to the traditional diviners. Even more subtle is the added fact that the client himself would not know which category of spirit is troubling him; however, this is clearly left to the discernment of the practitioner, who would then treat only "their kind" (whether *aljanu* or *iskoki*).[29]

Integration of Methods

Keeping this phenomenon in mind, the easy movement between Islamic and traditional practitioners is understandable. The two systems borrow from one another when seeking solutions to problems. Anxiety, fear, and guilt affecting the traditional community can be counteracted by Muslim practices. At the same time, traditional methods of neutralizing trouble are often sought by Muslims. Areas of greatest trauma to both communities are adultery, theft, plagues of nature, madness, and witchcraft.

It is among the open or open-traditional tribes where Muslim and traditional practices are mixed. It is different with "active-resistant" groups. The Tiv, for example, have a very complex scheme for dealing with infractions and aberrations, but there is no suggestion of Islamic influence. The same can be said for the large Birom tribe and smaller tribes such as Taroh and Kutep.[30]

The Mshelia clan of the Bura who live at Subwong told me that their mosque (see page 71) has always been the place where God is called upon when there is a plague. There was a very long drought in 1946 in

---

[29]The Muslim chief of Tsanyawa would allow for no distinction between *iskoki* and *aljanu*. He said these were two words for the same thing. But the Maguzawa chief said, "*Iskoki* are our spirits but *aljanu* are theirs (Muslim)."

[30]The Taroh woman who commits adultery and becomes pregnant will look forward to death unless she confesses to elders who the guilty man is. Truth is forced in Kutep by *ikia*, which is a tree fruit tied round with grass; when brought into the house, sickness and death will result if truth is not told. The *ubangta*, a forked stick planted in the center of the house, will force an adulteress to tell the truth.

spite of all efforts to end it,[31] so the elders finally called for sacrifice at their ancient prayer center. A ram was killed on the sacred rock located at the entrance of the mosque, the meat was distributed ritually, and prayers were recited. This act represented the highest appeal possible to God for relief. There seems to be no question in anyone's mind that they are calling on Allah at such times.[32]

Until recently an interesting Jukun celebration was kept annually among the Wapan villages around Wukari. The rite is called *watan gani*. It is a month-long activity of the Jukun-Muslim (*amgbakpariga*). It is practiced as a memorial to their original founder-saints, Sambo and Dibo. One Jukun man pointed out that the celebration has become less important in the last generation, because, he said, "Vaccinations have removed the need for it." It turned out that one of the main purposes of *watan gani* was the containment of smallpox. The fear of smallpox kept the festival going for generations. Through this community celebration an appeal was made to the Muslim forebears each year to save the tribe. A few years ago no one was found who would accept responsibility for the event, and the prediction was that as a result the town would be covered with smallpox.[33] The epidemic did not occur, and the *gani* cult suffered.[34]

In both the Bura and Jukun cases just cited a contemporary formula for the entire tribe had its origin in forms which were originally Muslim, though the models had been corrupted. The quality of the model, however, is not a relevant matter, especially when changes are taking place.

The "open-traditional" tribes have the most marked integration for resolving trouble. Traditional Pabir in the past had a particular tree or a fabricated clay god which was a center for power. One or both were

---

[31]The "efforts" were those of the usual traditional pattern--i.e., water was brought in special containers from the river and given special rites in each house--a mixture of sympathetic magic and religion.

[32]Malam Diko Shafa, April 4, 1970.

[33]Bitrus Angyunwe, at Bukuru, March 16, 1970.

[34]The connection of the *gani* cult with smallpox is similar to the *obwai* of the Kagoro tribe. This was a short-lived secret society with dancing, initiation, flogging, and ritualistic fines. It was inaugurated after a locust plague and was supposed to inhibit locust damage after planting. See Harold Gunn, *Pagan Peoples of the Central Area of Northern Nigeria*, "Ethnographic Surveys of Africa" (London: International African Institute, 1956), Part XII, p. 102.

used. When a red rooster was brought for sacrifice to either the tree or the household god, it would ward off calamity and bring good fortune. An old man, Tashkalma, said, however, that this archaic practice died out so that a more powerful ritual could take its place which would include the whole tribe.

What Tashkalma referred to is located at the place where the first Muslim, founder of the Woviri dynasty, reportedly "sank into the ground."[35] This figure bears the name Yemta-ra Wala. His myth is long and involved. He is the ideal catalyst for Muslim and traditional ritual, since his loyalty to Pabir tradition seems unquestioned, and he was a Muslim.[36] His traditional house at Sokifwi has a thatched covering and is surrounded by trees. The spot is highly regarded as a power center for the tribe. Here, in time of drought or plague, or whatever the need, the spirit of Yemta-ra Wala is implored through the resident priest. The ritual includes the sacrifice of a goat while cotton is scattered in the sacred area.[37] Yemta's grave is no longer used as a shrine, because the Emir of Biu says, "It is not fitting for our religion (Islam) now." But this is still an important place, especially in the village areas. Recent moves to bring tribal Islam nearer to orthodoxy have not affected the majority of the Pabir who live away from the towns and who still hold the shrine as sacred.

The dualism of *iskoki* and *aljanu* is not clearly differentiated except in groups where there has been a special connection to the Hausa-Muslim history. Yet Africanization of the Arabic *jinn* seems to be widespread, conforming readily to traditional concepts.[38] Hence the dark powers in traditional society and the harbingers of fear and anxiety in Islam have caused a symbiotic relationship to develop between *iskoki* and *aljanu*. Archaic indigenous practices, while rejecting the dogma, readily accept the innovations which Islam offers in order to increase and diversify the means for negating trouble.[39]

---

[35]See Meek, *Tribal Studies*, I, 140,162.

[36]*Ibid.*, I, 140,157.

[37]*Ibid.*, I, 162.

[38]The fusion of indigenous spirits and Arabic *jinn* is a phenomenon which has been demonstrated in much older Songhai Islam. See Horace Miner, *The Primitive City of Timbuctoo* (revised edition, New York: Doubleday & Co., 1965), pp. 99-105; also J. C. Froelich, *Les Musulmans d'Afrique Noire* (Paris: Editions de l'Orante, 1962), p. 124.

[39]The examples have obviously not been taken from such tribes as e.g., the Tiv, Birom, or Longuda which circumspectly reject Islamic innovations.

Traditional Society and The Muslim Image

The Impact of Social and Economic Change

W. M. Watt's study, *Islam and the Integration of Society,* describes both the unifying and the disruptive factors of primitive Islam within traditional Arab society of Muhammed's time.[40] He shows that there are social and economic laws at work when a new religion is developing. It is within the context of these laws that the religion is shaped, and it is against these laws that religion reacts. The study of medieval Islam in its original setting is germane to a constantly changing, pluralistic tribal society, such as Nigeria. Here socio-economic factors attached to the past intermingle and cause varying responses to religious change.

The dominant force in the original Islamization of the Hausa was that a monolithic tribal society became internally weakened through a proliferation of clans. In this way a new kind of state developed under Islamized chiefs. Watt dramatized, however, that for all the diversity in Islam, it has nevertheless been able to achieve some measure of harmony and integration.[41] Religious history in north Nigeria, as in ancient Arabia, illustrates that where non-religious factors are in a state of flux, society becomes maladjusted, and a variety of new religious patterns can result. Our study reflects that these complex social, economic, and political factors have, to the present, greatly determined the extent of Islam's influence in traditional religion.

The *Jihad* and After

Historically, Islam benefited greatly from the prestige and power which resulted from the influence of Uthman dan Fodio and his son Muhammed Bello. This was especially true in the areas where the Fulani were given political authority. However, the effect of the

---

[40]W. M. Watt, *Islam and the Integration of Society* (London: Routledge and Kegan Paul, 1961).

[41]*Ibid.,* p. 1.

heightened power of the Fulani also had its negative consequences among the pagan tribes to the south. The *jihad* itself flourished because of an economic and social malaise. This aspect has been dealt with in a number of sources.[42] It was only after the success of Shehu Uthman dan Fodio that the religious and racial aspects of the *jihad* became clear. In summary, it must be pointed out that nearly all the flagbearers (generals) of the Shehu were Fulani, and even the pagan rulers who had supported him, such as Zamfara and Zazzau, were displaced by Fulani. In this way the Shehu used the economic and political disruption which had long prevailed in the Hausa states as a means to Fulani-Muslim domination. This rule by a Fulani minority, especially among pagan tribes, was a long-standing controversy and figured heavily in the shaping of contemporary religion as well as the formation of the modern states of Nigeria.[43]

The rapid development of the religious teachers (*malamai*) as a respected and influential class resulted directly from the success of the great *jihad* of 1802.[44] Shehu Uthman and his son Muhammed Bello provided scholars with the model they needed for the serious pursuit of Islam. There was a literary dispute between Bello and Al Kanemi of Borno on what constitutes true Islam. This signaled a new era of academic sophistication among the royalty. The interchange gave a dignity to the Muslim upper class and sparked a wave of enlightenment among the *malamai*. This affected hundreds of tribes ruled by Fulani emirs. The importance of this movement in raising the consciousness for education and progress is reflected in the controversial work of Edward Blyden. He is to be commended for noting this positive side of Fulani rule even though he had an overzealous admiration for the benevolence of Islam.[45]

---

[42]See among others, J. O. Hunwick, "The Nineteenth Century Jihads," *Africa in the Nineteenth and Twentieth Centuries*, J. C. Anene and G. N. Brown, eds., (Ibadan: University Press, 1966), pp. 291-307; *idem., A Thousand Years of West African History*, J. F. Ade Ajayi and Ian Espie, eds., (Ibadan: University Press, 1965), pp. 267-88; M. G. Smith, "The Jihad of Shehu dan Fodio: Some Problems," *Islam in Tropical Africa*, pp. 408-24; K. Madhu Panikkar, *The Serpent and the Crescent* (Bombay: Asia Publishing House, 1963), pp. 179-86.

[43]Panikkar, *Serpent and Crescent*, p. 184. This is a scholar who writes authoritatively but without documentation.

[44]*Ibid.*, pp. 186-90. Reference to *malamai* here is to the "learned class" rather than a much wider use of the term referring in a colloquial way to "teacher."

[45]Edward W. Blyden, *Christianity, Islam and the Negro Race* (African Heritage Books, Edinburgh: University Press, 1967), Vol. I.

The pagan village possessing a Muslim teacher is always found to be in advance of its neighbors in all the elements of civilization. The people pay great deference to him. He instructs their children and professes to be the medium between them and heaven. . . . The Mohammedan, then, who enters a pagan village with his books and papers and rosaries, his frequent ablutions and regularly recurring times of prayers and prostrations, in which he appears to be conversing with some invisible being, soon acquires a controlling influence over the people.[46]

This statement claims to describe the period between the *jihad* and the coming of Lugard into northern Nigeria. A negative side to Blyden's statement is that, "Where the Muslim is found . . . he looks upon himself as a separate and distinct being from his pagan neighbor, and immeasurably superior in intellectual and moral respects."[47] To put it even clearer Obarogie Ohonbamu says in his book, *The Psychology of the Nigerian Revolution*:

The educated northerners were given the impression that their Islamic culture was so superior that they never had the urge to ape or imitate the white administrators.[48]

In addition to the image of enlightened superiority created by Islam there is a second factor which greatly affected the Muslim image. This is an attitude of fear and resentment held for the Fulani among pagan tribes due to slave trade. As late as 1970 I found references to the slave raids of the nineteenth century carried out by the Fulani as a lingering issue among traditional people. For example, hundreds of hill people among the Wurkum were forced into slavery under Fulani nobles. Whole families among various pagan tribes of central Nigeria can recount their history as slaves to royalty during the early colonial period.[49] It is regrettable that so little reporting has been done on this dark side of Nigerian Islam after the *jihad*.

I recall evenings during my residence of thirteen years in Gongola State (Muri), when the old men recounted stories they had heard from

---

[46]*Ibid.,* p. 176.

[47]*Ibid.,* p. 175.

[48]Obarogie Ohonbamu, *The Psychology of the Nigerian Revolution* (Devon: Arthur H. Stockwell, 1968), p. 171.

[49]An entire family of Muslims lives in the Wurkum town of Zelani. They were Bornu slaves and until thirty years ago remained with their master's family at Ibi. An entire section of the Longuda tribal area is given to the *ka-komo*, returned slaves, who by their history are considered of impure stock. The writer also met slave families in Lau, Jalingo, and Yola, all of whom can trace their history and identify their original stock.

their grandfathers about slave raids. Until very recently many of the old people lived in the hills where they were born.[50] Colonial pacification of the Wurkum tribes (1910-20) included an order for them to resettle in the lowlands. The hills had always served as their refuge, not only from local tribal enemies but from the Fulani raiders as well.[51] Six of the tribes we visited in connection with this study made references to nineteenth century Fulani slavery when discussing the negative influence of Islam.[52]

Two early factors, therefore, which had direct bearing on the modern problem were the power and status of the enlightened class of Muslim teachers on the positive side and, negatively, the resentment generated against Fulani rule in general and, in particular, the slave trade.[53]

The Colonial Period

Sir Frederick Lugard embarked on the colonization of northern Nigeria in 1900, committed to the principle of indirect rule. The philosophy of indirect rule did not, however, correspond to what actually took place.[54] Lugard himself was an enigma of humanitarianism and imperialism. His earlier years had been spent in fighting the Arab slave trade in Nyasaland and Uganda. This, in fact, was one of the assignments which brought him to Nigeria.[55] The system of

---

[50]See pp. 154-57.

[51]The old men told how groups of Kulung would band together during the raids and roll large rocks down on the Fulani warriors. This would have taken place in approximately 1840-1880, as the men received it from their own fathers.

[52]Longuda, Mumuye, Bachema, Kilba, Yendang, and Jen; all located in the general region formerly known as Adamawa.

[53]This is considered as evidence which puts a question on the amazing statement of Blyden, whose writings cover the period to which we refer. "The introduction of Islam into Central and West Africa has been the most important, if not the sole, preservative against the desolations of the slave trade. Mohammedanism furnished a protection to the tribes who embraced it by effectually binding them together in one strong religious fraternity, and enabling them, by their united effort, to baffle the attempt of powerful Pagan slave hunters," p. 186. This statement does not cover those tribes which did not "embrace" Islam.

[54]See the article by A. E. Afigbo, "The Colonial Phase in British West Africa, (iii), A Reassessment of the Historiography of the Period," Ajayi, ed., *A Thousand Years*, pp. 419-30.

[55]W. E. F. Ward, "The Colonial Phase," "(i), Political Developments," *ibid.*, p. 391.

indirect rule, by which natural rulers and native administrations carried out policy, is well known. The concept was not original with Lugard, but he put it into large-scale operation in northern Nigeria. Its greatest contradiction lay in the fact that he agreed to the continued rule over hundreds of animistic tribes by Muslim emirs, whom he found in power when he arrived. These, admittedly, are the natural rulers of the far North, of Borno, Kano, Katsina, Sokoto, and Zazzau.

The network of Fulani emirates among the pagan tribes to the south, however, allowed for indigenous leaders to function only at the local level. The Fulani were alien rulers representing a very small minority whom the traditional people did not recognize or accept.[56] Lugard's indirect rule was administered by a non-indigenous hierarchy of Fulani emirs. This anomoly set up explosive situations which have had sharp repercussions in religion as well as politics.[57] A. E. Afigbo, in giving an assessment of this period, notes:

> The exponents of indirect rule seemed to have conceived of the culture of African people as a loose connection of practices and institutions from which they could withdraw those institutions and practices of which they did not approve, while retaining unimpaired those which they did approve.[58]

The upshot was that cultural and religious institutions, especially of the non-Muslim masses, were constantly at odds with the protected rights of the Fulani hierarchy. If indirect rule had really meant the governing of people through their own institutions and authorities, it would follow that an indigenous chieftancy or local council would actually be given the right to administer through local custom. But, paradoxically, the very practices which would have been congenial to order and justice were subverted.

This raised the critical issue between traditional religion and institutional Islam. Afigbo comments:

---

[56]*Ibid.*, p. 394.

[57]A graduate student of African politics is unable to see the tensions set up by the rule of the Fulani among central tribes. John E. Means in his Ph.D. dissertation says: "Islam is the welding force struggling against the dissolution of the tribal system . . . the Islamic ideal . . . is the ability of Islam in the face of widespread migration out of the tribe into larger units, to continue to influence the tribal man in all his daily actions and thoughts, to continue to engender in him the notion that he still belongs to a universal community." "A Study of the Influence of Islam in Northern Nigeria" (Government), an unpublished Ph.D. thesis (Washington, D. C.: Georgetown University, 1965), p. 88.

[58]Afigbo, "The Colonial Phase, (iii) A Reassessment," Ajayi, ed., *A Thousand Years*, p. 425.

One would have thought that the first step in preventing a society from losing its identity under colonial rule should have been the preservation of its own religious system. The fact is, that the British were forced by circumstances (lack of staff and desire for economy, poor communications) to adopt a particular system of government and later set up philosophical justifications for the policy.[59]

Traditional practice was in conflict with a Muslim ruling class which could advantageously propagate their religion through the system open to them. These non-religious factors have taken their toll on the Hausa image. Many tribes across central Nigeria paid their first taxes (a hated exercise) to Muslim-controlled native treasuries. Traditional law became Muslim customary law, and the judge (*qadi*) who administered it represented a new institution superimposed over customary practices.[60] In towns where indigenous people lived and where village people came to do their marketing the presence of mosques elicited mixed feelings of respect and resentment.

Colonization by Britain was the combined result of many economic, political, and humanitarian factors, not all clear or of equal importance.[61] This carried another major factor of Islamic influence, which was the opening up of the land for trade and industry. The movement of supplies and raw material brought people into contact with each other. Tribal members were breaking out of their traditional environment for the first time. This set in motion a new rhythm of social relationships, one of which was the exposure of previously isolated peoples to the charisma of the Muslim community.[62]

---

[59]*Ibid.*, p. 426.

[60]In the past "law" covered three spheres--"customary," "Islamic," and "native" or "traditional." Islamic law was subordinate to both customary law and native traditions. See J. S. Trimingham, *Islam in West Africa*, p. 147. It is the kind of synthesis that results in native law being called "Muhammedan law and custom" or "Muhammedan customary law," even "Muhammedan lawful custom"; of J. N. D. Anderson, *Islamic Law in Africa* (Colonial Research Publication, No. 16, London: Her Majesty's Stationary Office, 1954), p. 4.

[61]Afigbo, "The Colonial Phase," "(iii) A Reassessment," *A Thousand Years*, p. 421.

[62]Meek writing in 1925 affirms this as follows: "By the opening of communications pagans and Muslims are coming into constant contact . . . (the pagan) soon realizes the narrowness of his own religion compared to the universality of Islam . . . this belief in evil spirits is not affected by his outward change of faith. He finds too that the Muslims are tolerant and that they have better houses, better clothes, and a better knowledge of the world than he." C. K. Meek, *The Northern Tribes of Nigeria* (2 vols., Oxford: University Press, 1925) II, p. 8.

The Hausa have always been ubiquitous tradesmen. They had been known for their long-distance trading expeditions long before the colonial period.[63] The trans-desert routes were given up after the mechanization of colonialism. But during the colonial period and up to the present, the transporting of textiles, cattle, cotton, groundnuts and other commodities to southern Nigeria has been dominated by the Fulani-Hausa. The upper class of the Muslim traders has become wealthy, and they have used their wealth in a number of ways to distribute their influence.[64] Thus the image of the Hausa has been formed over a long period. In social and business contacts they

> . . . express their own values, drawn from kinship, religion and political organization which themselves reflect differing stages of Hausa culture, history, and differ in their forms, functions and sanctions.[65]

The opening up of the country inevitably brought the Hausa trader into the rural villages. This provided opportunities for "unenlightened" rural people to attach themselves to Hausa traders, bringing them ultimately into the cities. Hence, the Muslim influence on tribal areas was from the Hausa traders and artisans who serve the markets and take up residence in the villages as well as from the sedentary (royal) Fulani who rule.[66]

THE EFFECT OF THE MUSLIM IMAGE ON RELIGION

These factors have had considerable influence on traditional thinking and the response to Islam. Certain post-colonial factors further shaped the situation which led to the civil war of 1966-70. These affected the ability of Islam to unite northern factions especially

---

[63]Reference to M. G. Smith's comprehensive treatment "The Hausa-Markets in a Peasant Economy," *Markets in Africa*, P. Bohannan and G. Dalton, Eds. (Garden City, NY: Doubleday & Co., 1965), p. 155.

[64]The Hausa (or Islamized tribesmen) who have made the *haj* make up a fraternity who share wealth and control large sections of the economy in trade, marketing, wholesale of commodities, and building supplies. Now their influence is felt in ways not possible before the civil war, which put businesses of the north into the ownership of northerners.

[65]Smith, "Hausa-Markets," *Markets in Africa*, p. 178.

[66]The Fulani are of two kinds: the *sedentary Fulani* who live in the towns and from which comes the hierarchy of chiefs, and the *bororo* who are the migrant cattle Fulani, nominally Muslim, but basically an animistic people. On local Hausa markets see Smith, *ibid.*, p. 131.

following the war.[67]   Various acceptance and rejection levels to the Hausa image developed as a result of the colonial period. The result has been fixed attitudes which are shared almost universally by the tribes studied. The answers which different members of a tribe would give when asked about the Muslim image were surprisingly consistent. The tribes which we have classified as "open" were the least critical of Hausa-Fulani religious elements, and, accordingly, there is a much higher degree of conversion to Islam within these tribes. The more introverted a tribe is, the more the dependence on its own traditional patterns, the less tolerant it is of the Hausa presence and the less open it is to conversion.

Trimingham identifies three basic stages of Islamization. These are *preparation, acceptance,* and *assimilation.* He seems to assume that any group which shows signs of the first stage will *ipso facto*, in time, develop into an Islamic community. This, however, does not follow. It is important to note that time is not the only factor which determines the extent of influence which the Hausa community may have in a given tribe.[68] Much more basic are the compatibility elements, the relevance or irrelevance of the conceptual system of Islam to the traditional religion, and the negative or positive images which the Hausa and Fulani have as a people. Following is a summary of the reactions given to the question of the Hausa or Muslim presence from the different groups classified in Chapter Two.

The Active-resistant Group

The elders of the Gyel clan, one of the largest of the Birom people, gave an account of how the first Hausa immigrants arrived in what would appear to be the beginning of the colonial period. Ndung Gyel, the father of the chief, related the following:

> A few Hausa men came to the chief and asked him for a place to live. This was during the time when five cowrie shells were worth a half a penny. The chief asked them why they had left their own tribe. They replied that

---

[67]This is related to the period of the late Sardauna (up to 1966), which will be considered in Chapter Five.

[68]Refer to P. J. A. Rigby, "Sociological Factors in the Contact of the Gogo of Central Tanzania with Islam," *Islam in Tropical Africa*, I. M. Lewis, ed. (Oxford: International African Institute, 1966), p. 272.

they had been moving about and that their tribe could be found everywhere. The chief led them to a certain place where, he said, they could build their houses. But first the *sarkin tsafi* (traditional priest) performed a ritual of purification in the ground and it was declared that from time forward no Birom should live on this "foreign ground" or ever plant a farm on it.[69]

When asked about the present feeling which the Birom have toward the Hausas who live near them,[70] they answered that they are accepted basically for their *kasuwanci* (marketing) but this has never included their religion. I asked Davou Jok about the indigenous Birom who have joined the Hausa community. He said he was personally acquainted with only one, but this man, "has very few visitors to see him and no one ever discussed Birom gossip with him."[71]

The Tiv have always been anti-Muslim. This has meant a nearly total rejection of anything that is Hausa, including, most forcefully, the Hausa religion. This negative attitude toward Islam has been part of what it means to be a Tiv. The self-awareness of the Tiv is a dynamic that can scarcely be equaled in northern Nigeria. Here is but a sampling of the way in which the antipathy developed.

It was the colonial administrators who brought the Hausas. They came to buy and sell and many of them were employed to translate for the British who knew only Hausa. They were looked upon as different, mysterious and secretive. Their writing was strange as well as their habits, but most objectionable was their religion. The Tiv looked upon them as having no real tribe, but as transients—traders, lazy and selfish. All Tiv know that our economy depends on hard work.[72]

Another Tiv man related the following:

Anyone who does *salla* is considered a Hausa man—he is no longer accepted as a Tiv. Why then would anyone wish to do it (become Muslim)? We know that converts to Islam are lazy people who have travelled about and in this way have become attached to Hausas. The "convert" must be rejected for the same reasons that the Hausa man is rejected. They are exclusive. They won't mix. Our women wouldn't marry them.[73]

---

[69]Ndung Gyel, at Gyel (Bukuru), December 12, 1969.

[70]Only isolated families, except for the mining town of Bukuru, where they live with various other tribes.

[71]Davou Jok, at Gyel (Bukuru), December 12, 1969.

[72]Jonathan Ukpekeh, at Bukuru, March 17, 1970.

[73]Jacob Yaaya, at Bukuru, March 22, 1970.

63

Among the Longuda there is an interesting connection with the internal slave-trading days which accounts for negative feelings about Muslims.[74] During the nineteenth century many Longuda were taken as slaves to Borno. Attachment to Muslim masters over the years resulted in their adopting Islam. When they returned, however, they were not accepted back into the tribe but were given special areas where they could live, quite apart. They have retained a negative image up to the present. Their people, though Longuda, are referred to as *ka-komo*, which means, "you returned" (e.g., from slavery). Since their customs and religion had changed, they were regarded by the majority of the Longuda to be more Kanuri than Longuda. When asked about the Hausa influence, the kinds of answers which the Longuda gave were:

I am not a slave that I should do the *salat*.
I don't want circumcision.
He (the Hausa man) is lazy; all he does is wander around on the road.[75]

One person said that even the young people say it is better to follow pagan rites than to do the Muslim prayers. In most societies only the older people would respond in such a conservative way.

The Open-traditional Group

As expected, the open-traditional groups are much more conciliatory to Islam and have allowed a noticeable penetration of the Hausa-Fulani into their villages. Correspondingly, more of the indigenous people have become Muslims. The Bachema invited the Hausa to live with them, provided they would fight on their side in tribal war. Muslims, they discovered, had effective "medicine" for war which would ensure victory. Especially valuable were the military charms which could make a man invisible while fighting. Many Bachema who claim to be Muslims, nevertheless, attend the Bachema festival of *Nzeanzo*.[76]

---

[74]David Windibiziri, at Bukuru, March 13, 1970.

[75]Villages around Guyok, June 10-12, 1970.

[76]The complex Bachema festivals in honor of the god *Nzeanzo*, have been covered by Meek (*Tribal Studies*, I, pp. 30-42) and reference Chapter One, p. 17 and footnote 75.

Rather than a negative Hausa image, in some tribes the opposite is true. The Mwaghavul (Sura) and the Kilba reported a positive side to the Fulani. The Kilba have an expression, "clean like a Fulani." While both the Kutep and Tiv men spoke disdainfully of the Muslim habit of washing their privates before prayer, this did not offend the Kilba. The way the Fulani prepare their food, carefully protect their clothes, and wash between their toes was admired by the Kilba.

Intermarriage with Fulani is not uncommon, and one of the Kilba men claimed that his whole family has contracted Fulani marriages.[77] The villages have been influenced by this openness to the extent that their leather workers copied the phylacteries (*laya*) of the Fulani, believing them to be more powerful than their native charms (*pelma*) which now they have put aside. The Mwaghavul accept even a nearest of kin who decides to practice Islam, without a break in family relationships. Among the Kulung, even though very few practice Islam in Bambur town, those who decide to "do *salat*" are not ostracized. The Eggon have felt a very strong Muslim influence coming from political developments of the past two decades, which they have not resisted. When asked why many of the traditional Eggon practices have almost fallen into disuse, they most commonly answered "*ikon kasa*" (the authority of the land). This refers to the Muslim-biased colonial administration and a brand of politics after independence which pressed the Muslim influence right down to the village level.[78]

The Open Group

Coming to the open tribes, much, if not all, of the rejection of the Hausa-Fulani and their religion has disappeared.[79] Nadel has covered in an illuminating way how social, political, and mythological factors were accommodated almost immediately as Islam developed among the Nupe.[80] Islamic practices had parallels with Nupe religion at

---

[77]Fatana Mubi, January 15, 1970.

[78]The subject to be taken up in Chapter Five.

[79]Nadel, for instance, shows that even though the Muslim factor was originally a military one, the shape of the religion was such and the sociological factors were such that to say opposition existed would be hardly accurate. *Nupe Religion*, pp. 232-58.

[80]*Ibid.*, pp. 232-36.

embrace the alien faith was, primarily, the prestige which the adherent gained through associating with the ruling class. As Nadel explains, it was not "spiritual preparation" which caused the change. Rather, "conversion to Islam offered safety from slavery and, secondarily, the patronage of mobility which peasants and craftsmen would seek for economic reasons, as well as to secure legal protection."[81]

When taking a walk about 6:30 p.m. through the Bura town of Shafa, I found clusters of Muslims gathered in groups at various places, singing and praying. They all wore the long white Hausa-type dress. The singing was enchanting, the gathering place dimly lit by kerosene lamps. I asked the guide about the exercise. He said,

> These are the Bura who first followed the traders into the Hausa towns of the North after the Europeans opened up the roads. This is why these people are Muslims. They were told by the Hausa where they would stay from night to night, that they would have to sleep and eat by themselves if they remained unenlightened pagans. The Bura pagan felt his great shame and was told that he didn't know God. After they became Muslims they were allowed to put their fingers in the same dish as their masters. Then they learned to pray.[82]

I asked him if some of these might be Hausas or Fulanis who were living in the town, but he assured me that they were all native-born Bura.[83]

It is apparent, therefore, that two major historical streams have converged. Both pre-colonial and colonial history have met in an ever twisting and unpredictable pattern of response as the tribes respond in ways which are unique to their own makeup.

VARIETIES OF INTEGRATION BETWEEN TWO SYSTEMS

Finally, we will observe how the cultural phenomena of both systems have mutually influenced ritual and myth. It is in the intimate expression of ritual that both form and content are revealed. The

---

[81]*Ibid.*, p. 235.

[82]Malam Diko, at Shafa, April 4, 1970.

[83]*Idem.*

extent to which the rituals change in the course of interaction with Islam is connected to the purpose of the rituals. These purposes change little when the community is able to resolve its needs from within the traditional myth and ritual. But once the traditional ritual has weakened, elements from Islam will be borrowed, and modifications of traditional religion will be the result.

The *Kano Chronicle* provides extremely valuable data about how religious change takes place once the traditional center has been weakened. At a very critical point the archaic ritual shrine located at Jakara was destroyed and a mosque was erected in its place.[84] In the conflict which followed, the more peripheral features of the new religion (Islam) were accommodated while the strong center of the traditional cultus was retained.

A more complete transition to the new religion came only after sociological changes became irreversible. The primary religion was then expressed through a new ritual pattern which reflects altered Islamic forms as much as it does the altered indigenous forms. Change follows this reciprocal way, and a sort of religious enculturation results. Islam is disfigured as it adapts to the local religion.

One might ask, When is a corrupt form of Islam, distorted as it often is by traditional forces, no longer Islam?[85] Or conversely, at what point in a series of changes effected by Islam can it be said that "pagan" society has become Islamic? The extent and type of Islamic influence on traditional religion falls into three categories: (1) traditional practice which continues alongside a non-integrated Islam, (2) traditional practice which becomes merged with a folk Islam, and (3) visible Islam which is overlaid on a traditional base.

---

[84]In the reign of Mohamma Rimfa, when Abdu Rahaman brought soil from Medina to Kano (1463); see *K.C.*, *ibid.*, p. 77.

[85]The distinction between the two converging systems is academic in most cases. There is a bias to Islam, regardless of how filled it is with traditional rituals, because of the universal norms (e.g., prayer, circumcision, and fasting). The pagan practices of the Muslim community are overdrawn and generalized upon by Meek, e.g., "The Koran is their fetish no less than the village idol, stone or tree, etc." *Northern Tribes of Nigeria*, p. 3.

TRADITIONAL PRACTICE ALONGSIDE
NON-INTEGRATED ISLAM

Where the cultus of the tribe has been retained in the interaction with Islam, it is because traditional religious features are more vital for the tribe than that which Islam offers. Among some groups the fixed rituals are intact to a remarkable degree today in spite of the eroding influence of secularization and education. This does not mean that these tribes have not undergone change, but that these changes have not been in the direction of Muslim practice.

Around 1976 officials of Benue State required the Jukun to modernize their traditional ideas of divine king. The royal rituals of the *Aku*, their king, symbolically regulate the lives of Jukun people. The king embodies totality, and the rituals symbolize the whole life of the tribe.[86] Therefore, any change in his status and role alters the religious life. The Jukun are a very special case.[87] They represent a major society where the traditional practice is aware of Islam—where Muslims, both Hausa and Jukun-born, live alongside of Jukun life. The Muslims are taken for granted by the Jukun as a part of their historical culture, but the integration is negligible.

The Birom readily accept that their *mandyeng* and *bwana* rites of sowing and harvest are practiced mainly by those closest to the traditional priest himself, although the intensity of practice varied from clan to clan. The Birom offer many reasons for the decline of fertility rituals. These include the coming of Christianity, education, and modern agricultural methods. Meanwhile, Muslim prayers and the fast are being observed everywhere around them, as they have been for years, and have no connection whatever with Birom religion. One Arabic school was started among the Birom during political pressures of 1964-67. It is located in one clan which was especially responsive to the religious pressures of that period.[88] But the school is located some

---

[86]The Jukun say, "The king stretches out his feet and all *tsafi* (traditional ritual) rests upon it."

[87]The phenomenon of the traditional *amgbakpariga* and recent converts to Hausa Islam will be taken up in the following chapter.

[88]A number of village heads became Muslims during the years of Ahmadu Bello's politics. Among the Plateau tribes numerous key people came to the side of the premier (see Chapter Five). Six Birom chiefs began Muslim practices, but only two have remained Muslim to the present. Of the others, one died, one became a Christian, and two are following *al'adun Birom* (the Birom customs).

68

six miles from the center of Bukuru town, and in 1970 had only a few students. The location and size of the Zawan effort shows how non-integrated Islam is among the Birom.

The Rukuba, a small tribe, and the Mumuye (numbering 250,000) still have active hunting rites and observe the rites of passage, especially initiation. But little deference is given to Islam, even though the Mumuye around Zing have a strong Muslim administration that was put in place by the British. In 1966 the tribe's highest festival, which is held in connection with the harvesting of yams, came in the month of Ramadan. The two sacred customs have nothing in common, and their simultaneous observance demonstrated the incompatibility between Mumuye religion and Islam.

Mention must be made here of the Hausa language, since it is the trade language used almost universally. The linguistic influence is perhaps one of the most subtle. Hausa has a very substantial Arabic source. It has been assimilated by the traditional tribes and used freely to express vernacular concepts. J. H. Greenberg notes that of the Arabic loan words in the Hausa language, by far the greatest number are from the category of religion (some 180).[89] Many of those which he lists are erudite Hausa expressions which would likely not appear in the speech of animistic people using Hausa as a second language. Further, the Arabic terms which are commonly used show that the Qur'anic or Sunni concepts are rarely taken over. These expressions are, rather, adopted back into the culture and given a local coloration.[90]

TRADITIONAL PRACTICES MERGE
WITH A FOLK ISLAM

Nadel in his assessment of Nupe Islam, and Baxter, who reports on the Islamic factor among the Boran, both have reservations about the shape of the Islamic models which the traditional society first

---

[89]Joseph H. Greenberg, "Arabic Loan-words in Hausa," *Word*, 1947, pp. 85-97, see *Religion*, 9.94.

[90]For example, *addini*, Ar. *din*, religion; *imani*, Ar. *iman*, faith; *zunubi*, Ar. *sanb*, sin; *annabi*, Ar. *nabi*, prophet; *salla*, Ar. *salat*, prayer; *sujada*, Ar. *sujud*, prayer, to mention some of the more common.

confronted. When one cannot know the precise form of the new religion that first reached a particular community, it becomes difficult to describe the direction which the confrontation took. As Nadel says, the extent to which a ritual system reflects the reaction of the primary forms toward the new creed, or merely their "faithful acceptance of a new creed loosely and confusedly taught is difficult to say."[91] Baxter takes the position that it is not possible to view Islam as a normative or coherent system, nor can one take the Somali ritual "as a whole, but the varying *elements*, conditioned and subsequently changed again." Both the traditional side and the Islamic side "give the impression that, in general, Islam has been re-interpreted in the form of a number of Somali culture traits."[92]

Folk Islam emphasizes the altered forms of Islam which traditional society develops for the benefit of the society. It is found most commonly where a weak and poorly structured Islam has existed alongside a highly ethnocentric community. What Watt has to say about the influence of Arabic animism on the formation of Islam is relevant here. Muhammed, at first, did not see that his religion was incompatible with the pagan shrines. The decisions as to which pagan practices could not be allowed in the new monotheism were made over a long period.[93]

> As animism had provided most of the existing cultic mores, it is more prominent in the form of the Islamic cult. Animistic symbols and practices could easily be taken over and given an Islamic interpretation—because they were already "superstition"—something left over rather than elements in a living religion. The most important example of this is the acceptance of the Ka'aba or sanctuary of Mecca as a shrine of God.[94]

The influences acting back and forth between Islam and traditional religion result in imperfect models of Islam, similar to early Islam in Arabia. The same kind of assimilation and change take place in traditional structure. The difference between the situations in this study and in Muhammed's time is that Islam had already been altered

---

[91]Nadel, *Nupe Religion*, p. 244.

[92]P. T. W. Baxter, a paper presented to the Fifth International African Seminar, "Acceptance and Rejection of Islam among the Boran of the Northern Frontier District of Kenya," *Islam in Tropical Africa*, p. 248.

[93]Watt, *Islam and Society*, p. 188.

[94]*Ibid.*, p. 187.

by the time it reached West Africa. Islam was not being formed, so to speak, but had taken on African features along with its history.

The unusual ritual practices by the Mshelia families at Subwong village illustrate in a remarkable way how Islam is taken over by indigenous ritual and made to serve the traditional myth. The history is well known by local people.[95] The original Damatapa tribesmen received a Fulani stranger, Afyama, who had left his home near Song after being disinherited by his father. Afyama brought with him a branch from his own Muslim compound and planted it on the Subwong hill. There he practiced his prayers and circumcised his children. He kept the fast faithfully without any other Muslims present or a teacher of any kind. The indigenous people ridiculed his ritual and totally rejected his personal habits. His sons traveled to Song to get themselves Muslim wives and brought them back to Subwong hill. After three or four generations, however, the extended family of Afyama agreed to stop doing the *salat* in order to conform to the Mshelia religion. This shows how dysfunctional the Muslim practice had become, since the *salat* would be the last element in Islam to be surrendered. The indigenous people despised circumcision, but the Fulani stubbornly retained this as a sign of their cult.

In referring to Subwong earlier, it was pointed out that the need for wives for the Fulani descendants motivated them to give up the *salat*. Intermarriage then created a new pattern. The central observance of the new religion was a perversion of the Ramadan. Through the new ritual, cyclic rites of the tribe were carried out. Circumcision was never adopted but the traditional mosque of Afyama is still the Sacred Place. This is the place of highest appeal to God on behalf of the tribe. A folk *Id il Fitr* was carefully described by the villagers. It is performed inside Afyama's mosque, which is a ring of trees that were planted from the original tree he brought.[96] It is a mixture of Muslim

---

[95]The account from personal visit made to Subwong on April 4 and 5, 1970.

[96]In summary, the people gathered outside the ring of trees marking off the mosque. Three elders (*limami*) officiated inside. They "read" verses from the Qur'an (by memory passed on from three generations); the people all responded with "*amin*" at various intervals. A sheep or goat is killed at the "sacrificing rock," the blood drained, and the animal is cut into pieces; the pieces of meat are thrown to the congregation as a *sadaka*.

and pagan elements, so fused that to isolate them or to observe them independently is impossible.[97]

How widespread these indigenous forms of Islam are would be hard to say, but evidence of this kind of synthesis appears in other places. As noted previously, the *watan gani* was a communal celebration of the Jukun and was inaugurated by the Jukun-born Hausas as a memorial to their Muslim fathers, Sambo and Dibo. The celebration of *watan gani* is of a month's duration, as is Ramadan. It elevated the figures of Sambo and Dibo to the position of great ancestors, having a function close to that of patron saints (*wali*). The *watan gani* practice was so widespread that when "true" Muslims arrived at Wukari at the beginning of the colonial period, they condemned it as pagan and began to instruct the *amgbakpariga*. However, the practice was so advanced as an indigenous form that the influence of the Kano Muslims caused the *amgbakpariga* to break up into three groups. One group remained as they were, and a second group "converted" to "true Islam," while a third opted for pure Jukun practices, leaving all Muslim forms.[98]

VISIBLE ISLAM OVERLAYS A TRADITIONAL BASE

A third pattern in the modification of ritual moves us closer to what might be described as an "Islamized" society. The society may *appear* to be Muslim, but on closer observation the cultus is clearly non-Muslim and the rhythm of the festivals and rites is indigenous African religion. There is, however, such a harmonious utilization of the major Muslim rites that a *symbiose animisme-Islam* , of which Monteil speaks, can be said to exist.[99] The two religions have had an association over a long period, and the traditional peoples have

---

[97]As recently as 1940-45 an effort was made to show the natives of Subwong that theirs was the earliest form of Islam in Buraland. Consequently, a *liman* was appointed and orthodox instruction begun. But the pattern was so foreign to Islam that the "purification" process did not materialize. The true Muslims live in Shafa town, three miles away.

[98]From an interview with a leading *amgbakpariga*, Ibrahim Usuman, at Wukari, April 18, 1970.

[99]V. Monteil, *L'Islam Noire* (Paris: Editions du Seuil, 1964), p. 43 with reference to the Dyola from L. V. Thomas, *Les Diola* (Dakar: Afrique-Documents, 1960), pp. 486-508.

allowed the Muslim community to develop quite freely with an acceptance of their Islam as a whole.

The Maguzawa show that certain institutions of Islam are accepted as a regular part of life while others are practiced only sporadically. The wedding which I observed provided the opportunity to discuss rites of passage with the Maguzawa elders. The marriage ceremony had been performed by the local *liman*. He said his position was a hereditary one, going back six generations. As a *liman*, he did not live with the Maguzawa, but came and went from their compound from nearby Tsanyawa, when his services were required. The *liman* attended the Maguzawa festivals on the day following the marriage ritual. When asked if he condoned the heavy beer drinking and other pagan festivities, he replied that he had only come to watch and that he was used to seeing such things. Neither the bride nor the groom attended the wedding ceremony, only the parents. However, the marriage ritual was no different than for any Hausa Muslim.[100]

There are, correspondingly, naming ceremonies for infants which the Maguzawa seem to practice uniformly. The circumcision rite was described in detail. It is practiced on boys between the ages of six and eight, and the practitioner must always be the Muslim barber. At Madaurare there was some contradiction as to whether a Muslim burial is expected of all Maguzawa or of those who were known to be Muslim. The first report said, "The Muslims have a right to name our children and perform our marriages, but when it comes to burial, this is done without the *liman*, for a man is what he is when he goes out of life."[101]   However, the village head, himself a convert, said that Muslim burial rites are practiced by all. He said that this was an innovation which was introduced during the period of the late Ahmadu Bello, Sardauna of Sokoto (d. 1966). If, indeed, the burial is done under Muslim patronage, all the major rites of passage have been covered. Thus, the Maguzawa give the appearance of being an Islamized society. It is, however, a veneer which seems to guarantee the security of Islam while the strong traditional center still governs

---

[100]After the witnesses gather (approximately 7:30 p.m.) the bride price is announced by the family head. The *liman* then recites selected portions from the Qur'an concluded by the *Fatiha*. Following this, all do *shafawa*, which is a movement of the open palms on the face, downward from the forehead. All participate in the *shafawa* even though they may not be Muslim. Concluding the ritual is the declaration of marriage.

[101]A brother of Gelo who was unnamed.

73

their life. During the three days which I spent there, I did not detect that anyone was praying in the Muslim fashion. Maguzawa have no part in the Ramadan, though a number of the village men have been known to spend the month of the fast in Kano. One confessed that it is impossible to fast when the women are constantly preparing food.

Some of the observations which Horace Miner made with respect to the Songhai would be true among the Pabir.[102]   As with the Songhai, there is a strong loyalty to Pabir tradition and there is continued traditional religious practice. In Biu and other smaller towns, the Hausa dress, the prayer beads, and prayer circles were all very evident. The regularity with which the Muslim rituals are adhered to varies greatly with the individual and his place in the society. The *salat* is widely practiced. The more specific Muslim mores such as preferential marriage, Muslim life style, medicines, and personal habits are options which are open to all. But it is only the few who became totally involved by regular prayer at the mosque and by studying the Qur'an. The society finds its unity in being traditionally Pabir. The royal elite and their clientele have become quite orthodox through the *malamai* who are attached to the king's court. But the influence of Islam on the rest of society has been that of an overlay.

A further kind of relationship could be summarized as a society which quite universally conforms to the Muslim ritual but still has the traditional core as its center. By all standards the Nupe seem to be the most regularized as an Islamic society. When Nadel states, however, that "integration is complete only when it bears the ethos of Nupe religion," he is referring to dominant rituals which are of indigenous origin.[103]   One such is the *navu*, a "pagan" ceremonial which has a possible parallel to the Muslim *Muharram* but bears specifically Nupe features. It is, in fact, a pre-Islamic festival which has been reintroduced into the new religion. While the *navu* is practiced by all as a symbol of Nupe unity, it has little or no Muslim character. The *salat* is observed by the masses but without understanding the meaning of the Arabic words. Even the Friday services have the imprint of Nupe life. There are Nupe prayers which are said in addition to the prescribed Arabic ones. They are spoken in Nupe and reveal the dynamic of the indigenous core and a surprising reference to Nupe

[102]Miner, *Timbuctoo*, p. 78.

[103]Nadel, *Nupe Religion*, pp. 257-58.

cosmology, which has never been lost. These prayers are spontaneous, and as Nadel observes, they "show the familiar looseness and variability of phrasing which no orthodox Muslim prayer permits. Above all they invoke *Soko*, not Allah, and thus wholly recapture the content and style of the pagan invocations."[104]

[104]*Ibid.*, pp. 238-39. "Prayer at Harvest": from Lemu town, "The harvest is cleared: Soko protect us from fire; Soko protect us from smallpox; Soko protect us from the heat that dries up everything."

"Prayer at the Beginning of Rains": from Bida town. "Soko may he give rain in plenty. May he give food that thrives beautifully; Soko send us rain which falls down upon man. And the man who is in a canoe on the water, and the water in the bush, protect them also for all of us."

CHAPTER THREE

CHANGING SOCIETY AND
RELIGIOUS DECISION

CHAPTER THREE

CHANGING SOCIETY AND
RELIGIOUS DECISION

For the African, the tribe is the matrix in which his religion takes shape. It is in group life that the meaning of myth is communicated, and it is in community that a person's sacramental relation to nature is experienced. Any change in society will directly affect the individual. The individual becomes disoriented when separated from his environment and will have to struggle for adjustment.

The history of Islam in Kano shows that the alien religion capitalized on a serious fragmentation of tribal institutions which was already underway. Erosion of the social structure did not mean, however, that the new way was taken over systematically. On the contrary, the tribe continued to hold tenaciously to the old symbols of its life. When these symbols were challenged by the new system, recombinations of old and new forms appeared which reorganized the tribe. Tensions leading to disunity began as clan heads and vocational guilds formed new groupings. Within three or four generations this process resulted in a pluralistic society. It was in this milieu that Kano Islam was shaped.

The *jihad* of 1801 changed the situation. The traditional strength which was centered in the tribe had already dissipated, and the time was ripe for a strong leader.[1] The *jihad* established the massive northern areas of Nigeria as an African Muslim society, with Sokoto as its center. When, therefore, we think of Islam today, it is important to remember that influence was from the Hausa-Fulani North upon the animistic peoples living in the central region. The same can be said

---

[1]Cf. Watt, *Islam and Society,* who in his discussion of competitive Arab and Jewish groups at Medina speaks about a situation which "tends towards the acceptance of a strong leader (Muhammed)," p. 17.

with respect to the ancient Kanem-Borno Islam. The Borno area, with Maiduguri at its center, is a proud Islamic society. The Bornuese kingdoms were famous before the formation of the Hausa states.[2] Islamic influence, therefore, refers primarily to the impact of Hausa-Fulani Islam on the peoples of Plateau, Niger, and Kwara states and of Kanuri-Borno Islam on the tribes of Bauchi, Gongola, and Borno states.

This Islamic North has undergone changes as well. There have been adjustments of Tijaniyya and Qadariyya Islam to secularization, political upheaval, and formal education.[3] Great numbers of non-Muslims who have lived among the Muslims in the northern states (Ibo, Yoruba, and other non-Muslim peoples) have had little effect on the Islamic pattern.[4]

In this chapter we are concerned with tribes in the so-called pagan areas of the middle North, where pressures are similar, in a modern context, to the pre-*jihad* confrontation in the Hausa states. The form of Islam which interacted with the traditional groups in recent history is ideologically and politically the Islam of the Sokoto caliphate with its widely distributed network of emirates. In evaluating the impact which Islam has made on the tribes in their religious context, significant questions arise: Has tribal religion been making a satisfactory adjustment to secularization, and, if not, does Islam offer a practical alternative? Are the united factors of tribalism still strong, and if so, does Islam support or break down this will to unity? Does Islam build a community which can fill the vacuum created by the forces of de-tribalization?

---

[2]The Borno antecedent for the history of Islam in the Hausa states is contained in the Bayajidda legend. See also H. R. Palmer, *Sudanese Memoirs*, Vol. II, p. 13. For a history of the conflict between the Sau and the Berbers (Beri-beri) during the Sefawa dynasty (all antecedent to Hausa Islam) see S. J. Hogben and A. H. M. Kirk-Greene, *The Emirates*, pp. 307-12.

[3]In recent years the Tijaniyya have become an elite brotherhood, especially of the younger and more progressive Muslims. This has had its effect on the traditional Qadariyya ruling class. A number of the emirs have joined the Tijani order. Where emirs have wanted identification with the "new elite" this change has been advantageous. Cf. Trimingham, *Islam in West Africa*, p. 92.

[4]For this reason the attention of our study is not on the fairly consolidated tribes of the Hausa and Borno regions where the non-Muslim element is relatively insignificant.

The word "tribalism" is associated with a variety of meanings so needs to be defined carefully. We do not mean a pejorative use of the term so prevalent in journalism and politics, though some of these overtones cannot be avoided. Lloyd's political description of tribalism is fair. He says tribalism is: "Loyalty to one ethnic group which parallels or transcends loyalty to the new state."[5] The term "ethnicity," as understood by sociologists, carries the force of what is meant. A term which translates best as "tribe" occurs in all of the languages of the groups studied. While it carries some objectionable association for some sociologists and anthropologists today, Africans, generally, still use the word with a great deal of conviction.

Dr. Obarogie, in writing on the Nigerian Civil War, sees the "tribalists" only in large language blocks (Ibo, Yoruba, Hausa, etc.). He refers to the entire North as a Hausa-Fulani region and in doing so commits the same error of most Westerners who fail to see the pluralism of peoples in the North.[6] The many language groups (over 200) are improperly referred to as "Hausa" only because they speak the Hausa language. They are distinctly different from each other. It is this blind spot which has detracted from the value of the studies done by scholars who come to Nigeria just for a short time. John Means, for example, erroneously assumes that all of northern Nigerian can be studied from Kano City. Kano, he said,

> . . . is a place where one can observe without too many complications and difficulty the magnitude of Islam's penetration in depth. There one finds varying degrees of Islamic influence among the inhabitants.[7]

It is precisely the complications and difficulty one meets in pluralistic tribal society which give the true picture of the influence Islam is having.

One value of tribalism is its integrative quality. It provides a solid center of reference for individuals who by nature must have a

---

[5] Lloyd, *Africa in Social Change*, p. 289.

[6] Obarogie Ohonbamu, *The Psychology of the Nigerian Revolution* (Devon: Arthur H. Stockwell, 1968), pp. 114-34.

[7] John E. Means, "A Study of the Influence of Islam in Northern Nigeria." Unpublished Ph.D. dissertation, Georgetown University, 1965, Chapter iii, p. 138.

community. Yet tribalism has been described by a national leader as the "bane of Nigeria."[8] The statement was made by Chief H. O. Davies in the *Sunday Express* before the Nigerian Civil War. In light of the devastation of the Civil War, what he said seems almost prophetic.

> Tribalism is to make a fetish of one's own tribe and to support the members of that tribe at all times whether they are right or wrong. It follows that the tribalist is the fellow who sees nothing but good only in his tribe's people, who supports, defends and encourages his tribesman even if palpably wrong, who joins in a fight for no other reason than that someone is fighting a member of his tribe; who as a Minister, Board Chairman or Manager, awards jobs, contracts or scholarships on the basis of tribal origin and not on merit, efficiency or entitlement. Such a one is the Tribalist.[9]

While this statement was made in the context of a civil government which was less than two years from collapse, still, description of tribe as the force which dominates all aspects of life is well taken. In Chapter One we observed that traditional religion caters to the whole tribe. Islam, by contrast, is supra-tribal, providing an option for disoriented tribal members and creating a new religious identity which is often more meaningful than the tribe of birth.

RELIGIOUS RITUAL AND SOCIAL UNITY

Tribalism can be disruptive when a country is working for national unity. At the same time, the symbols of the tribe hold the community together and give meaning to its life. This is the dilemma of pluralistic tribal culture. The most important values of the society must be maintained if there is to be unity; yet these values are highly ethnocentric and tend to polarize tribal groups. This polarization, in turn, conflicts with national unity. The situation which developed in Nigeria just after the Civil War reinforced the fact that "tribalism still reigns supreme."[10] Nevertheless, modern forces which drive people from the tribal-centered life into a more pluralistic society are many. These, in time, can be harmonized into a true federation. Unity of this

---

[8]Chief H. O. Davies in the *Lagos Sunday Express*, March 21, 1965.

[9]*Ibid.*

[10]From an article by Effiong Etuk in the *New Nigerian*, June 6, 1969, p. 5. "Tribalism still reigns supreme in Nigerian society and every effort, it appears, is being geared towards a negation of the very concept of righting the ills of the past that plunged the nation ino its present predicament."

kind is, however, a slow process, since ethnic loyalties are more powerful than national loyalties.

Following the Civil War (1970) there were those who argued for a military government to continue indefinitely. Those who were for military rule talked frequently about the ethnocentric makeup of the many Nigerian tribes and religions. This highlighted the problem that tribalism raises for civil government. The issue at hand is that particular groups want to maintain their own identity above that of the state. Ade Adenusi had this point in mind when his article appeared in a northern newspaper:

> I should like to make it abundantly clear that my opting for continued military rule after the war does not in any way emanate from a loss of confidence in our civilian rulers. Rather it is from my deeprooted conviction that Africa . . . is not ripe for practice of democracy which some people look upon as an ideal political system.[11]

We have emphasized from the beginning that the involute nature of tribal life lies at the bottom when there is tension in religious change. Where ethnocentrism is less marked, there is more openness towards new religious forms. Where there is a high degree of cultic activity, exclusiveness and resistance to change prevail. It was said that in the ancient city-state a stranger was one who did not belong to the religion of the city; he was likewise one who had no access to the rituals or protection from the gods.[12]

TRADITIONAL CULTUS AS AN ORGANIZING CENTER

When the word *unity* is used to describe a society, it does not mean that there is complete agreement on all features, nor is there participation by everyone to the same degree. But unity does signify a high level of agreement among the major segments of the society touching its most important values and aspirations. The ability of symbols and myths to survive in a modern African society depends upon how closely they uphold the highest values of the society and

---

[11]M. Ade Adenusi, "Do We Need a Civilian Regime After the War?" *New Nigerian*, June 6, 1969.

[12]Refer to Fusel de Coulanges, "The Ancient City." *Reader in Comparative Religion*, p. 93.

whether they are in relative harmony with the forces of modernization.[13]

Secularization has pushed traditional religions into new configurations, liberalizing most, but not all. As change takes place, peripheral features[14] are usually sloughed off, while the unifying symbols and rites at the center are retained. Watt has observed that the primary function of worship is to maintain and increase the physical energy available to the tribe.[15] To the extent that the traditional pattern can provide this energy depends upon how much meaning and cohesiveness can be drawn from the ancient symbols.

An example of such a strong center is the Kutep figure, *Kukwe*. This is a man, not a spirit, known and recognized by all. His value for religion is that he is a symbol of the tribe; his function is on behalf of the whole community, giving cohesiveness to the tribal structure. Each clan has a *Kukwe* since no single man could be on location physically for the whole tribe. This is not a contradiction since *Kukwe*, irrespective of his physical makeup, idealizes the totality of the clans. There are not, therefore, seven *Kukwes*, but there is one. The seven individuals, all recognized as *Kukwe,* represent a unity which symbolizes all the clans of the Kutep.[16] Restrictions placed on *Kukwe* are for the good of the whole society. His health and well being is a symbol of the health of the community. The meaning of his name is "the man with power." As such,

> He never eats from an imported dish but only from the traditional calabash. When he eats or drinks he always leaves a bit remaining in the container to ensure continuing food and drink. Kukwe cannot spend the night on the farm but must return home, else the village will be attacked by beasts or disease. Kukwe seldom bathes and when he does it is only a little, for if he removes all the dirt from his body the crops will fail. No one ever says Kukwe is hungry else famine will come to the people. Kukwe never drinks pure water because if he does the people of the hill will turn pale with

---

[13]It was stated repeatedly in nearly all tribal areas that education and Christianity have been the greatest factors of change. This may have been a biased response considering my role. The links between Christianity and colonialism are well known.

[14]E.g., local festivals, clan rites, and activities which were not integrated into the *mythos* of the entire tribe.

[15]Watt, *Islam and Society*, p. 183.

[16]The "hills" of Kutep-land are localizations of the clans, and each *Kukwe* is identified with one of the hill groups which, taken together, are the tribe.

sickness. In the time of drought Kukwe spreads his blue cloth out on the roof of his house so the clouds will gather and bring rain.[17]

Not only is the figure of *Kukwe* himself the personification of myth, but in times of crisis affecting the whole tribe the seven *Kukwe*s gather, as though one man, to determine what ritual action must be taken to correct the trouble.

The central figure of the cultus differs from tribe to tribe as do the levels of weakness or strength of the cultus itself. The myth of the ancient priest at Dukil of the Longuda tribe, once so vital, now only carries power in one area. Dukil is still the figure which confirms the right to rule upon new chiefs. Most of the former power of Dukil has been transferred to Guyok, and the rituals have been greatly modified.[18] Yet this traditional priest figure continues as an ancestral reality, and his office is a vital link with the past. He is an impressive sight as he moves about with his cane and long locks.[19]

A similar situation exists at Bambur among the Kulung. In spite of the education of the young people and the growing influence of Christianity, the *Basali* cult was still intact in 1970. While some lesser rites had disappeared in the preceding two decades, Basali still regulated the *rites de passage* for many families.[20]

ISLAM AS A FACTOR OF UNITY

Islam penetrated the traditional cultus of the fourteenth century due to factors that were non-religious for the most part. Watt's observations confirm that the breakup of society is an important factor for Islam.

Changes have been most drastic in the sphere of worship, for the ancestral cults have been replaced by Islamic forms. The success of Islam here, however, is not necessarily due to its own attraction, but is probably the

---

[17]Timothy Tukura at Bukuru, March 17, 1970.

[18]See Meek, *Tribal Studies II*, pp. 332-36 and cf. Chapter Five, pp. 137-138.

[19]David Windibiziri at Bukuru, February 20, 1970.

[20]Samuila Bako at Bambur, April 10, 1970.

result of the disappearance as effective social units of the groups with which the old cults were associated.[21]

The disintegrative factors of traditional society are manifold, and the struggle of the archaic pattern to adapt itself to modernity is erratic. But the question needs to be asked whether Islam is a positive and creative force in the maintenance of tribal unity in a time when the traditional structures seem to be coming apart. J. R. Means, as we have said, viewed Islam from Kano and made his generalizations for northern Nigeria from that vantage point. It was this limitation which led him to record the following:

> Islam is a welding force, struggling against the dissolution of the tribal system . . . . The new religions, Christianity for example, Westernization, and the aftermath of colonial control threaten now the dissolution of the tribal system, as no forces have ever before and they pose a real threat, not to Islam itself, but to the Islamic ideal, that is the ability of Islam in the face of widespread migration out of a tribe into a larger unit, to continue to influence the tribal man in all his daily actions and thoughts, to continue to engender in him the notion that he still belongs to a universal community.[22]

Here Means has confused two quite different issues. He speaks of the integrative force of Islam which is struggling against the dissolution of the tribe. But he speaks also of an "Islamic ideal," which is to give a sense of tribalism under a new aegis to those who have become detached from the tribe.[23]

Both of these factors, seen in their proper relationship, are important. First, the question whether the religion of Islam acts as a cement for holding together the tribal cultus must be answered with a qualified "no." The history of the pre-*jihad* Hausa demonstrates how cyclical and linear religious structures do not reinforce one another unless other non-religious factors have prepared the way. The tendency of the tribe to cling to its indigenous integrative symbols is almost universal. Where these have survived and there is an active pull to the past, Islam will have a negligible effect.

---

[21]Watt, *Islam and Society*, p. 137.

[22]J. E. Means, "Influence of Islam," p. 58.

[23]"Christianity aims at dissolving tribal ties, while Islam, by nature conservative, seeks to retain them in all their forms." *Ibid.*, p. 89.

Yet, Islam is able to forge a body of new religious people when ties to the traditional center are not strong and the dynamics of the Muslim community can reorganize them under new loyalties. There are obviously indigenous features among the Nupe, for example, even though the overall impression is Muslim. The Nupe identity with the Hausa Muslims is greater than with the surrounding non-Islamized tribes. The Nupe respect for community appeals to the Islamic ideal of cultural and religious unity. The new community (*umma*) represents material security and social standing. But the change came through a combination of social circumstances and the readiness of Islam to fill the vacuum left when young people were turning away from the traditional cults for political and economic reasons.[24] Islam became the beneficiary of a social upheaval which left the old forms empty. As a charismatic community Islam was able to capitalize on the disintegrative process and at the same time to contribute to it. The appeal of the *umma* in its African social context cannot be overemphasized as an influential factor presenting itself to whole tribes who see it as superior to the old way.

Notwithstanding, the turning of whole communities to Islam in the past 55 years has been rare.[25] The appeal of Islam is much more on the individual basis. Islam is attractive to individuals who have been separated from primary tribal loyalties because in this new religion they can find a reorganizing center for life. The sense of superiority provided by Islam meets a real need of the tribal person who feels culturally inferior. He truly feels that it is a great privilege to belong to this community. He embraces Islam often on these grounds alone, which act becomes a kind of salvation for him.

We have said that traditional religion, centering in the cultic symbols, is a powerful uniting force for the tribe. Some tribes are more richly endowed with these powers than others. On the other hand, what is meaningful to the particular tribe in its local setting can separate and divide when unity is needed in the larger pluralistic society. When this happens, Islam has proved its ability to reorganize a faltering system around new symbols, often in addition to the old,

---

[24]See Nadel, *Nupe Religion*, p. 251.

[25]The movements into Islam through the political approach of Sir Ahmadu Bello showed some initial signs of massive conversions, but the results subsequently proved this not to be the case. See Chapter Six, p. 169 ff.

and it thus becomes a factor of unity for many disoriented tribal members. There is yet a third observation which is a striking adaptation of the problems which alien systems confront.

THE INTEGRATION OF TWO SYSTEMS

The Jukun Hausa, dating from the Kwororafa period, are still very much a part of the Wukari Jukun society.[26] Like the Maguzawa they have developed a resistance to absorption into mainstream Islam. The *amgbakpariga*[27] might be described as a sub-culture of the Jukun which predates any colonial contacts with Islam and which ethnically falls somewhere between the traditional Jukun and the Hausa. The name is symbolically part Jukun and part Hausa. The first three syllables are the Jukun designation for "long folding," and *riga* is Hausa for "gown." Hence, the reference is to the long, full gowns of the Muslim (Hausa) in contrast to the customary Jukun dress for men, which is a single large cloth draped over one shoulder. The *amgbakpariga* represent an innovation of Islam, which, like the Bura at Subwong, has been intimately connected with life in traditional society. The adaptations which developed changed not only the Muslims themselves but the indigenous Jukun religion within which they were living.

Ibrahim Usman is a member of this group and a highly respected leader.[28] He recalled in detail the history of the *amgbakpariga*.[29] Hausa people were living at Wukari when the Jukun left Kwororafa about the eighteenth century.[30] These Hausa, who became the *amgbakpariga*, allowed the Jukun to settle with them even though they were greatly outnumbered by the Jukun. There was added to this Wukari Hausa group a second wave of Muslim Hausas from the Kano

---

[26]See Meek, *A Sudanese Kingdom* (London: Kegan Paul, Trench, Trubner & Co., 1931), pp. 22,23,29 *et passim*.

[27]For this careful spelling I am indebted to Wm. Evenhouse, a linguist who worked with the Wapan (Jukun) in 1971.

[28]A leading businessman of Wukari, formerly chairman of the Board of Posts and Telegraphs. He is Christian, not a Muslim, but an *amgbakpariga*.

[29]"The Jukun of Wukari claim that the *amgbakpariga* are the descendants of Hausa people who were carried away by the Jukun from their homes in the North during raids on Hausaland." See Meek, *Sudanese Kingdom*, pp. 29,30.

[30]*Ibid.*, p. 22.

area. This latter group settled in with the original Hausas. The two groups then lived together and became known by their Jukun name after they began to marry the Jukun women. In this way they became truly Hausa-Jukun. As Ibrahim Usman explained, concessions were made by the Hausas in marriage as the patrilineal Hausa custom came into conflict with the matrilineal Jukun society.[31] This was worked out by a number of uncharacteristic compromises on the part of the Hausas. One was the removal of the Hausa gown by a husband and the donning of a Jukun garb in the presence of his wife's mother. This deference to the mother-in-law shows how flexible the relations were between the Hausa and Jukun.

The passage of time brought the Hausa-Jukun (*amgbakpariga*) under full authority of the Jukun king, to whom they gave respect as any other Jukun. Nevertheless, they continued to hold their own Muslim ceremonies and to live quite separately from the indigenous Jukun. The exposure to a more true Islam came during the colonial period when Hausa traders from Kano began coming to Wukari.[32] These immigrant Muslims disclaimed the *amgbakpariga* due to the high degree of accommodation that had taken place with the Jukun. This attitude caused many of the *amgbakpariga* to embrace true Islam of the Hausa teachers. But the greater number remained as Muslims who have a strong identity with the Jukun tribe up to the present.

The true Hausas in Wukari have only a peripheral identity with the highly involuted Jukun culture, while the *amgbakpariga* have almost full privileges as Jukun. They do not serve on the *Aku*'s (king's) council of Jukun elders, but their participation in the life of the tribe otherwise is not noticeably limited. A number of the group are leaders among the businessmen of Wukari, and they are as active as any other Jukun in the local administration. Some live in special units of the town, but most of them are scattered throughout the Jukun community. They still keep the abdominal markings of the Hausa indicating a high degree of self-awareness. It is not uncommon for a Jukun who practices Muslim prayers but who is not a part of the Hausa community to be treated as one of *amgbakpariga*.[33]

---

[31]The matrilineal Jukun society is discussed by Meek, *ibid.*, p. 37.

[32]The Hausa "strangers" were spoken of as *masu tuwon waje* (the eaters of "outside" or foreign food). Bitrus Angyunwe, at Bukuru, March 11, 1970.

[33]*Ibid.*, at Bukuru, August 20, 1970.

The presence of the "true" Muslims in the Jukun towns marks off the *amgbakpariga* as being Jukun. Some of the group have actually left their Muslim tradition,[34] but the greater number are practicing Muslims. The absorption of this historic Muslim group into the Jukun community indicates that if Islam is to function as a force for unity within the traditional societies, the Islamic mores will be recast into near indigenous forms. The *amgbakpariga* are an unusual case, due to their history and their modern role in Jukun life. However, other similar illustrations show that Muslim Hausas who live with tribal groups and mix with them in marriage will tend to take on the texture of tribal life. The result is that cardinal Muslim practices are sublimated and may even fall into disuse.[35]

THE INDIVIDUAL AGAINST THE COMMUNITY

LOSS OF TRADITIONAL CENTER AND RELIGIOUS CHANGE

We have already said that one of the direct influences leading to Islam occurs when a person becomes detached from his indigenous home and people. Islam can then become a new organizing center for his life. Forces that combine to break up the tribe press in from all sides. Wilfred Cantwell Smith speaks of Islam's ability to give security and refuge when society becomes fragmented:

> (Islam provides) communities into which any stranger may enter, and where he can meet on equal grounds with the people of other tribes . . . universal religions . . . serve a useful social function in giving a faith to live by in providing against insecurity. They help in employment, sickness and death. While they do disintegrate to some extent, they also seek to re-integrate society and to "destroy and overthrow," to "build and to plant."[36]

The highest conversion rate to Islam takes place among two social groups: (1) those who for various reasons have abandoned their tribal

---

[34]Quite a number are Christian.

[35]The Subwong Bura, as an example, where circumcision was retained but the prayers were abandoned.

[36]W. C. Smith, "Islam in the Modern World," *Current History*, 32, No. 190 (June 1957), p. 44.

center and (2) those who live in the cities and towns. Loss of status or disorientation from the natural group brings apprehension. Levy-Bruhl observed that the individual who does not belong to a social group counts for nothing; hence, "when a stranger dies in a Thonga village and no one knows him, 'he does not matter.'"[37] Since the African personality is communal, it is through the group that an individual finds his self-awareness. A common expression is, "I am because we are." Colonization contributed to the breakup of the tribe as a center of orientation. The social and economic forces which came with colonization soon intensified,and the process of disintegration after the 1950s has been alarming.

Seeking security and fulfillment, however he may define it,often leads the tribal person away from his own roots. This loss of confidence in the old way puts him in a vulnerable place. One of the striking episodes connected with the *Kano Chronicle* finds two members of the Dalla tribesmen quickly joining the side of Tsamia, the Muslim chief of Kano, after he destroyed their "pagan" shrine. Tsamia asked Makare and Danguzu, the two unbelievers, "Why do you not run away?" They replied, "Where are we to run to?" "Praise be to God," answered the Tsamia. "Now tell me the secret of your God." And the *Chronicle* records simply, "They told him."[38] Here is a primitive illustration of what has happened in many northern tribes. When the prestige and influence of the tribal cultus loses its holding power over individuals and groups, a vacuum is created which Islam can fill, and in time the old structure is dismantled.

The dynamic images of the Muslim faith are unclear when the stranger views Islam from outside.[39] But to one who has felt the loss of identity with his primary society, these images begin to have great appeal. Colonialism opened a door eighty years ago with Lord Lugard's arrival. Freedom of movement came with the governing setup, giving Africans exposure to a new kind of world. To enter the door of Islam by simple conversion meant a lift to higher levels of life when compared to the restrictions of the tribe. The massive movement

---

[37]From Junod, quoted by Levy-Bruhl in *The Soul of the Primitive* translated by L. A. Clare (London: George Allen & Unwin, Ltd., 1928), p. 72.

[38]*K.C.*, p. 69.

[39]"An ideational system such as that of Islam contains a number of dynamic images and because some men are chiefly moved by one and some by another it is possible to have separative processes within a wider integrative process." Watt, *Islam and Society*, p. 114.

to urban areas resulted in the breakup of once strong rural communities. When kinship structures break down, Islam can give coherence across tribal lines. Watt makes an appropriate observation about Islam when he says, "Islam is essentially a religion for individuals who have been uprooted from their community or whose communities have vanished under their feet."[40]

RELIGIOUS IDENTITY AND SOCIAL STATUS

There is a malaise in contemporary tribal religion because of the conflict which the systems have with education and modernization. The tribal person is quite secure with his traditional ways as long as his life is kept within the prescribed limits. But today with the ease of movement which is open to all but the most rural villages and with education available in even the most isolated places, tensions with the old way are acute. The ability of the religion of the fathers to keep its hold on the young people depends not only on the strength of the religion but on the modern economic and political factors that put pressure on it. Structures from tribe to tribe vary so greatly that, given identical social and educational factors, one tribe may retain a hold on its people while another moves radically away from traditional forms.[41]

In the larger towns there is a group which might be called the quasi-elite. This group tends to look down upon farmers and village craftsmen, while most of this "elite" group are, themselves, just a step away from this kind of life.

> Whilst they deny any fundamental difference between themselves and the remaining members of their groups, they are training their children to occupy an elite status, giving them the best schooling and often restricting their interaction with children of humble parentage.[42]

---

[40]*Ibid.*, p. 137.

[41]The Tiv have kept a tight identity even in the cities, while the Gwari have responded in varying strengths to Christianity as well as to Islam, many becoming absorbed into the larger Nupe culture, and with little tribal identity in the towns. For Gwari see M. Shuaibu Na'abi and Alhaji Hassan, *Gwari, Gade, and Koro Tribes* (Ibadan: University Press, 1969).

[42]Lloyd, *Africa in Social Change*, p. 318.

Likewise, in the villages it is not uncommon to hear young men especially speak disparagingly of the religion of their birth. A very common Hausa expression is *Tsofon hanya ba ta ciyad da yau ba* (the old way cannot nourish today). Certain elements of the old religion may be retained, but for the sake of respectability the more obviously "pagan" rites are put aside. The Mumuye teacher will usually respect the harvest laws, but will treat the *dodo* masquerader as a joke. The Jukun man will honor his ancestors in family rites but tends to reject the *aku ahwa* festival of communicating with the dead.[43] This selectivity by the younger generation is everywhere and in varying degrees.[44]

Against this background the Muslim community presents an appearance of being progressive. The individual desires the respectability of the new religion, but his ties to the tribe restrain him from wholesale adoption of Islam. It is in this dilemma that we have observed the greatest range of self-assertion by tribal members. The individual may not be primarily affected by the religious appeal of Islam. Rather, it is the desire to get ahead and find whatever means will assure status in the shortest possible time which is most important. Some react to the tension in one way and some in another,[45] but the power of Islam to separate the individual from his traditional peers is very real.

During my nine years of residence in Bambur (Gongola State) a private *masalaci* (Muslim prayer enclosure) was the only evidence of Islam in the village. It belonged to Ibi Kagal. It was surrounded by grass mats, because he said he wanted to keep his times of prayer without distraction from unbelievers. The townspeople claimed he was keeping pagan rituals, yet he claimed firmly that he was a Muslim. He entertained the Hausas from the nearby village of Mutum Daya and encouraged them to make use of his private mosque. The conversion

---

[43]Bitrus Angyunwe from Wukari, commenting on the ceremony described by Meek in *Sudanese Kingdom*, pp. 238 ff.

[44]Over and over, when young people were asked about principal traditional festivals and practices, they would preface their answers by the remark *Tun ba mu waye ba* (before we understood or were enlightened). The older men as a rule did not have this reservation.

[45]E.g., Christianity and the educational institutions, or movement to cities, moving from place to place, learning a trade superficially, etc.

was for Ibi's own status and his need to be seen by the rest of the clan as one who was progressive and modern.[46]

Kisiki Gambo of the village of Jigawa is one of the Maguzawa who joins the other Muslims on Friday for prayer. He said that during the political pressure just before the Civil War he was offered the job as tax collector for three villages with a stipend of eight pounds ($20.00) per month. But a condition was attached to the position. The district head stated that these positions should go to men who "recognize God and who would bring *sadaka* (alms) to their local *imam*." Gambo agreed. He had already lost his chance to be chief of the Maguzawa village due to clan rivalry, and he said in summary, "I don't feel bad about leaving them."[47]

Malam Lawal of Mayo Belwa had no education until he attended an adult literacy class of the former Northern Nigeria Regional Government. After he learned to read and write the Hausa language, he was asked to become one of the teachers in the same literacy program known as *Yaki da Jahilci* (War on Ignorance). The program was sponsored by the Office of Enlightenment of the Government.The program was dominated by Muslims, and the opportunity to become teacher meant one must first convert to the Muslim faith. All of his brothers were traditional Bachema except for one who was a Christian. But among them only the Christian could read. He knew his family would despise him if he became a Muslim, so he left his family because of his new position and said simply, *Samun matsayi ya kawo haka* (obtaining the position caused this to happen).[48]

Such cases are many, but the significant factor running through all of them is that personal fulfillment was not being realized in the traditional framework. This need, in addition to some measure of prior disorientation from the group, in many cases, resulted in religious change.

---

[46]Ibi Kagal, known personally, and with additional information from Samuila Bako at Bambur.

[47]Kisiki Gambo at Jigawa, March 14, 1970.

[48]Lawal Ndiko at Mayo Belwa, January 10, 1970.

When investigating this dynamic among the Tiv, I discovered that there are a few Tiv-born Muslims who live in the major towns, such as Gboko and Makurdi. Information about them was scant, but the Tiv men generally agreed that these Tiv Muslims "do not want to work,"[49] and that they had been "travelling in the North and were exposed to Hausas."[50] I found one Tiv man at Makurdi, however, who told me that his reason for "joining" the Hausas was because they had offered him a girl for marriage and he had no way of meeting the prices demanded for girls in his own Tiv families. Further, after marrying the girl, he was given a sum of money (amount not disclosed) to "buy some goods." So he felt that he could be successful with the help of the Hausas.[51] He went against the community for personal reasons that he felt were legitimate, even though it meant rejection and loss of status among his own people.

However little the individual knows of Islam when he aligns himself with the Muslim community and however minimal his outward expression of Islam may be, he may, nevertheless, have full privileges in the new religion. He can also maintain some measure of identity with the old at the same time.[52] Hence, the individual who turns from his father's religion may gauge his activities in the new community to suit his special situation. The ability of Islam to accommodate to an animistic sub-stratum is well known, and this makes it suitable as an African religion.[53] The attitude of the tribe to the individual who converts may vary. For example, the ability of the Mwaghavul and Kilba families to integrate those who have gone over to Islam shows that Islam can "fit" the need of the person and yet be compatible with the local structure. However, not all feel at home with their brothers once they have gone against the community.[54] Especially in urban

---

[49]Jacob Yaaya at Bukuru, February 10, 1970.

[50]Jonathan Ukpekeh at Rukuru, February 13, 1970.

[51]Ahmadu Orshi at Makurdi, January 18, 1970.

[52]Nadel tends to oversimplify when he observes, "The final step of conversion changes it (the outlook) but little; indeed, it can hardly be otherwise since conversion is so loose an affair and not a real 'step' at all." *Nupe Religion*, p. 253.

[53]Watt, *Islam and Society*, p. 189.

[54]One Kutep man told me of his brother who dies of a disease, and the brothers of the family whould not bury him; even though there wer no Muslims closer than five miles, they refused his burial. Iliya Madaki, January 22, 1970.

areas, Islam is capable of forming a new kind of society where religion is the adhesive, displacing the weakened ties of kinship.[55]

URBAN STRESS

Nigeria's towns and cities share features and problems with urban societies everywhere. Yet there are certain characteristics which are typically African in the urbanization of Nigeria. With a few exceptions the cities and towns are composed of different groups based on both tribe and religion. A town need not be large but is always an area of concentrated population, usually the seat of administration of the local authority, a center of marketing and a residence of the chief or emir.

A distinction should be made between tribal towns such as Wukari, Numan, Biu, Takum, or Bida—and the more cosmopolitan centers such as Jos or Kaduna. The tribal towns have a higher degree of a unity, because here one tribe dominates. This means that the officials and politics tend to serve the majority group,[56] and the secondary groups fit into this dominance. In the larger towns there is a heterogeneity that recognizes the interests of various clusters of people, the diverse languages, religions, vocations, and economic strength.

Lloyd shows that the greatest number of residents in West African urban areas are recent immigrants who are looking for something which the towns and villages cannot offer. He observes that only a minority are urban born; hence, the lack of civil spirit. The special interests of the tribal communities inhibit organized administrative unity.

---

[55]For the forming of a religious society in the city of Medina, but which would not have been possible among the tribes themselves without religion, see Watt, *Islam and Society*, p. 18.

[56]E. U. Essien Udom, in a paper presented to the Institute of Church and Society, "Unity in a Pluralist Society," given at Zaria, April 1970. "The term 'unity' should be qualified. By unity one does not mean complete agreement on all matters of detail by all members of the society. Rather, unity signifies the presence of a high degree of agreement among a vast segment of the society on the most important values and aspirations of the society." It is the domination of a major cultural group in a town which designates a town as "tribal" by our definition.

The immigrant usually claims that he intends to return to his own home village in his old age, if not earlier, insuring that his rights to land and political status do not lapse through his presumed renunciation of his group.[57]

In both the tribal towns and the more cosmopolitan cities one fact is very important: It is here that the Muslim communities thrive. In the tribal towns the Hausa-Fulani sections are traditionally apart from the local people, and the indigenous converts to Islam will often resettle in these Muslim neighborhoods. There is another difference between the tribal town, such as Wukari, and the cosmopolitan city of Jos. In a city like Jos there is relatively little contact with the "old religion." Even where tribal units live together, indigenous ritual practice is minimal. In the tribal towns traditional practice is not greatly altered and may, in fact, be enhanced when certain festivals or shrines are centered there.[58] These towns are in rhythm with the villages nearby, since the steady circulation of the rural people into the town keeps the town relatively intact, as far as religion is concerned.

THE MUSLIM URBAN PRESENCE

Islamic history shows that the strength of Islam always has been centered in the towns. Muhammed found the base for his new religion among the scattered, disunited tribes of the desert. However, it was among their urban kinsmen in Medina and Mecca that the religion was established and from whom it found momentum.[59] The city of Kano, founded by Gajimasu in the twelfth century, was brought to its greatest power by Muhamma Rimfa. It was in this city where the factions could be welded together and the economy controlled. Here impregnable walls could seal off the opposition while an urban ethos developed. We have already seen that among traditional people the greatest influence of Islam is in the towns. Islam dominates the open-traditional towns. It has considerably less influence in the tribal-oriented towns and all but disappears in the open rural areas.

The Kutep are highly traditional. When asked about their history with Muslims, they speak of Takum town, where their chief resides.

---

[57]Lloyd, *Africa in Social Change*, p. 290.

[58]E.g., Fare, the ceremonial grounds for rituals of the Bachema god, *Nzeanzo*, located near Numan or Puge, the sacred grounds of the Jukun king near Wukari.

[59]See Watt, *Islam and Society*, Chapter ii, esp. pp. 4-20.

He is Muslim, as are most of the people who have official rank. However, Islam is virtually non-existent in the villages. The Mumuye are well informed about Islam through their Muslim contacts in Jalingo town and nearby villages, but there are practically no signs of Muslim influence in the Mumuye villages themselves.[60] And so the pattern continues throughout the central belt of Nigeria. In the more traditional northern states, the dominant groups are Muslim. The smaller groups from traditional tribes live among the Muslims in varying degrees of strength. This strong urban quality of Islam is widely recognized and is integral to its very life. Syed Abdul Latif concluded:

> (Islam) cannot exist in its distinctive form without towns and only townspeople can conscientiously follow its principles. The farmer instinctively resists it as a disintegrative factor; on the other hand in the town where life and personal relationships are more secularized, Islam is an integrative factor. Town life and trading involve abandoning the local religion; Islamic law can operate over a wider field of social relations; qadi's courts can function and teachers attract pupils from a wide area. In the townsmen class are occupational groups, clergy, men of business such as merchants and traders, craftsmen, shopkeepers, vendors . . . and finally artisans and manual laborers. The heterogeneous characteristic of towns, however, derives from differences of ethnic origins rather than from divisions of labor. Islam with its power to call the jami for Friday prayers is the only integrative factor.[61]

This ability to organize and flourish in the city is an historical fact of African Islam. For centuries the royal religious cults of old Songhai saw Islam grow beside them.[62] Timbuktu successfully put three distinct ethnic groups together under Islamic governance. While the three streams maintained social and ethnic distinctives, it was the Islamic religion which formed their mores and provided the most notable characteristics.[63]

---

[60]It can be said that virtually no Muslim lives among the Mumuye in their villages and hamlets. (1970) They are only found at the Mumuye trading locations and markets, usually located on main roads or near the more populous villages and at the political town of Zing.

[61]Syed Abdul Latif, *The Mind al-Qur'an Builds* (Agapura, Hyderabad: The Academy of Islamic Studies, 1962), p. 6, cited in Means, "The Influence of Islam," p. 99.

[62]See J. O. Hunwick, "Religion and State in the Songhay Empire, 1464-1591," in *Islam in Tropical Africa*, pp. 296-317.

[63]See Horace Miner, *The Primitive City of Timbuctoo*, pp. 11-31.

Businesses in the towns are the backbone of the Hausa economy. Trade at the most expansive wholesale level and with the seller of assorted wares on the street is virtually controlled by Muslims. This was always the case, but it became even more so after the repatriation of the Ibos in 1967. Before the Civil War a great percentage of the transport business in the North was Ibo controlled. But beginning with the seventies this control shifted to affluent *alhajis*,[64] who opened up northern-based markets between Kano, Sokoto, Zaria, Kaduna, and the cities to the southwest and southeast. Muslim businessmen have contracts in all of the northern cities, allowing them to buy regional goods and ship them to southern cities for marketing and export. On return trips the lorries are filled with the hard-to-find consumer items, building supplies, and imports which in turn are retailed to local traders at prices which are more or less controlled by the transporter himself. The small retailer in Jos is often connected to the Hausa community by his trade. The wealthy Muslim traders are often willing to provide capital for enterprising retailers. This creates a creditor relationship which the Hausa *alhaji* uses as a source of influence.[65]

Islam, on the other hand, is not so adaptable to the rural agricultural life. Here the life cycle is set by the rhythm of seasonal changes and fertility.[66] Islam's more sophisticated system with its emphasis on such things as the unity of God and the sacred community have negligible relevance to the farmer.[67] The rituals of the nature cycle are less congenial to Islam than the secularism of the city. The Jos market depends on the farmer who brings his produce and cattle for

---

[64]Those who have made the pilgrimage to Mecca enjoy special status, which is to their advantage socially and economically; the title *alhaji* has, in most places, become synonymous with wealth.

[65]Levy-Bruhl's observation pertains: "It is clear that even in societies without a high technological or economic development, there is a definite economic system, in which the religious society helps to motivate, guide, distribute and validate the productive and distribution energies of the individuals in it." *The Soul of the Primitive*, p. 137.

[66]"Religious beliefs and attitudes were assuredly not created either by methods of food production or by some mechanism of exchange. But they did grow up together with them, and it was the economic system that made certain constituents and certain forms of religion relevant at one period and others relevant at another." P. Radin, *Primitive Religion*, p. 41.

[67]The Muridiyyah movement is an attempt to make idealistic Islam relevant to the soil, and in so doing the form of Islam is distorted. See Hunwick, *Islam in Tropical Africa*, p. 313.

sale each day. The movement of his goods and the price he will receive is very much in the hands of the Hausa trader. Therefore, even though there is a symbiosis benefiting both groups, little of the Muslim religion ever leaves the environs of the city or town.[68]

Disintegrated Tribesmen

S. A. Latif speaks of Islam as an "integrative factor" in the urban areas.[69] By this he refers to the fact that often converts to Islam come through the door of disintegrated tribalism. Motivations for moving to a city are varied. Most common would be employment and seeking a more successful life. Along with this is the desire to leave the tribe's inhibiting environment. When a young man comes to the city without solid contacts among friends and kin, he can become disillusioned and poor. Soon his sense of security is undermined, and he feels disconnected. In this quite desperate situation new social and economic contacts have to be made. I talked with two young men in Jos, one a Gwari and one a Basa, who were working for Hausa traders. Both of them are in debt to their Muslim employer and both are being fed and housed by him. Both admit that they would not leave Jos now to return home and could not, even if they wanted to.

It is very difficult to evaluate the urban influence on immigrant tribespeople. However, I had the chance to interview various people during the 1970 celebration of *Id il Kabir* , which fell on February 12. This is a day when the entire Muslim community in Jos roams about the city in colorful dress and in very high spirits. I found them very approachable. I attended the morning prayers at the traditional communal prayer grounds near the river. There was a crowd of at least 5,000. Before and after the communal prayer I had opportunity for conversations. I asked 32 people the same questions: "What is your tribal background?" and "When did you begin to 'do *salat*'?"— that is, become a Muslim. The second question was asked especially of those who admitted their background to be of a non-Muslim tribe.

---

[68]Keeping in mind, however, the Muslim retailers who are residents of the small villages, especially along the roadsides between the town suppliers.

[69]See footnote 59.

100

Including the day before *Id il Kabir* and the day itself I was able to contact 63 people.[70] The statistics developed as follows:

1. Of the 63, 41 claimed a Hausa or Fulani parentage, of which 30 were born in Jos. The others came to join relatives here during the previous five years.

2. Of the 22 who answered that their tribal roots were other than Hausa-Fulani, the following tribes were represented:

Mwaghavul	6	Taroh	1
Gwari	4	Nupe	1
Eggon	2	Mada	1
Katab	2	Jarawa	1
Idoma	2	Koro	1
Seyawa	1		

Of these 22, 15 agreed that they began to perform Muslim prayers within the past ten years and in each case since coming to Jos. The Gwari, the Nupe, and two of the six Mwaghavul men said they came to Jos as Muslims from their homes.

This is but a sampling, of course. Nevertheless, the pattern shows that a high ratio of people who were influenced to follow Islam through city associations reacted to the frustration they felt in the tribal society.[71] It is also significant that where large tribal groups are living in the city, the tribal identity is higher and can hold the tribal members together more meaningfully. This group is less open to Islamization. The Birom, for example, would have little reason to Islamize, because their tribe comprises all the area of the town of Bukuru to the west. The Tiv, likewise, would have little incentive to Islamize. This is not only because of their antipathy for Islam , but also because there were many Tiv living in Jos at the time, and they are

---

[70]The interviews were done as quickly as possible, on the streets, at resting places in the Hausa section of the town, and while going to and from the celebrations. Most were quite cooperative, though the *liman* of Jos did ask what the inquiry was about. This required a personal visit to his residence for an explanation.

[71]See Watt on sociological motivations for religious change, especially in the cities. *Islam and Society*, p. 137.

very ethnocentric.[72] It is estimated, however, that over 160 tribes of various strengths are represented in the city, so the ability of any one tribal group to hold its members varies. Many are completely cut off from tribal ties. These factors taken together illustrate why Islamic influence in the towns is a unique phenomenon.

DISRUPTIVE FACTORS AFFECT RELIGION

The cities are growing incredibly fast, and there is a steady flow of young people into the urban areas. This causes two major problems for the tribal person, which in turn may affect his religious practice.

Social   Controls   and   Family

Habila Aleydeino, who was Commissioner of Social Welfare for the former North East State in 1970, stated:

> The influx of people (into the cities) is due to a number of reasons: some come in search of employment, others in search of a new, glorious life, others to join relatives, etc. One thing which is common to all comers into the urban area, however, is that they are leaving something behind—they are leaving a set of rural values based on age old traditions and customs. There, one had elders who guided one and helped one to plough through life along a well-beaten path proved generation after generation with little changes over the year . . . There are inhibitions and prohibitions. In fact, the rural life is a straight jacket into which everyone is born, and into which everyone must fit . . . With the disappearance of the inhibitions the distance of ear-pulling elders and the formalizing of means of social control (local authority) people find that they can be able to experiment on modes of behaviour which would perhaps be unthinkable in rural areas.[73]

There is a new freedom in marriage found in the towns in contrast to the much stricter marriage in the tribal setting. In rural areas men usually choose their wives from nearby villages and almost always from the same ethnic group.[74] Where in rural areas ancestral

---

[72]Their numbers are large enough so that they can function without learning the Hausa language, and they are able to maintain social clubs and Tiv agencies on behalf of the tribesmen. They worship as Tiv in their own congregations and make use of the Tiv vernacular.

[73]A paper presented to the Institute of Church and Society by Habila Aleydeino; read at Zaria, April 13, 1970. "Rapid Social Change in Urban Areas," pp. 3-4.

[74]Lloyd, *Africa in Social Change*, p. 287.

attachments are very strong, these are broken down in the cities where tribal identity is no longer an absolute basis for marriage. Urban freedom of this kind is usually intentional. The individual, in many cases, has already decided to go against his own community and leaves now the traditional life behind and forms new associations. It often happens that these associations are not made at the kinship level, but the status and economic security they bring is very important. This urban person and many others like him will experience what is known as the "city washing" (*wonkan birni*). This idiom refers to someone who for these and other reasons turns to Islam upon moving into the city.

From Rural to Urban Economy

There are no strict forms in the cities. The cyclic life of the village centered on the sowing of the seed and the harvesting of crops. However, this routine meant more than simply the planting and eating of one's own crops. The rural ritual depended on familiar groves where trees are habitations of good and evil spirits. It centered on familiar rocks and shrines, the sound of the shaman's whistle, the piping and dancing of the seasonal rites, the drumming and the singing. Practically all the sights and sounds that are the very life of the village are blotted out and stilled upon coming to the city. Lacking success in one city job, the tribal person tries another. The supply of manpower is often greater than the demand. The work available is new to the rural person. Many jobs require some kind of mechanical experience which he or she has never had. Even those who have some education come to the city and find that others are better prepared and already hold the positions they are suited for.

When these educated persons lived in the village, they were looked up to as the elite. Now in the city they are treated as mediocre, even with disrespect. This is demoralizing. More than this, instead of occupying a clean-swept village house, a man must pay rent for a poor room—often sharing it with others who are not of his own tribe. He may have to buy all his food and cook it himself or pay an additional price to have it cooked for him.

These circumstances can be made more tolerable by close relatives who are already oriented into the life of the town. But considering the masses who move about, many people do not have such attachments. These lonely persons often find an open door to eat and even lodge in the Muslim quarters. Here the *umma* makes its impact on the detribalized. Here is a new tribe offering fraternity, as it were, the promise of a "beaten path" at a time of frustration and much fear.[75]

So the cosmopolitan town is a mix of many social units. This being the case, these groups either band together to survive in a weakened form, or cease altogether. Where Islam tended not to be relevant in the village because of its alien ideology and the ethnocentrism of the tribe, new factors now take over in the city, which bring religious change. Adherence to Islam does not demand renunciation of tribal ties. Therefore, the urban tribal person may participate in both worlds without feeling disqualified. But in time, Islam usually gains the upper hand. This is due not only to its own appeal but also because it fills the vacuum created by the loss of traditional society and the mores which were associated with it.

THE LIVING AND THE DEAD

THE ANCESTRAL FUNCTION

The attitude of the living toward the dead is bound to be an area of conflict when Islam confronts African religion. The respect which African societies give their ancestors is one of the few universal features of African religion. When these two religious systems interact, the voice of the ancestors could well have the last word.[76]

Our study among twenty tribes shows that ancestors are not regarded as divine. Their relationship is one of mediation between the living and the dead. Generally they are actually feared by both family

---

[75]See Watt, *Islam and Society*, pp. 174-75, for a discussion of brotherhood and the *sunna* as valuable factors of "religious tribalism" for the displaced.

[76]Functioning through control and mediation. Control by: "calling the living (Kilba)," "revealing the truth (Jukun)," "special power for special acts (Tiv)," "moving about at night (Tiv, Jukun)." Mediation by: "sleeping on their graves which opens up communication (Jukun)," "healing only comes through the ancestors (Mwaghavul)," "the oldest person ranks next to the dead (Tiv)," "ancestors require sacrifice (Longuda)," "laws concerning the ancestors must be kept for health in the tribe (Kutep)."

and clan.[77] Where Islam is a major factor in the community, ancestors who have high rank and have become figures of power will usually be accommodated into the new system in some way. Yet the recent dead are also important to the religion. They represent various levels of power and are the center of intense rituals. How, therefore, will this strongest single feature of African religion adjust to Islam, which officially allows no compromise with the unity of God and gives no place to a power that competes with God?

The function of the ancestors cannot be reduced to a simple statement. Ancestor worship (or veneration) confirms Eliade's statement that primitive life is always complex.[78] John Taylor refers to the role of the dead in African society as "the tender bridge."[79] This thoughtful expression carries with it the idea of reciprocity between life and death and suggests that a fragile relationship exists between the living and the dead. The relationship may be tenuous and fearful, but it is real. Here is a bridge, a way over and a way back, a way to speak and to be heard, as well as a way to listen and wait.

Ancestors do function as sources of power and regulators of morality, but it is their social control which dominates. Middleton believes that the only role which the dead have is to serve the family.[80] Durkheim built his whole thesis on the idea that the ancestors are symbols of the social function of religion.[81] Generally, the supreme being is so distant from real life that the dead spirits replace him as something close to the people.

---

[77]"Fear" as ranging from a profound sense of respect to actual precautions taken not to incur their anger. All are evident in footnote above. See J. G. Frazer, *The Fear of the Dead in Primitive Religion* (2 vols. London: Macmillan and Co., 1933).

[78]"The simple and one-dimensional presentation so often found in the works of synthesis and popularization depends entirely on the author's more or less arbitrary selectiveness." Mircea Eliade, *Patterns in Comparative Religion* (Cleveland and New York: The World Publishing Co., 1958), p. 32.

[79]John Taylor, *The Primal Vision* (Philadelphia: The Fortune Press, 1963), pp. 154-71.

[80]The ancestor cult is "of indirect significance, however, in that it increases the sense of group solidarity among the members of the lineage." John Middleton, *Gods and Rituals* (Garden City, NY: The Natural History Press, 1967), p. 40.

[81]Durkheim generally is very skeptical of the reality of the ancestors and their tribal function in any primitive society. He asks a contradictory question when he says, "How could a vain fantasy have been able to fashion the human consciousness so strongly and so durably?" *The Elementary Forms of the Religious Life* (London: Geo. Allen & Unwin, Ltd., 1915), p. 70.

The theological issue does not seem to arise as long as Islam lives alongside the ancestors. Part of the reason for this is that the Islamic insistence on the worship of God is so strong, filling the vacuum of the African high god, that ancestors, by contrast, take on quite a different function.

Lewis reaches the conclusion that ancestor cults "may be accommodated effectively and persist in a Muslim guise." Mediation is not a strong theme in Islam. The ancestors help in this area, for in the indigenous cosmology they carry the honored place of being prayed "through" rather than being prayed "to."

CUSTOMARY PRACTICE AND ISLAMIC INFLUENCE

The ancestor issue, however, does trouble the conscience of the Muslim. The danger of *shirk* runs very high in certain societies where honoring the dead is practiced openly. Even the most simple Muslim does all he can to avoid the conflict. If Islam has a strong influence where there was once an active ancestor cult, the practices that center on the dead will be modified to fit the Muslim pattern.

Special illustrations of this come from the Pabir and the Jukun. The Pabir once had complex rituals of ancestor remembrance, but the society is now highly Islamized. The Jukun, on the other hand, has an active ancestor cultus which has a significant Muslim feature.

Muslim Dominance: Pabir

The basis for the Pabir ritual of the dead was the annual festival known as the Mambila. The word itself means "ghost," and the festival was what the name implies—a feast in honor of all forefathers but especially the fathers of royalty.[82] According to the Pabir, when a man dies, his soul goes to his predecessors, but it is allowed to return once each year at the Mambila feast. In pre-Islamic days the chief himself took a prominent part in the feast. A white bull was sacrificed on behalf of the chief's father. The chief officiated while offerings of heart and kidney from the sacrifice were presented with prayer before

---

[82]See discussion in Meek, *Northern Tribes,* I, pp. 160-61.

106

sacred pots.[83] When asked about the ancient tradition, a Muslim man explained that God would not forbid the Mambila, but the chiefs of the past thirty years preferred not to participate and arranged for someone else to represent them. So the character of the Mambila was greatly altered since its locus was the chief and his closest ancestors. As a result, the ancestor ritual has become a family affair where the father of the home officiates in "feeding the ancestors," requesting them to mediate with Allah concerning problems which arise.[84]

Tribal Dominance: Jukun

The adjustment made among the Jukun is significantly different from that of the Pabir. In this case the Muslim element does not dominate so does not have enough influence to alter the original form.

Even though the ancestor institutions are most resistant to change, there has, nevertheless, been a decline in the Jukun practice of *aku-ahwa* in the past thirty-five years.[85] Angyunwe of Wukari explained that the principal features of the ceremony were still being carried out. Food is taken to the bush on behalf of the dead ancestors. In the heat of the dancing, the participants are able to "speak" with the dead to get their counsel on behalf of the living.[86] Voices are said to be heard as well as grotesque sounds of every variety which, it is believed, are the dead actually speaking. The old fathers are called up first, and then the more recent dead speak.

This direct, public form of conversation with ancestor spirits has always been objectionable to the Jukun-born Muslims. The Hausas strongly opposed it and would allow only that the *aku-ahwa* spirits have something to do with the Muslim *jinn*. The Jukun Muslims, however, found it difficult not to participate in the ceremony. It carried several benefits for them associated with a need to dominate their wives and secure the father's place in society. The dilemma was

---

[83]Tashkalma Biu, at Biu, January 10, 1970.

[84]*Idem.*

[85]The rite of dancing combined with speaking with the dead, discussed on pages 110-11 and treated by Meek in *Sudanese Kingdom*, p. 238.

[86]Bitrus Angyunwe, at Bukuru, February 14, 1970. The widows must contact the dead husbands and give them tokens of respect in order to have health assured.

solved by Muslims arranging for substitutes who participated in the *aku-ahwa* on their behalf. The substitute was usually a non-Muslim family member who was often paid for this service.[87]

On the other hand, the masked ancestor figure (*dodo*) has always been prominent in Jukun society. This symbol of tribal ancestry has been duplicated by the Jukun Muslims. They have their own *dodo*, called *Ashama*, who makes his appearances at annual festivities commemorating the ancestors of the original Hausas who lived at Wukari. The *Ashama* is one of the major Jukun impersonations of the dead and is prominent in the installation rituals of the Jukun kings.[88]

With the Jukun, therefore, we have seen that where the strong ancestor cultus cannot be appreciably modified to suit Muslim ideals, the pattern will be officially rejected. Then compromise measures will be taken to sustain continuity with the dead within a Muslim setting.

---

[87]*Idem.*

[88]See Meek, *Sudanese Kingdom*, pp. 139-51.

CHAPTER FOUR

PRIESTS, POWER, AND RELIGIOUS RESPONSE

CHAPTER FOUR

PRIESTS, POWER, AND RELIGIOUS RESPONSE

The term, "religious power," refers to the means available within the ritual system for personal and community problem-solving. Religious power includes both methods of treatment and the practitioners who mediate help. Obviously, in seeking for power to solve problems, African people are no longer restricted to traditional methods. Western influence and participation with the outside world have greatly enlarged the field from which solutions come.

THE SHAPING OF RELIGION

There are certain kinds of problems that cause people to think in a religious way. Religious thinking seems to take place on the spirit-world level rather than on the rational level. Granted, this is not an easy distinction to make within the African worldview, but the two levels need to be recognized. Traditional African societies exercise a common sense approach to most crisis situations. This suffices quite well until a special set of circumstances arises that, as Horton says, "can only be coped with in terms of a wider causal vision than common sense provides." At this point, Horton claims, there is a "jump" to "theoretical thinking"—that is, to religion and spirit.[1]

The role of various kinds of practitioners is extremely important when we study African religion. The *Kano Chronicle* describes an important transition in the role of the ancient pre-Hausa leader, Barbushe. It shows that his priestly function had disappeared from tribal life by the time a stranger called Bagoda arrived. Bagoda

---

[1]Horton, Robin, "African Traditional Thought," *Africa*, XXXVII, p. 60.

symbolized a primitive form of Islam that began to develop around the year 1000.[2] The expansion and diversification of the new tribe resulted in a further decline of power at the traditional center of Dalla. As the Hausa society begins to take shape, the division between religious and political rule becomes marked.

The hold which the priest/king Barbushe originally had is recalled by his own words to the people as he entered the "sacred place."

"I am the heir of Dalla, like it or not, follow me ye must perforce."
And the people said, "Dweller on the rock, Lord of Mamale, we follow thee perforce."[3]

But the situation was greatly changed during the rule of the *Ha'be* kings (1000-1450). Rulers could no longer draw upon a spiritual continuity over their subjects for the traditional right to rule. The political function of religion became prominent. The kings began to oppose traditional structure. At times this took the form of open hostility, which resulted in an advantage for the enemy or, again, in his defeat.[4] In other cases a reasonable adjustment was made. In one extreme case a chief saw that he had no alternative but to capitulate to tradition. For that entire period he was an "indigenous" ruler.[5] But whatever the outcome, a prominent role was always played by the clerics, both traditional and Muslim, as they divined, consulted, and intervened with the king on behalf of the people.[6]

During times of crisis, especially in wars, both traditional and Muslim clerics were consulted. The *Kano Chronicle* records that Yaji called on the Muslim clerics of the Warangawa "to make prayer" so that he could conquer the Santolo. But Kanajeji counselled with the

---

[2]D. S. Gilliland, "Religious Change Among the Hausa, 1000-1800," *Journal of Asian African Studies*, July-October 1979, Vol. XIV 3-4, pp. 241-57.

[3]*K.C.*, pp. 63,64.

[4]Gugua (1247-1290) was "liberal, eloquent, wise and magnanimous." But, even so the pagans hated him because he tried to discover the "mystery of their God." Gugua, however, was blinded by an encounter he had with the pagan apparition holding a red snake. This victory for all the pagans was balanced by their defeat under Tsamia (1309-1343) who successfully destroyed the *Tchibiri* shrine. *K.C.*, pp. 67-69. Also see Chapter One, pp. 36 ff.

[5]As in the case of Kanajeji (1390-1410) who denounced Islam and capitulated to the side of the *Sarkin Tchibiri* and received the traditional paraphernalia. *K.C.*, pp. 73,74.

[6]See esp. Gugua, Tsamia, Yaji, Kanajeji, Daudu, Mohamma Rimfa, Abubakr Kado, Mohamma Zaki, and Alhaji Kabe.

head of the pagan cult, *Tchibiri*, and heard him say, "Whatever you wish for in this world, do as our forefathers did of old."[7] Mohamma Rimfa's reign is remembered for the visit of Abdu Rahaman and the spectacular influence which the "learned men" had on the policies of the chiefs.[8] Yet very soon after Rimfa's reign the animistic-Muslim practices of *Tchakuwa* and *Dirki* were instituted. These syncretistic practices were encouraged by the Muslim clerics who had by this time become adept in magic as well as in prayer. Even the Arabic scholar Sheik Abubakar of the Maghreb made a suspicious promise to Mohamma Zaki. "If you wish to repel the men of Katsina," he said, "I will give you something to do it with."[9]

These religious priests continue to influence African society. The highly developed clerical class of the Hausa as well as traditional groups represent religious power of first rank. They know the characteristics of each ethnic community and are expert in developing the particular means to cope with felt needs. The orthodox Muslim cleric may officially forbid connections with "pagan" rites, but, as Greenberg notes,

> The Mohammedan learned men . . . entertain an actual belief in the power of these (pagan) spirits, and these create a condition which permits considerable survivals of the *iskoki* cult among the mass of Moslem Hausa.[10]

The conclusion of Greenberg's study (*The Influence of Islam on a Sudanese Religion*) shows that the Muslim practitioners do not maintain a clear distinction from their animistic peers. [11] There is a high degree of interaction between the two. Islam, says I. M. Lewis, cannot be too rigid about the service it renders its clients, because many are seeking "relief from affliction which the orthodox rituals . . . of Islam have failed to remedy."[12] The factor of immediacy, so important in African religion, has given a highly utilitarian quality to Islam in its West African setting.

---

[7]*K.C.*, p. 73.

[8]*Ibid.*, p. 77.

[9]*Ibid.*, p. 83.

[10]Greenberg, *The Influence of Islam*, pp. 68-70.

[11]*Ibid.*, p. 70.

[12]Lewis, "Islam and Traditional Belief," *Islam in Tropical Africa*, pp. 69-70.

Every important crisis implies a strong emotional upheaval, mental conflict and possible disintegration. The hopes of a favorable issue have to struggle with anxieties and forebodings.[13]

Means for maintaining balance and power for the society are provided at various levels by priests, whether Muslim or traditional. They find it to their advantage to work in a mutually respectful way, borrowing from each other and admitting to limitations which each has.

TRADITIONAL AND MUSLIM CLERICS

Radin takes quite a secular view of the way in which religious specialists develop. This grows out of his functional view of religion which he sees as the means of stressing and maintaining the life values of the society. The "religious formulators," as he calls them, are, therefore, those who "manipulate the psychological correlates of the economic-social realities."[14]

TRADITIONAL PRIESTS — MAJOR AND MINOR

Radin believes that priests are motivated most by personal gain, so that they devise all kinds of ways to manipulate the public. In fact, these practitioners have much more integrity than Radin's view permits. These special offices developed right along with the tribe. The ways in which the priests function follow the structure of the tribe. For one community the priesthood is centered around the seasons and the crops.[15] Where a particular crop is important for the whole tribe a designated family holds the special rites in trust and are a center of power. Or when rituals of the tribe focus on the ancestors, the original family holds the symbols and controls the rites connected with the dead. The heads of these special families become priests and continue this function for the whole tribe.

---

[13]B. Malinowski, "The Role of Magic and Religion," *Reader in Comparative Religion*, p. 12.

[14]Radin, *Primitive Religion*, p. 15.

[15]For example, the Birom whose major rite is of sowing (*myendeng*) and harvesting (*bidushe*); or the Kulung, whose Basali priest sets the sowing time.

The full status of this office seems to be reached once it becomes hereditary, so that the rites and sacred paraphernalia are handed from father to son. This family, and the priest in particular, have a personal identity with the sacred emblems of the office and the spiritual rights associated with it. This, then, is a priest of the highest order, held in special honor by the entire tribe.

> He is the repository of the tribal traditions and therefore presides at initiation ceremonies. He receives and makes offerings on behalf of the people. By virtue of his intercourse with the spirits he obtains esoteric knowledge of powers by which he can drive out wicked spirits.[16]

This major priest can be the ritual head of a tribe. Examples of this are the Vabo priest of the Mumuye and the traditional Dukil fathers of the Longuda. But the major priest may also be the head of a special cult which functions on behalf of the whole tribe. This is illustrated by the chief of Fare, guardian of the sacred grounds of the Bachema god, *Nzeanzo*, and by the priest of Tilla Lake, where the sacred crocodiles of the Pabir are cared for.[17] So it is with the "Rainmaker," who has such a powerful place among the Mumuye.[18] Further, mention could be made of the priest *Ma* among the Jen and the head of the Kulung *Basali* cult. The feature which these priests have in common is that they act on behalf of the whole tribe, symbolizing a universal myth. These positions are always hereditary, linked to the great past of the tribe.

A quite evenly distributed group of practitioners are more concerned with the everyday fears and ills of individuals. These we might call "minor" priests when compared to the above. These specialists have the sanction of the community, because over a period of time they have demonstrated their knowledge of spiritual powers and have proved their ability to resolve personal crises. These minor priests are distinguished from a class of diviners who thrive by the clever use of magic formulas with very little or no reference to

---

[16]Meek, *Northern Tribes*, p. 43.

[17]See Meek for the priest of Fare, *Tribal Studies*, I, 28 ref., and on Tilla priest, *ibid*, pp. 166 f.

[18]The great "Rainmaker" is in a separate category of function within the Mumuye cosmology, since his appeal is direct to the Supreme Being, *La*, who alone can give rain. The "Rainmaker" thus does not perform ritual acts through the priest of Yabo, the religious head of the tribe.

religious myth.[19] These minor priests are of a more local type and are described by a Kilba man for his tribe.

> Some have unusual power because at one time a whole family set them aside saying they have been born with a right from their grandparents. Some became priests by dreams which the people respect and receive as facts or as having come from the god of the family. Some gain the awe of the people by doing usual things or making truthful predictions about family troubles. When certain men can get power over bad spirits they are accepted as being in the god's power.[20]

These local priests are distributed widely in African traditional society, and it is mainly with this group that the interaction with Muslim clerics occurs.[21]

MUSLIM CLERICS IN THE TRADITIONAL COMMUNITY

Among the tribes of our study the term *malam* (Ar. *ulama*) long ago fell into a corrupted usage. The indiscriminate use of the word generally described anyone, especially in rural areas, who could read and write and had some status as a result. So the word *malam* has been taken over by all Hausa-speaking peoples to describe men who are literate, even though they are not teachers. We wish to use the term in its more specific, historical sense, referring to the learned class that has always accompanied the spread of Islam. These persons not only teach Muslim dogma but also advise on ethical practices and dispense cures (*magani*) of various kinds. The *malam* of the traditional village is a folk doctor, less sophisticated than the *malam* of the centers of historic Islam, such as Sokoto, Katsina, and Kano. But, as Greenberg says, it is evident that

> There are wide variations in the degree of importance and financial status of different *malams*, with which the varying degrees of learning, ranging from a mere knowledge of the Koran and a few medicines, to what may be a considerable knowledge of Arabic grammar, law, astrology and medicines are roughly correlated.[22]

---

[19]Almost without exception the spokesmen for the tribes made a clear distinction between the practitioner who acts through myth, accepts sacrifices, and appeals to religious symbols, in contrast to the magician-diviner whose whole system is self-contained.

[20]Ishaku Kwambila (Kilba), in an interview at Bukuru, February 6, 1970.

[21]See discussion by Nadel on the Nupe *gunnu* priest in *Nupe Religion*, pp. 72 ff.

[22]Greenberg, *Influence of Islam*, p. 66.

In this discussion we are concerned with the less "orthodox," usually self-styled and semi-literate *malam*. Granted, these *malamai* (pl.) may perform daily prayers and can recite from a few to many chapters of the Qur'an. But along with this they have learned certain divining methods, and they both make and sell Qur'anic charms (*laya*). Nadel describes this ubiquitous group as a "medley of incongruous bits of information," making no attempt to imitate the more formal methods of the higher class of priests.[23] This local Muslim "doctor" is readily available both to Muslim and non-Muslim. He is not a proselytizer but renders services for a living. Here, away from the controls of the large centers of Muslim life, interdependence and accommodation take place. Even in a city like Kano, the more scholarly *malamai* admit their interest in pagan cults, and I did not find it awkward to discuss *Bori* practices with them. *Bori*, the Hausa possession cult, does not seem to be in conflict with the Muslim acceptance of the spirit world.

There is a tendency on the part of the Maguzawa *malamai* to view the Maguzawa beliefs and practices with a fair amount of tolerance. In the large tribal areas about which we have been writing, this kind of tolerance expands to outright participation in certain forms of traditional practice. Intermarriage by Hausas with village women has not always resulted in raising the children as Muslims, as is generally thought. The Muslim husband is often bound to traditional customs and sanctions which, in many cases, he respects.[24] The freedom of Muslims to visit in "pagan" homes and vice versa has changed considerably the exclusive character of Islam among village people.

EXCLUSIVENESS AND INTERACTION

IN MUSLIM AREAS

There are limitations, however, within which traditional priests and Muslim clerics work and which determine who makes up their

---

[23]Nadel, *Nupe Religion*, pp. 246-47.

[24]This is especially noticeable where the Hausa Muslims marry into matrilineal societies such as the Jukun. The deference shown to the mothers of wives, such as gifts and manual labor, is not the custom among Muslims.

clientele. The presence of Hausa *malamai* in many traditional communities is a comparatively recent development, though none seems to remember when there was no "Hausa medicine" available. The difference in status and role of the Hausa *malam* of the northern states compared to the middle belt areas has already been pointed out. The Hausa-Fulani states of the north do have their minority peoples, both the so-called "strangers" and the "pagan" Hausas.[25] People who have needs among these groups tend to seek for the help which is available to them from within their own community. Yet in these areas where the Muslim customs dominate, the minorities give a place of second importance to their own practitioners. The Birom and Mwaghavul who live in Kano reported practically no contact with their own traditional medicine and have little continuity with tribal customs. They are forced to rely on means provided for them by the Yoruba, a much larger group who occupy parts of the Sabon Gari ("new town")[26] section of Kano. This would be unthinkable were they living in the indigenous setting. The tribes of the middle belt areas (Benue, Plateau, Kwara, Niger, and parts of Gongola and Kaduna States) are such a minority in Kano that little tribal dependence is necessary since "most are educated and are in the city to pursue employment."[27]

But where the non-Muslim Hausas are concerned, the situation is much different. Here there are two distinct roles, one for the local priest and the other for the Hausa *malam*. Which priest shall administer for which situation touches on content as well as method. The Maguzawa admit freely that they do seek help from the Muslim *malamai*. The fact is that the ills and problems which arise from the sphere of Maguzawa spirit cosmology can be solved by their own Maguzawa practitioners (*bokaye*). All others must be referred to a Hausa *malam* for suitable "medicine" (*magani*). This distinction was made by Gelo, chief of Madaurare.

> When a woman comes to our own priests and complains of barrenness, she is asked many questions, in the Maguzawa tradition. There are certain

---

[25]"Pagan strangers" (*bakin arna*) are the non-indigenous tribal people who live in Kano in great numbers, whereas the "pagan" Hausa refers to the Maguzawa and the few Kutumbawa who have not become Muslims.

[26]Also the greater part of a large Christian constituency live here. The "old town" is almost totally Muslim.

[27]From an interview with Adamu Gwari (Gwari tribe), in Kano March 19, 1970.

"tests" which the diviner can give as help to know what has caused her trouble. If the herbs and smoke do one thing to her the diviner knows he can continue to help her, but if it does something else he must dismiss her. Only the diviner knows the difference.[28]

Gelo referred to the divination of spirits and said a distinction is always made between *iska na gida* (spirits of the village) and *iska na waje* (spirits from the outside). He understood that the client never makes a distinction himself; he only seeks help. But he is willing to go to either the Muslim or the traditional practitioner.[29]

The usual Hausa practice was described as follows: The *malam* writes verses of the Qur'an on a writing board (*allo*) which is then washed off. The client drinks the water with which the board was washed. Or, just as common, verses from the Qur'an are written down, the written verses then rolled into a ball and covered with leather and worn according to the *malam*'s directions.[30] The Maguzawa priest relies on herbs, bark, roots, *turari* (smoke of various fragrances), and spoken incantations. But it is the Hausa *malam* who has the right to administer ritual at Maguzawa ceremonies of birth, marriage, and death. It is only in the past thirty years that the Maguzawa have been buried as Muslims.[31] The influence of the Muslim clerics on Maguzawa religion, then, is important not only for these *passage* rituals but also because they provide cures for troubles caused by "alien spirits" (*iskokin waje*). It is worth noting that Muslims were not coming to Maguzawa diviners or priests. The influence seems to be very much in one direction.

IN TRADITIONAL AREAS

The way in which the Maguzawa use the services of Muslim practitioners can also be seen in other traditional areas. The Muslim community may be small, so the consensus is on the side of traditional practices. Consistently the active-resistant groups had the most negative attitude when asked about the usefulness of the *malamai*. The

---

[28]Gelo, at Madaurare, March 14, 1970.

[29]The traditional man usually visits the traditional priest first, since the "patient understands his own medicine the best." *Idem.*

[30]Miner, *Timbuctoo*, p. 93.

[31]Begun through the influence of the late Sardauna of Sokoto, Ahmadu Bello.

Longuda and the Mumuye have retained traditional practices which control the young people in many ways. This is especially true of the Mumuye. This is also true among the Tiv, where any form of Muslim practice or seeking for Muslim help is practically non-existent. However, the Jukun, while resenting institutional Islam, are not adverse to seeking the help of Hausas who have established a reputation for "powerful medicines."[32]

It is not easy to establish the circumstances which guide the traditional man to one or other of the practitioners, whether Muslim or his own. There is a simple pragmatic approach to things. People will go where they can get help. The religious question often does not even enter in. Sara, a Gwari student, gave the rationale for going to one or the other as follows:

> The pagan will go to the pagan priest when he considers his trouble to be caused by usual things which he can understand. But for unexplained things or things which do not respond to the usual medicine he goes to the Hausa *malam*.[33]

Bearing this observation in mind, I talked to Malam Sule, who is a Hausa man living in a "pagan" town.[34] He described the major problems which "unbelivers" have when they come to him for help. In frequency of occurrence, he felt the first two were almost equal. These are: (1) boys and men (rarely girls) who are seeking marriage, and (2) means for many kinds of good luck or quick money. Following these he gave barrenness as a problem usually brought by men on behalf of their wives, but also being sought by some women. When I asked him why these particular problems form his main service to the traditional community, he said, "The people think that Allah has more power to give them these kinds of things than do their own pagan sacrifices (*tsafi*)." This was an obvious answer, so I pressed him further. His reply was, "They do not need Muslim medicine for the diseases which their own religious workers understand."

---

[32]Bitrus Angyunwe stated that he knows of some who have actually joined the *amgbakpariga* as a result of their effective medicine.

[33]Sara Kwara, Gwari tribe, at Jos, December 11, 1969.

[34]The term "pagan" is in contrast to "Muslim" to reflect the Muslims' own terminology, e.g., *kafir* or *arna*.

The conversation with Malam Sule confirmed what the Gwari student had said: phenomena which are outside the domain of the traditional and familiar are referred to the Hausa *malam*. When asked about referrals in the village of Bambur, a spokesman from the Ba'ngai clan denied that they go to Muslim *malamai* for barrenness, because, "We have our own ways to help our women get pregnant." His reference was to the local Basali cult and to rituals at special shrines set aside for this problem. But on the issue of seeking for mates and for obtaining good luck or quick money, he admitted that many do go to the *malamai*.[35]

The field of available power has definitely been enlarged by the presence of the *malam*. Since the service he renders is extremely valuable to him as a source of income and personal prestige, he is lenient when it comes to "orthodoxy." Malam Sule said the important thing is that the *malam* knows what he is doing, since he cannot expect the "pagan" client to understand. His answer when asked about "bad spirits" which must be driven off was, "The Qur'an does not forbid methods of exorcising spirits." Hence, here is the grey area where, perhaps, the greatest amount of mutual contact occurs between traditional and Muslim priests. Lewis feels this collusion arises directly from the Qur'an:

> The Qur'an itself provides scriptural warrant for the existence of a host of subsidiary powers and spirits. These may not all be equally legitimate, but their existence and effectiveness, whether malignant or beneficial agencies is not disputed.[36]

This fraternity between the two systems is discussed by Froelich covering Francophone West Africa in terms of what he describes as *un veritable dualisme religieux*. A true religious dualism exists in Senegalese society where Islam has dominated for five centuries. He refers to the Hausa as a people who have accepted both the *marabout* and the *feticheur*, because they see the two as quite necessary for the equilibrium of the society.[37]

---

[35]Nyala Ba'ngai, at Bambur, April 10, 1970.

[36]Lewis, "Islam and Traditional Belief," *Islam in Tropical Africa*, p. 60. He also adds, "Muslim theology is equally tolerant in its attitude towards divination, magic, witchcraft and sorcery. It condemns the illegitimate use of the last two but does not question their efficacy." *Ibid.*

[37]Froelich, *Les Musulmans d'Afrique Noire*, p. 104.

LEVELS OF ORTHODOXY IN RELIGIOUS PRACTICE

INTERACTION OF MUSLIM PRIESTS WITH TRADITIONAL PRIESTS

If the *malam* and traditional priest were to compare the means open to them, the traditional priest would have the advantage. The non-Muslim priest has a far wider range of techniques he may use.[38] Islam can, however, find ways to accommodate to traditional society. The basic issue for the *malam* is to be reasonably sure that his methods have some kind of a Muslim precedent. How far a *malam* can go towards animism in his technique is unclear.[39] From what one can observe, especially in the villages, it seems that the *malam* can do almost everything the traditional priest can do. The *malam* fits his methods into an Islamic rationale. However corrupted folk Islam may be, it is still Islam. What a Muslim *malam* does is never identified with animism in the mind of the client.

Traditional treatment is carried out through forms controlled by tribal ritual, while Muslim treatment, whatever its appearance, is within the sphere of Islam. The issue of "doctrine" or "orthodoxy" never arises in the mind of the client. The client is seeking for help and rarely thinks about the source of that help—whether it is orthodox Islam or not.

When a *malam* erects a shrine in a "pagan" village as the center for his services, it must be remembered that in primitive Islam it was not easy to differentiate between "orthodoxy" and traditional practice. Watt speaks of the evolution of "islamic ideation" in Mecca and the fact that many pagan shrines were abruptly taken over and used as centers of power for Muhammed.[40] African Muslim practitioners use local places and local terminology for performing their services. Illustrations from Timbuktu today, for example, show that even with the passing of centuries the practices of the *malamai* do show very little

---

[38]Ranging from his own variations on traditional rites to magico-religious methods.

[39]See Lewis, "Islam and Traditional Belief," *Islam in Tropical Africa*, p. 65.

[40]See Watt, *Islam and Society*, p. 188.

awareness of orthodoxy. The methods of the *marabouts* have always accommodated to the Songhai-Bella culture. Horace Miner writes:

> After prolonged drought some marabouts pray continuously in the mosques, and others, with their students, chant prayers as they go through the sandy streets and visit tombs of saints . . . . Still another means of securing the benefit of the sacred word is commonly used in cases of illness. . . .The marabout writes the Arabic passages with charcoal on a wooden writing board . . . the words are washed off with water into a calabash. The patient drinks thrice of this water and his body is washed with the remainder.[41]

These practices are very much in the tradition of Islam. But Monteil shows that exorcism introduces much more questionable methods. In *L'Islam Noire* he describes women who are possessed of spirits. These spirits have to be driven out by dances and divination. The description Monteil gives is similar to *Bori* practices in Nigeria. *Bori* produces convulsive states by dances and chants, through which it is alleged that the *spirits* inhabiting the person can be identified.[42] But I learned that among the Maguzawa only the diviners are prepared to deal with spirits which cause harm. The *malamai* agreed that these local practitioners have better "medicine" for certain traditional spirits.[43]

As already stated, the extent to which the *malamai* employ methods based on traditional structure is often considerable. I refer to an episode which occurred in 1962. A Yendang man (Gongola State) had been studying with me but had to drop from school because of a chronic abdominal disorder.[44] When all medical help failed, he went to the town of Lau for treatment by a Hausa *malam*. The diagnosis and treatment were strikingly indigenous. The problem was laid to a certain evil wind or spirit (*mugun iska*) which he said had "blown in" from Bauchi town. The treatment,which lasted for two weeks,

---

[41]Miner, *Timbuctoo*, pp. 84,93.

[42]Monteil, *L'Islam Noire*, p. 44.

[43]Stated by the *liman* (*imam*) who performed the Maguzawa wedding. Though he would not allow that there are certain categories of "spirit" which are distinct from *aljanu* (e.g., *iskoki*), he did, nevertheless, agree that there are "worthless spirits" (*ruhohin banza*), with which the *bokaye* can communicate.

[44]The subject referred to is Barnaba Panti, a native of Didango (Yendang) who had been treated for over two months for abdominal gastritis at the mission hospital at Bambur.

required the drinking of "sacramental water"[45] (*ruwan albarka*) and the tying of various charms to his arms and waist. The patient was also required to listen to readings from the Qur'an at appointed times. The results were beneficial, even though the client professed to be a Christian. When the *malam* was asked why his practice could help "unbelievers," he replied, "God is no respecter of persons." The provocative feature about this treatment was the *malam*'s admission of an "evil wind" (*mugun iska*) as the cause. This is a term which belongs to the spirits of the "pagan world." Here the Hausa practitioner openly used terminology that would make the patient feel comfortable and employed methods of treatment that were familiar. The special feature of the treatment that he would not have from his own healers was the reading of Muslim sacred scriptures.

The Lau incident could be duplicated many times to illustrate the wide use of local methods by *malamai*. The ancient fusion of Islam and traditional religion among the Bura at Subwong, for example, included a "truth tree" where pagans and Muslims alike consulted the Muslim priest of the great Baobab.[46] When truth is sought in connection with any kind of wrong-doing, a peg is driven into the soft bark of the Baobab. The person who has done the injurious act, whatever the nature, must break off the peg as a confession. If he refuses to do this, he knows that bad consequences will follow.[47]

Incidents of what appear to be a kind of sympathetic magic among Muslims are not uncommon. The long drought of 1965 was taken seriously by the Qadariyya *malamai* of Bauchi. I came upon them one

---

[45]This is the water which is used to wash the Qur'anic verses off the writing boards. *Baraka* (Hausa: *albarka*) is the supernatural power available through Muslim holy men, sacred words and objects, and is supremely important in North Africa and less in Senegal and Mali. Here *albarka* does not function as a kind of "mana." It would be more accurate to say that it means "blessing" of a salutory kind. The North African model of *baraka* is discussed extensively in E. A. Westermarck's *Pagan Survivals in Mohammedan Civilization* (London: 1933), pp. 87-144.

[46]The *kuka* tree (baobab) is twelve feet across at the base and is a veritable collection of metal and wooden pegs, some protruding and others being enveloped by the fleshy bark.

[47]Various "truth-telling" devices are scattered throughout the tribes. One such is the *ubangta* of the Kutep, which is a forked branch planted in the floor of the house. A woman accused of adultery fears the "seeing-power" of the *ubangta*. A rope is let down through the roof which she may cut if she wishes to "tell all." If she does not tell, illness, even death, will follow. A powerful *ubangta* held by an old man can be sold at his death if the price is met.

124

day marching in the roundabout at the center of the town. They were chanting in the name of Allah. They interrupted their slow movements at least twice to spit on the ground. This was done in unison. All were turbaned and dressed in white gowns. The sight was unforgettable. I asked the meaning of the ritual and was given the same answer by three people; they were imploring Allah for rain.[48]

The methods change from locale to locale, but one thing is consistent. There is no other power apart from that of Allah, even though the means by which it is invoked vary greatly. But the core of Islamic practice is retained, such as prayer, scripture recitation, almsgiving, and the fast. But the wide interaction with traditional practice is the point which needs to be emphasized. The tribe recognizes the services of both. The *malam* must resolve his ideological dilemma by practicing what is condemned in theory, because it meets the needs of people on their own terms.

ISLAMIC AFFECTATION BY TRADITIONAL PRIESTS

The *Kano Chronicle* gives considerable evidence of the clerical Muslim class employing traditional practices, especially just preceding the *jihad*. But there is little to illustrate that traditional priests tended to adopt Muslim practice at this time. Indeed, there is little known of the non-Muslim practitioners after the time of Rimfa (1499). The *Chronicle* gives the impression of a rather systematic progression to an Islamized society, where obviously pagan practices were done under the guise of Muslim ritual.[49]

Traditional religion, however, does on occasion, borrow and imitate forms which belong to others. The imitative techniques of traditional priests are usually found between neighboring tribes and clans. For example, one of the major features of traditional religion is the *dodo*. This masquerader, which has been referred to before, is a physical representation of the ancestors, the "first father" of the

---

[48]This occurred in Bauchi in the month of July, 1965.

[49]Significantly, the stubborn pagan element, the Maguzawa, had already been dispersed by Bugaya (1390) who ordered that they "scatter themselves through the country" *K.C.*, p. 72. Such action would have dissipated their strength as a counteractive agency to the developing Muslim society.

125

tribe.[50] It is the sort of institution which develops directly from the primitive myths and has no dependency on later religious models such as Islam.

It can be shown that the *dodo* is a cross-cultural phenomenon. The *dodo* has been adopted, altered, and even surrendered as tribes interact with each other. Some *dodos* are active in fertility rites, others appear at initiations; some are rarely ever seen while others seem everywhere present, policing uninitiated boys and women. The traditional priest takes the function of the *dodo* into account, since his role is highly integrative with fixed rituals and the calendar of sacred festivals. Imitations and adaptations of the *dodo*'s role are clearly affected through intertribal contacts. For example, the Yendang have no *dodo* of their own, so they make use of certain functions of the *dodo* of the Mumuye, a neighboring tribe, even though very little else is borrowed. The *dodo* of the *Aku* cult of the Kulung is similar in name and identified with that of the Jukun, who have left their imprint on Wurkum tradition.[51] Other rituals involving special shrines and unusual appeals to "foreign ritual" (*bakon tsafi*) give evidence of traditional ritual being imitated and borrowed.[52]

There is, however, no widespread evidence that Muslim techniques have been adopted into traditional practice. The Muslim practitioner in the traditional tribes finds it to his advantage to be as liberal as possible on the side of local tradition.[53] The reverse of this, while not widespread, does exist and bears comment.

---

[50]While the *dodo* phenomenon is a major feature of African religion and cannot be overlooked, it has not been dealt with extensively in this text since its origin seems not to be related to Islam, nor has it been appreciably affected by Islamic influence. It is strongest in the "active-resistant" tribes, and, indeed, does not even exist in some of the more open tribes, e.g., Sura and Pabir.

[51]This influence by the Jukun is impressive as contacts are made within the boundaries of the old Jukun kingdom. As with the *Aku* cult, an arm-slashing cult of Mam is found among the Kulung and surrounding tribes as far east as Jen. It is known among the Kulung as *Gabra* or by the Hausa name *Bori*. Its manifestations can be traced to Wukari, where it would have been logically brought from Kano through contact during the Kwororafa raids (approximately 1670-1700).

[52]Cf. the borrowed cults among the Nupe, especially that of the *Sogba*, which is an innovation taken from the Gwari and described by Nadel. *Nupe Religion*, pp. 210-13.

[53]See the discussion on the integration of this masked cult with Islam and Nupe society, and the historical activity with the Fulani and emirs of Bida. *Nupe Religion*, pp. 192-94.

Traditional priests of the "open" tribes show the most Muslim features, such as the priests of the Pabir and Nupe and, to a lesser degree, the Kilba and Bura. The shrines of the Pabir have served both Muslim and non-Muslims but are under the jurisdiction of their special hereditary priests. Because of the nature of the dual clientele, Muslim features are evident. Muslim prayers are done in the compounds of the priests, and alms are given in support of the priest.

Nupe Islam has not been uniform in its integration with traditional ritual. The priestly systems of the Nupe continue to function, and the major cults of the *gunnu* (especially that of the *ndako gboya*) have Muslim sanction.[54] The priests of *ndako gboya* are becoming harder to find in the past thirty years, but this cannot be laid to pressures from Islam.[55] The priests of the *navu*, the pre-Islamic Nupe festival, observe Muslim rites but continue with their customary functions. This is also true of *ndako gboya*, which continues without any sign of deference to Islam or question whether the ritual meaning is inappropriate within Islam. Both the *imam* who performs at the great Muslim *salat* and the *navu* priest are accepted as persons of status, and both are respected as supporters of Nupe ideals.[56]

The more spectacular use of Muslim paraphernalia is by what might be called "secondary" practitioners. These are not cultic priests who are of the hereditary type, but are those who have received individual status by reputation within the tribe. While it is not common, there are interesting adaptations of Muslim practice performed by these village practitioners among the Kilba and Mwaghavul. These are magico-religious uses of Muslim artifacts which have been associated with the *malam*'s power. The *luguji*, it is recalled, is a Fulani practice and is used for divining the future.[57] While it is of Muslim origin, it became a well known institution among the non-Muslim Kilba. The *luguji* has been given various adaptations by local Kilba priests, but the effectiveness of these adaptations was very hard to trace.

The most widespread imitation of the practice of the *malamai* by traditional practitioners has been what is known as counterfeit charms

---

[54]*Ibid.*, p. 195.

[55]*Ibid.*, p. 257.

[56]See pp. 74-5.

[57]See discussion on *luguji*, Chapter Two, p. 45.

(*layar jebu*). These phylacteries (*laya*) which are of Muslim origin are often fabricated by village practitioners and sold for various illnesses or to give personal protection from a variety of dangers. They are usually found in the rural areas. But instead of a Qur'anic verse, the leather packets are filled with sand or some other useless material, while the binding appears to be that of the "true" *laya*. In villages among the Piya people, I found a large collection of these counterfeit charms. However, there was no knowledge of the fact that Qur'anic verses were supposed to be written down by a *malam* and then placed in the leather packets. It was the *form*, the outward appearance of the *laya*, which was supposed to effect cure and give protection. The local priest may have known what a *laya* really is, but since his clientele did not know and readily accepted his substitute, there was little need of raising the issue.

This same type of adaptation has been found in the uses made of the Muslim prayer beads (*cazba*) for divining.[58] Even copies of the Qur'an (or what are said to be copies) were the major artifacts used by two local priests among the Wurkum. These books were reputed to have strong "medicine" which could effect "good cures" by hiding them in appropriate places. A copy of the Qur'an was used as an anti-witchcraft device in the case of one Gwomo man on behalf of his daughter, whose illness was diagnosed as a curse.[59] The same man mentioned other cures where the tribal priest had used "the book" with success.

An unofficial relationship of consent exists between the *malamai* and the pagan priests. The capacity to accept the reality of all forms of spirit, both good and evil, is inherent in Islam and provides a tolerant base from which Muslim practitioners can operate in traditional society. The Islamic source from which their methods take shape is not important, as long as it is agreed that their practices are beneficial.

---

[58]In the village of Wuroleca, Old Muri District of Muri Division, one old man showed me some prayer beads which he kept hidden in a ram's horn. The beads were used only as his vehicle of diagnosis. He said that he had purchased them from a Hausa *malam*. They were employed by throwing them on the ground, after which he "read" the pattern. He said they were more powerful than his "polished stones."

[59]The girl had been subject to catalytic seizures since a small child. Her speech was often affected for two or three days. The trouble was traced to evil action generated by a local family. The Qur'an was hidden in the ground inside the house where the witchcraft was thought to be located.

The *malam* quite openly gives consent to and employs variations of traditional forms.

The traditional practitioners must be viewed at two levels. One is as a class of high tribal priests, who are guardians of tradition. These classic priests are exclusive to the particular tribe and have little contact with outside practitioners. But on the lower level of magico-religious services there are local priests who diagnose personal troubles and mediate ritual cures. These show a much greater integration with the Muslim *malamai*. They are aware of their own limitations and imitate some of the methods which have a Muslim source. This indirectly gives credibility to their Muslim counterpart. But since the Muslim borrows traditional practices, the relationship becomes one of mutual recognition, with factors of acceptance evidenced by both sides.

CHAPTER FIVE

THE ROLE OF KINGS
IN RELIGIOUS CHANGE

CHAPTER FIVE

THE ROLE OF KINGS
IN RELIGIOUS CHANGE

The connection between politics and religion in the northern states of Nigeria has always been complex. Islam dominated politics during the colonial years and immediately after. But with Christianity gaining in numbers and influence, and with the formation of states (1969), the situation has changed. We shall discuss the recent developments in the next chapter.

African "politics" refers to a vast and ancient system. It includes the governance of small rural tribes, large chiefdoms, as well as the administrations of state and federal government. The Western idea of separation between church and state is in fundamental conflict with the African worldview. The African has always accepted spiritual power as a quality that gives the right to rule. It is no wonder, therefore, that anyone with political ambition looks upon religion as an ally.

The *Kano Chronicle* illustrates time and time again that ancient royalty, both Muslim and non-Muslim, used religion as a means of service to the state. Barbushe, the leader of the ancestors of the Hausa, was a classical priest-king. He was the embodiment of both the judicial and religious elements of community life. He was a type of primitive leader whose right to rule derived directly from his contact with the source of religious power.[1] It was of highest political importance that the ruler was a master of the spiritual forces available to him. He knew

---

[1] The Wazirin Kano reinforces the myth of super heroes when he records that this Barbushe could "kill an elephant and carry it for ten miles on his head to his house." *Gaskiya*, Sept. 1, 1969, p. 7.

he could institute change only if political factors were in a state of flux and if the religious institutions were also in a period of readjustment. The sensitive role of the religious factors has always been of fundamental importance to politics.

One is led to ask a question, How important is the relationship between politics and religion? On the one hand, the utilitarian ways that rulers use religion for political ends seems to relegate religion to the purely secular level. On the other hand, the habitual use of religion by politicians shows that it is religion which truly moves people. The high function of religion in African society must be reckoned with if the politician is going to be successful.[2]

TRADITIONAL CHIEFS IN AFRICAN RELIGION

There is as much diversity in the types of local rule from tribe to tribe as there is in religious practices. The term "natural ruler" refers to those leaders who rule at all levels, by virtue of a particular cultural history and with the consensus of the ruled. The range of power which a chief has and the strength of his influence in the community is related to the particular function he has as chief.[3] Perhaps no other single factor so consistently affects the form which religion may take as the role which the natural ruler plays in society.

THE DEVELOPMENT OF LOCAL GOVERNMENTS

The system of local rule was highly developed by the time the British began to administer the former northern provinces. The various types of political structures ranged from loosely federated village groups to complex kingdoms such as that of the Jukun and the sultanates of Sokoto and Borno. But the backbone of traditional political power was, and still is, the governments of hundreds of hamlets and villages. Here, likewise, are "the formulators of

---

[2] See the discussion by Watt in *Islam and Society*, p. 178.

[3] Where the role of the king is traditionally one of primary importance to the myth of the tribe, the personality of the chief has a higher impact on religion than in other cases where the chief's role is not so integrated.

religion,"[4] the traditional priests, who symbolize the political authority which is attached to religion.

The village head (local chief) was always the key figure in this network of rule. Traditionally, he was the final political and judicial authority. In the larger communities several headmen represented the major families. The chief, in these instances, acted only in consultation with the heads of family.[5] A single extended family could, in fact, make up an entire tribe. In such a case the head of the family would be the mediator between factions in the family and was invested with rights which were binding on the whole group.

Originally, the simplest political unit was the family. With the passage of time, the families were forced together for various economic and defensive purposes. This movement, along with the natural proliferation of family units, resulted in large federated communities. In such a federation it could develop that a single family, once autonomous, would become a separate ward, or *anguwa*, as the Hausa term describes it. Thus, a high degree of diversity is found in the makeup of the given tribe, and the interests of the historical local units are protected by a hierarchy of leader-figures. These come into the picture as chiefs, variously constituted, who are responsible for the conduct, tradition, and public behavior of their subjects.

Or the society could take another direction. This was when a large family broke away from a village to found an independent exogamous community.[6] The head of this village would, as a normal rule, be the head of the family which first occupied the site. These historical figures and families are the key to understanding what is often a complicated maze of religious and judiciary figures. In nearly every case the origin and sociological situations that gave rise to the tribal

---

[4] A term used by Radin in *Primitive Religion* which refers to a special class of "priest-thinkers" in every primitive community.

[5] The head of family (clan) is the *mai unguwa*. In many rural communities where the compounds are scattered, he actually becomes the real person of power, while the chief, often living some miles away, is a figurehead.

[6] For example, the people of Ballasa were partitioned from Bambur (Kulung tribe) and set up their own chieftainship to the west of Bambur on the other side of the "great hill." In time, the bulk of the people returned to the Bambur area, but the chief of Ballasa has always resided on the original site, continuing to represent the families who migrated.

families will explain the various levels of authority and their overlapping functions. For example, the historical right of an original family to land claim is recognized. Even more important, special religious functions are held within the original family, for they are "the keepers of the keys," so to speak. The right of the head of a particular family to rule included his ownership of the sacred symbols of office. He held the secrets of the myth and was a warden of the calendar of festivities. Meek says that this religious rite derived from the fact that it was the priest-king who "first entered into an alliance with the *genii* of the place."[7]

THE DUAL ROLE OF THE TRADITIONAL CHIEF

This leads us to consider the chief as a religious priest and dispenser of magic power. The tribes studied give evidence to the fact that the right of leadership is both judicial and religious. It is common now to find that the religious powers of the chief have been separated from his political function. But this was not always the case, and in some tribes a very high degree of spiritual power is still vested with the traditional chief.[8] This distinction is made by the Hausa terms "ritual chief" (*sarkin tsafi*) as opposed to "chief of the town" (*sarkin gari*) or "chief of the land" (*sarkin kasa*).[9] Originally there was a single chief covering both the religious and the judicial spheres. He was the "first father," so to speak, the hereditary personage. If it should develop that the hereditary chief was not a capable administrator, or should the tribe become too large, he could be relieved of his civil function, and this would then be taken up by another. However, he would still retain his position as "ritual chief" (*sarkin tsafi*), for he alone could manipulate the religious symbols on behalf of the tribe.[10]

It is common today to find the "ritual chief" as a well known and distinct personage who holds office quite apart from that of the civil chief. This relationship is of high importance, and the factors that

---

[7]C. K. Meek, *The Northern Tribes*, Vol. I, p. 245.

[8]In the large tribes, such as the Jukun, and smaller hamlets of the Mumuye.

[9]*Sarkin tsafi* is the chief or leader of traditional ritual, while *sarkin gari* is the chief of the town (*gari*) or *kasa* (land).

[10]A case of this kind of history is demonstrated by the Zing Mumuye where the priest is now an active figure for religion only. In Jen the priest of the god *Mam* formerly held complete power.

contribute to unity between the two functions or which separate them may be closely related to the influence that Islam has in the community. An additional cause of the separation between civil and religious chiefs was that Muslim tribes did not wish their ritual chief to have direct dealings with their Muslim conquerors. In attempting to conserve their cultus in the face of domination by aliens, these tribes would select intermediaries who, in turn, became the civil heads. This pattern prevailed among many of the indigenous tribes who came under the rule of the emirs and district heads who were usually Muslim. The ritual chief (*sarkin tsafi*) was thus shielded from secular political affairs while the "chief of the land" (*sarkin kasa*) could move freely in political circles without endangering the historic cultic pattern.

The functional distinction between the *sarkin tsafi* and *sarkin kasa* became more pronounced during the colonial period when the British administrative system called for a chief who could represent the people to district councils. The traditional leader was often not a suitable person to meet the demands of this more sophisticated function.

An illustration of the strong religious leader who traditionally ruled the tribe comes from the Longuda (Gongola State). Longuda immigrants originally settled at Dukil, situated in the north of the tribal region. The head of Dukil was the spiritual father and acted as chief as well, since the moral and judicial control of the tribe was centered in his person. He mediated with the ancestors on behalf of the entire tribe, and as chief he also decided on secular policies such as declaration of wars. One of the highest offices among the tribes in the region, known as Adamawa,[11] was that of the "rainmaker." The chief of Longuda was well known as a "rainmaker" and as such he attracted people from neighboring tribes as well.

Some forty years ago the center of power shifted from Dukil to the civil chiefdom located at Guyok. The relationship that exists between Guyok and Dukil is a sensitive one, for traditional practices are diminishing and political prestige has been enhanced. Yet Dukil is still the center for consultations on matters of first importance such as the appointment of chiefs. The direct influence of the traditional or ritual

---

[11]Demonstrating the absolute priority of the land and its use in connection with crops as being the content from which the structure is formed.

chief on the community is negligible. But the spiritual connection between political activity at Guyok and the ancient center of power at Dukil demonstrates a continuity with the non-Muslim Longuda tradition. This firm tradition has successfully resisted a political shift to Muslim-dominated politics which carried other tribes into Islam.

A comparable situation developed in the Jen tribe but with a different result with respect to Islam. Among the Jen the ritual chief was always the ruler and official head of the community. As the priest of the high god, *Ma*, he was given to seances in order to communicate with the divine spirit. As chief he was the hereditary owner of the land and ritual overseer of all the fishing rights in the Benue River. As priest he was custodian of the moral behavior and spiritual welfare of his people. This unity, however, gave way under pressures of the colonial administrators. The Jen elders were asked to appoint a chief who would be free to function in legal matters only.

The framework into which such a chief would have to fit was that of the Fulani emirate. The emir resides in Jalingo and in 1970 was overseer of twelve districts. Each district was administered by a Muslim district head who, in turn, supervised all the local chiefs. There had always been pressure put upon the local tribes to appoint Muslim chiefs. This was an intense situation in the years just preceding the military coup of 1966. At the time, the chief of Jen was an ambivalent person who ostensibly served the traditional institutions but who, at the same time, was known to engage in Muslim prayers. Hence, what had been a strong and unified cultic personality now, for political reasons, became identified with both traditional religion and Muslim political interests.

THE DIVINE KING

We have observed these examples of the separation of religious and political authority. Developments that affected the *Aku Uka*, King of the Jukun, illustrate the conflict which can arise when the king continues to function as a symbol of the totality of life.

The divine king of the Jukun is a myth born out of an exciting history of the widespread Jukun kingdom, at one time centered at Kwarorafa.[12] One of the Jukun leaders summarized what the *Aku* has always meant for Jukun people. He is the executive head of the tribe, the head of the religion, and the continuing symbol of the tribe's origin.

> He is truly head of *tsafi* (religious ritual). When there is no king everything stops. So it is that the head of each family, the father, is a "king," who always eats first and then the children follow. So our king always eats first and no one will take food until the king has finished his own.[13]

One Jukun elder said, "The king is the only tradition which the village people know. Take away the king and these persons have no way to 'steer their life.'"[14]

In November 1969 it was publicized that the then current *Aku*, Adi Bwaye, must submit to a "traditional death." This expected demise of the king every seven years is highly controversial. It seems a fact that this was the custom years ago. The king historically lasted only seven years. His demise was never really spoken of as death but as a transfer of authority. The details were always kept a mystery. Whether or not this modern *Aku* would "die" in 1969 generated wide controversy. Non-Jukun people and state officials became involved. Adi Bwaye did have political adversaries, so his "death" would serve their interests.

---

[12]The subjects were known by the same names and appear prominently in wars of Kano and Borno. A full treatment of the figure of the Jukun king may be found in Meek's *Sudanese Kingdom*. Jukun men who have read Meek vouch for its accuracy. Much of what Meek did in his *Tribal Studies* was done from secondary sources. *Sudanese Kingdom*, pp. 120-77.

[13]"The king is totality. He is fertility. No one dare say he is dead even though, in fact, he may be; and when he dies he cannot be buried until the sowing. He is said to have died with the old grain and the sowing is for the new king. It is for this reason that the dead king's body must be preserved, irrespective of how long it might have been since he expired." This quote, and that in the text, by Bitrus Angyunwe of Wukari, March 10, 1970. See also Meek, *Sudanese Kingdom*, pp. 164-77. The refusal of the late *Aku's* family to carry out the Puje burial (five months after death) is a significant modern innovation.

[14]Solomon Gambo, at Wukari, April 19, 1970.

This was an important test case because the ingredients of change were religious as well as social and political.[15]

The climax of much newspaper and radio publicity concerning the case was that in February 1970 the death of the *Aku* was announced.[16] His death was assumed by many, naturally, to be an act of subversives who used the traditional myth to get him out of the way. I spent time in Wukari after the *Aku*'s death and talked to enough people directly concerned with the *Aku*'s personal service to be convinced that he did die of natural causes, however untimely his death may have been.[17] It was, however, a test for the viability of the divine-king tradition in a modern African state. The royal customs following his death were kept intact. For example, it is taboo to ever speak of the king's death, and "conversations" with the late king were carried on from behind a grass mat. The ambivalence with which many educated Jukun involved themselves in these events testifies to the tension they felt. There was sincere loyalty to a much-loved tradition which had now become inconsistent with the modern age.

John Mbiti sees the divine king of this type as a political anachronism, which he attributes to the lack of a "future time" concept. If the office of these rulers had messianic elements with a future "hope," we could expect these sacred rulers to enter into the stream of modern African history.

> The most they can now expect is that with the dissolution or diminution of their office a strong mythology will almost certainly build around them and their office.[18]

---

[15]*The Lagos Sunday Times* carried a banner story with the caption, "Should this Man Surrender His Head?" Under the caption was a picture of the late *Aku*. Typical of this provocative article were such statements as, "Having reigned for seven years the custom of the tribe demands that the ruler must die." "The ruler's death is said to be witnessed only by very old male elders and in a sacred place." *The Sunday Times*, November 23, 1969. This kind of newspaper publicity raised the case to national issue. It was reported that the *Aku* kept guards at his bedroom doors, and he did, in fact, become very ill. The state government declared firmly that it would not tolerate any kind of activity that would endanger his life, even in the name of custom.

[16]Such public announcements of death or admission of death are again a radical break with sacred tradition.

[17]The coincidence of his death with the publicity the death-tradition had been receiving was a timely event for certain traditional Jukun factions, for political enemies, and for those who benefited by the publicity which they had created--e.g., *The Sunday Times*.

[18]Mbiti, *African Religions*, p. 22.

140

The overall impression among the Jukun is one of deep respect for a great myth, against which are thrown the inevitable forces of progressive politics, modernity, and education. While this incident did have a bearing on Islam, our primary purpose is to illustrate how real the unity is between priest and king. What happens in the king's court has a direct connection with the religious environment.

The Jukun present an example of kingship and religious power, neither of which has been affected appreciably by Islam.[19] Muslims have never been represented in the king's inner council. Not even the Jukun-born Muslims (amgbakpariga) have ever been included.[20]

Pabir

In contrast to the Jukun, the king of the Pabir is a divine figure with quite a different influence, in that it is set in the context of Islam. The shrine of Yemta-ra Wala, referred to previously, combined the interests of both the "pagans" and the Muslims of the Pabir tribe.[21] However, it is generally agreed that the twentieth chief, Ali Pasikur, was the first "true Muslim," even though the Pabir religion in the royal family persisted along with Islamic practice.[22] Similar to the Jukun, and until very recently, the Pabir chief was said not to have died, but to have "gone away for a time."[23]

---

[19]The *New Nigerian* of Friday, August 22, 1969, carried an article telling of a new mosque which would be built in Wukari costing $280,000.00.

[20]All matters connected with the continuity of the kings have been handled by a highly esoteric and secretive council whose principle is the *Ku Vi*. Participation of the Jukun Muslims in the kingly rites is done by their keeping a sacred *buka* (hut) at the king's palace, along with many other clans and cult groups. These "huts" are a part of the "sacred enclosure," symbolizing the right of the king to rule over all the people. The Muslims also make their own contribution of beer to enter at the Puge ceremonies for the king's coronation. (See Meek, *Sudanese Kingdom*, pp. 144-52.) These gestures of identity with the king by the Muslim community illustrate the difficulty indigenous Muslims have in breaking with the strength of the traditional center.

[21]See Chapter Two, p. 54.

[22]Noted by Meek in *Tribal Studies*, Vol. I, p. 139, and concurs with our own interviews.

[23]Near Biu is a serene volcanic lake (Tilla) where the "king's crocodile" lives. The rites connected with this sacred lake in the past were all centered on the "king" motif. At the king's death the crocodile would leave the water and present itself to the priest of the lake for sacred rites. See Meek, *ibid.*, pp. 166-67.

141

An old man who lives at Biu claimed that tradition connected with the ancient kings is no longer honored, because "God has enlightened our heads." This man was a close relative of the royal family and spoke as a practicing Muslim. But there is little doubt that the sacred rites traditionally centered around the chief have been altered simply to conform to Islamic practice. The striking difference between the Jukun and the Pabir is that while in both cases the chief-king is the central figure in forming religion, the Islamic element has not been an influential factor with the Jukun. However, with the Pabir, Islam emanating from their king, has radically altered the course of tribal religion. The controversy over the death of one *Aku* and installation of the new *Aku* demonstrated the strong consensus still centering around a tribal myth. The progressive Islamization of the Pabir shows the transformation of the traditional cultus formed around the king. This process of Islamization has significant historical precedents.

THE ISLAMIC FACTOR IN AFRICAN RULE

HISTORICAL PRECEDENTS

Study of the *Kano Chronicle* shows that when the Wangarawa arrived from Mali, a massive conflict between the Islamic and the Hausa religions was inevitable. The kings were always the central figures as the pendulum of power shifted from "paganism" to Islam and back again. Usually the Muslim king (*sarki*) was able to hold the pagan forces at bay, but frequently a reactionary king would lead a movement back to the traditional rituals and the old symbols. This was also the erratic pattern which characterized the older Songhai kingdom. It took many years before Islam became the religion of more than a few from the royal class.

Hunwick gives a summary of the reciprocity between religion and the state in Songhai between 1464 and 1591.[24] As early as 1098, Al Bakri recorded that when a new ruler was installed at Gao, "he was

---

[24]J. O. Hunwick, "Religion and State in the Songhay Empire, 1464-1591," *Islam in Tropical Africa*, pp. 296-314.

given a sword and a shield and a copy of the Qur'an that was said to have been sent from the caliph at Baghdad as an insignia of office."[25] Hunwick adds further that "the king was called Kanda and professed Islam, never giving supreme power to other than a Muslim." But he goes on to say:

> This pattern of Islam as the official royal religion with the mass of the populace remaining pagan, and with a largely pagan court ceremonial, remained the general fashion up to the end of the period examined here (1591) and is an indication of the very delicate balance which always existed between Islam and the indigenous Songhay religious structure.[26]

Kings and leaders have openly used religion as a means to keep the upper hand, whether traditional religion or Islam.[27] When "true" Islam took up its cause against "paganism" for reform, it was always the chief who was at the center. The power struggle between traditional chiefs and the hierarchy of Islam has been a modern version of the ancient dynamics so obvious in the *Kano Chronicle*. The rule of Bello, following Uthman dan Fodio, established the emirates located in centers where the *jihad* (1804) had been victorious. But, except for the far northern states, these emirates never represented natural rule or the consensus of the tribes.[28] Even with a Fulani emir, the traditional chief still has considerable influence. The conflict caused by a Fulani Muslim hierarchy vis-a-vis the tribal chief who symbolizes the natural right to rule has always posed a dilemma.

---

[25]*Ibid.*, p. 297.

[26]*Ibid.*

[27]Sunni Ali demonstrated with the Songhai kingdom (1464-1492) the manipulation of religion for the state, thus both encouraging and containing Islam. The syncretism which developed found Islam providing many of the necessary and useful elements of Songhai culture. His attempts to keep the religious forces in balance are modified by the Askias, who carried their involvement with the *ulama* much further. They gave status to the *ulama*, yet continued to maintain the traditional institutions. The result was little popular support for Islam while, at the same time, Islam had considerable influence in the urban areas and among the elite.

[28]J. E. Means' characterization of the emirs is inaccurate. He says, "There are two contradictory forces at work in Nigeria producing tension. One is the tribal spirit which urges divided people to reunite under hereditary tribal leaders (the emirs). The other is a deliberate full scale effort to obliterate the tribal system." *The Influence of Islam*, p. 91. The Fulani are not hereditary tribal leaders by any definition except in the Hausa history after 1450 and by the history of the *jihad* in the "middle belt" tribes after 1810. But here (in the "middle belt" Fulani were never the *indigenous* leaders even though their rule is "hereditary."

The political situation in which most of the non-Muslim peoples found themselves after the great *jihad* could not be described as a theocracy. The Muslim minority had the power, but the heterogeneous tribal groups, among whom lived relatively few Muslims, produced what might better be described as an imperial cult.[29] A theocratic Muslim state means that the rulers hold their position not only because they are Muslim, but because they were forceful, charismatic personalities as well. This was the situation in Nigeria during the nineteenth century after the *jihad*, especially during the time of Bello and al-Kanemi. But attempts at a theocracy in Nigeria failed because of the nature of Islam as well as the African religious society.

> The concept of State as an independent political institution is just as alien to Islamic thought as to African thought. Islam in theory recognizes only the existence of the *umma* (and protected communities) with the *imami* as the leader. The constitutional principle of the state is the unity of the political and religious community.[30]

So there was no basis for such a state, for not only was the Islamic power structure formed from above without support from below, but the factions of a disunified African society gave no basis for the Islamic ideal. The religious integrity of the state ultimately depends upon the masses who conform to the ruling ideology. Even the theocratic Muslim units of government which developed from the *jihad* did not owe their organization to Islam in the classical sense. The sultanate of Sokoto kept the Hausa political structure and gave it the general appearance of Islam.[31] Such so-called theocratic states would point to the position of a ruler as justification for the term. In what was formerly known as Northern Nigeria there was only a superficial adherence to Islamic law. Its weakened influence at present "makes it certain that it must have been more limited in its application to the

---

[29]"Imperial cult" is a term used by Trimingham to describe "present day states which include a majority or a significant portion of pagans but whose chief is a Muslim." *Islam in West Africa*, p. 140.

[30]*Ibid.*, p. 133.

[31]Watt makes this point in *Islam and Society* in which he says the Sokoto state had a "veneer of Islam" (p. 135), and he also refers to a communication from Trimingham which affirms that older states, especially Masina (*diina*) were based on more solid Islamic tradition.

nineteenth century."[32] The notion that Uthman dan Fodio was the *imam*, while the *umma* was represented by all the people, was short lived. It was a situation in which "submission" and "conversion" came to mean the same thing.[33] As the system of emirates moved away from the great centers of charismatic Muslim leadership into the traditional tribes of the middle belt and to the south, the notion of a theocracy became even more unstable.

> The revolution was accomplished only in a limited way. The leaders of the *jihad* were rarely capable of effecting the transition from military rule to civil administration. They had no experience of a Muslim state, but had in view an idealistic model gained from reading law books.[34]

The failure of the theocratic state lay in its inability to adjust to the cultural and religious problems presented by a heterogeneous traditional society. With the sultan stationed at Sokoto, anarchy within the widespread empire was everywhere. Slave raids and feudal taxation were carried out freely without interference from Sokoto.[35] The abuse of justice was widespread, and even Islamic ideals were put aside. Muslims were frequently declared to be infidels on trivial charges.[36] The situation which the British found, and upon which they built, did not carry a consensus for Muslim authority among the "pagan" tribes, nor was it based on orthodox Islam. This was because there was no *community* of religion (no *umma*), even though the emirs continued to acknowledge the religious authority of the *imam* of Sokoto.[37]

The tension which the state encountered in Nigeria is that the emirates, exclusive of the far Muslim North, were organized on a contradiction. Islamic theory recognizes only the existence of the *umma* (and protected communities) with the *imam* as leader.[38] Unity of the political and the religious was never realized except perhaps in

---

[32]*Ibid.*, p. 133.

[33]See Trimingham, *Islam in West Africa*, p. 142.

[34]*Ibid.*

[35]"The theocrat (Uthman dan Fodio) resigned his duties as head of state to devote himself to religion, and the elements of anarchy were so predominant that within a few years his empire had degenerated into an assemblage of slave-raiding and tax-extorting fiefs in practical independence of the titular overlordship of Sokoto." *Ibid.*, p. 142.

[36]See Watt, *Islam and Society*, p. 135.

[37]See *ibid.*, p. 133, and Trimingham, *Islam in West Africa*, p. 142.

[38]Trimingham, *Islam in West Africa*, p. 139.

the ancient Borno states and areas located close to Sokoto. The Hausa themselves distinguish between those who are Muslim among them and those who are not. They speak of two realities in their own ranks when referring to *musulunci* (the Muslim way) and *maguzanci* (the pagan way).[39] The factors of disunity were even more critical where the royal elite who were Muslim had authority over the "pagan" (*kafirai*) who were their subjects.

The attempt to bring a pluralistic traditional society into line with an imperial Islamic cult has had negative repercussions. The emirs attempted to use the external trappings of Islam to give the appearance of the ideal Islamic community. But in fact, the internal structure has always revealed a great diversity of traditional peoples who care little for Islam.

POLITICS AND THE SHAPING OF RELIGION

It is taken for granted that the colonial administration gave strong support to Islamic institutions. Lugard's policy was one of assent to the Muslim right to rule, which left very few barriers to Muslim consolidation.[40] Lewis points out:

> . . . many elements of the traditional Muslim political organization in the (colonial) administration of indirect rule naturally enhanced the status of Islam and encouraged its wide dissemination.[41]

As Islamic influence grew, the traditional chief was caught in a hopeless situation within the Muslim hierarchy. When the British arrived, they found that Islam was enforced through a wide distribution of emirates. Besides being the system which was in place, Islam provided a linkage between the introverted tribal community and the incomprehensible colonial machinery. In this way the Islamic tradition became a bridge which could mediate "between the narrow particularism of traditional society and the wider impulses and

---

[39]For the cultural notions which are "Mohammedan" and included in the idea of "*musulunci*" see Greenberg, *The Influence of Islam*, p. 11.

[40]Cf. Lewis, *Islam in Tropical Africa*, p. 77.

[41]*Ibid.*

requirements of modern life and economic interests."[42] The non-Muslim masses had entree with the colonial administration, provided that the traditional leaders worked through the Muslim authority. Since Islamic leaders bestowed upon African rulers the right to rule, and since association with Islam enhanced the status of the traditional ruler, the traditional ruler found Islam to be beneficial.[43] A traditional ruler usually accepts Islam for the benefits it can bring to him in terms of personal power.

This political form of religion is precarious indeed, because the religion of the ruler does not have the consensus of his people. Such a chief will have to "guide his ship" between the forces of Islamic innovations imposed on his own system, the powers of traditional conservatism, and the unpredictable responses from those over whom he rules. Given the Muslim hierarchy, the extent to which a traditional chief may align himself with Islam is unpredictable. The extent and type of alignment by "pagan" chiefs with Islam took many directions in Nigeria after independence (1960). The position which the chief takes is highly influential in shaping the religion of the people, so we must observe some of the variations.

POLITICAL EXPEDIENCY AND RELIGIOUS AUTHORITY

There is a strong tendency for a traditional leader to consent to the appearance of Islam, because it is politically expedient. It is true that the administrative prestige which developed from the Fulani Muslim Empire was not felt everywhere, nor was it equally impelling. The former Northern Region of Nigeria could be divided generally into three areas with respect to historic Fulani ties. There are still the uncontested Muslim areas both of the Borno (Kanuri) and Hausa/Fulani empires. This area is defined today by the states of Borno, Sokoto, Kano, and parts of Kaduna, Bauchi, and Gongola. The second area is the large "central North" (formerly called the

---

[42]*Ibid.*, p. 80.

[43]This is a feature of African indigenous rule in Songhai and is reflected in many ways throughout the *Kano Chronicle*.

Middle Belt).[44] These people have always been subjects of the Fulani emirates but may or may not be Muslim (and generally are not).[45] Today this would include parts or all of Kwara, Niger, Kaduna, Benue, Plateau, Bauchi, and Gongola States.

A third category is also in what can be called central Nigeria. It includes the areas which did not come into the Fulani conquest (mainly Plateau, Benue, and parts of Gongola, Niger, and Kwara States). Here, as a result, Islamic influence has been felt in more diversified and indirect ways.[46] The observations which follow come from both of the last two groups and would generally not apply to the first, since there the chiefs are Muslim among Muslim subjects.

Muslim District Heads and Traditional Village Chiefs

Until quite recently the greatest amount of administrative conflict which affected non-Muslim people was at the village and district levels. The colonial Native Authority system[47] was organized along the following lines: The emir was at the head and directly under him were administrative districts. The appointment of district heads was determined by the emir and his council. Only exceptionally would the district head not be a Muslim. In most cases he would have some historical right to the post (e.g., family succession). The greatest amount of interaction between political figures occurring on the day-to-day level was between a Muslim district head and the traditional village chief, who may or may not be a Muslim.

---

[44]This term refers to what was formerly called the "pagan belt" of North Nigeria in contrast to the "Christian" Eastern and Western Nigeria and the Muslim Far North. The "middle belt" was politically a very strong platform for non-Muslim northerners, and it was thought after independence that it might become a fourth major administrative region. But the proposition failed, and the political advantage went to Ahmadu Bello and his Northern Peoples' Congress (1964).

[45]This would include large and historic emirates such as Bauchi, Gombe, and Biu, where the major towns are overwhelmingly Muslim, but where the tribes who make up the constituency are numerous and basically animistic.

[46]Such as, for example, Benue, Plateau, and Kwara, which are massive areas, generally under traditional chiefs, but also usually classed with the "Muslim North" by virtue of the Hausa *lingua franca* and the former identity they all have under the northern regional government (Kaduna). With present state-system of government, these misnomers about the Hausa-Muslim "north" need to be corrected.

[47]Since 1968 the native authorities have been known as local authorities.

148

A typical example of what can happen when these political religious forces meet was illustrated in the Muri Emirate of former Adamawa Province, now part of Gongola State.[48] The most notable figure in the last generation was the Emir Muhammadu Mafindi, who died in 1953. He was so respected that the non-Muslim Mumuye spoke of his death as the passing of the great ancestor figure (*babban dodo*). Mafindi is remembered for his courageous trek across the desert to Mecca in an old model car at a time when very few were even attempting the *hajj* from Nigeria.[49] The very high regard which the "pagans" (*kafirai*) had for him is witnessed by the fact that the Mumuye "rainmaker" at Yoro was given a district headship.[50]

The reign of Muhammadu Tukur, Mafindi's younger brother, and that of Tukur's son Alhaji Umaru Abba (since 1966) marked a period of increased and, at times, serious tension between village heads and district heads. In 1971 there were eleven districts in Muri,[51] varying in size and in numbers of people. All of them were predominantly non-Muslim in spite of the strong Muslim groups and increasing numbers of Christians.[52] A closer look at one of these districts (Wurkum) as it was in 1970, with its headship at Karin Lamido, will demonstrate the competitive religious forces that affected the lives of people every day.

The indigenous religions of the Wurkum tribes are as diverse as the tribes themselves. In the Wurkum District (approximately 1200 square miles) there were seventeen tribes ranging in numbers of members from as few as 400 to 6,000.[53] It is hard to find a more heterogeneous situation. The only real unity the tribes had was a jurisdictional one which was centered at the office of the district head at Karin Lamido. Jalingo, the residence of the emir, had always been a

---

[48]A reliable but short history of Muri is to be found in S. J. Hogben and A. H. M. Kirk-Greene, *The Emirates of Northern Nigeria* (London: Oxford University Press, 1966), pp. 447-64.

[49]*Ibid.*, p. 452.

[50]*Ibid.*, p. 453.

[51]Wurkum, Lau, Kwajji, Zinna, Mumuye, Malingo, Muri, Mutum Biyu, Dakka, Bakundi, Gassol. The 1963 census showed a total population of 599,270 in Muri division, of which 154,725 are Muslim, and 409,360 are pagan.

[52]Considering that there is also an established Christian Church in the area, making up some 5% of the total population.

[53]Bambuka and Jen.

structure was located at Karin Lamido. It was to the district head that the village chiefs had to give account.

During the early days of independence, strong pressures were being put upon the village heads to become Muslims. This was especially true during the elections of 1964. It was to the advantage of the local chiefs to do so, especially from the standpoint of personal prestige. At the same time, the people of the indigenous villages were repelled by Islam because of mounting taxes and legal injustices.[54] The village chief who put on the Muslim facade had an advantage with the Muslim district head. In turn, the district head would tend to favor the community that the chief represented. This was to the advantage of the people. Such a village head would adopt Muslim dress and certain Muslim customs in exchange for whatever benefits he might derive for himself and his subjects.

In the early 1960s, chiefs in the villages were either "traditional" or "progressive." The "progressive" chiefs rushed to the support of Sir Ahmadu Bello, who was then the Sultan of Sokoto. His party, the Northern People's Congress, was the official "northern party." When local chiefs supported the NPC, this was virtually the same as declaring themselves to be Muslim. Such action was rewarded with amenities and promotions that enhanced their prestige. From 1962-65 several examples can be cited.

Bambur town (Kulung tribe) and Mutum Daya town (Kwanchi tribe) joined each other in what was then the District of Muri. The Bambur chief, Jatau Tabulo, was a traditional Kulung who scrupulously kept to the rites of the Kulung religion. He was not literate, but as a chief he was, in every way, a symbol of the people. Jatau gave much respect to the traditional institutions and recognized that his right to administer was dependent on his faithfulness to tradition. Mutum Daya is the market serving Bambur. There the village head had become a Muslim, had adopted the Muslim dress, and had learned the Fulani language. This chief had attempted to restructure his local court around Muslim law (*shari'a*). Both of the tribes are about the same size, and in both the people were equally

---

[54]For example, local taxes which were not paid by a terminal date brought, in some areas, beatings with a cane by policemen of district heads; several reasonable cases for the district court were turned down because of the political commitment of the plaintiff.

committed to traditional custom. The Muslim chief of Kwanchi, however, became a favorite of the district head at Karin, who was called the Ubandoma. They travelled together on local visits. The chief of Kwanchi received gifts from the Ubandoma, and he became the stand-in for the district head (*madadin sarki*) when he went on long tours, including his pilgrimage to Mecca.

As the pattern developed between the two chiefs, the Bambur people were more and more unable to get action through their chief, Jatau, when he requested help from the district council. Petitions for village wells were always refused, and court hearings were hard to secure. This became a serious source of tension. Kwanchi, on the other hand, received most of what they asked for, and this enhanced the status of their Muslim chief, even though the people were animists. The chief of Kwanchi always gave credit where it was due — that is, to the fact that he was a Muslim. This same pattern could be seen over and over again. Where the traditional head was relatively independent from the people, this, coupled with a weakened traditional religious system, resulted in an influential Muslim community gathering about the chief. But, just as noticeably, where the chief served the interests of the past and followed the consensus of his elders, a resistance to Islam would develop.

When Jatau died in Bambur in 1964, the Bambur elders judiciously selected one of the oldest teachers, respected by all, but who had converted to Islam from Christianity. The logic was clear enough. It has not worked out that Bambur people have embraced Islam as a result, but the change from a strong traditional chief to a Muslim chief had its salutary effect on the community. The overall effect on religion has been a continued slowing down of traditional customs and festivals. The attitude of Yawai, the present chief, is to permit all religions, but the power of a direct connection between chief and tribal religion is no longer present. The bias, rather, is on the side of Islam, and tribal members are free to choose it without repercussion.

In another case the tribal chief of Jen reportedly was doing the *salat* while still claiming to be loyal to the "tribal" religion. This produced a series of problems for him, both on the side of the Muslim hierarchy and among his own people. One afternoon in 1954 a large group of traditionalists and Christians banded together at the head's residence to make their demands. Their resentment of the Muslim district head had reached the flash point. Their demand was for a "son of the land" (*dan kasa*) to be installed as district head.[55] The resentment to Muslim Fulani rule was widespread, and the move on the headquarters of the district head was countered by soldiers of the British district officer. The riot was forcibly put down, and many were put in prison.

When Nigeria received her independence (1960), it meant that the district head would be elected rather than appointed. During his public speeches for election as a Fulani Muslim, the incumbent district head promised that people could once again practice an ancient possession cult (*Gabra*). This cult had been officially banned by the colonial regime.[56] Such deference to the secret Gabra society by a Muslim leader was well publicized, and, as a result, much of the "pagan" opposition to the Muslim candidate dropped away. Traditionalists supported his election and never questioned whether his compromise with blatant "paganism" was right or wrong. That a Muslim district head should actually encourage the reinstatement of a radical pagan rite shows the pragmatism of the Muslim religion in political situations.

Chiefs and Their Subjects

Traditional village chiefs who were under the emirs tended to steer a course between the customary and the Muslim expectations. While there was no fixed pattern, these local chiefs tended to disregard the religious aspect of the Muslim hierarchy. Where local chiefs turned to Islam for political reasons, it very rarely followed that this had a proselytizing effect on the people. A Muslim chief who rules non-Muslim people must cater to the religious practices of his subjects if he is to rule effectively. This results in a model of Muslim rule which is neither revolutionary nor authoritarian.

---

[55]The riot of 1954 included Jen people as well as many from various tribes and resulted in imprisonment for many.

[56]A Kulung version of the *Bori* which was borrowed from the Jukun and modified to fit the Kulung cultus. Its objectionable features include the cutting of the arms in excited states of dancing.

The long-standing Zing chieftainship, also located in the old Muri Emirate, is a case in point. The Zing area is inhabited by Mumuye people who have held closely to one of the most conservative models of traditional religion to be found anywhere in Nigeria. While some of the educated and certain other fringe groups have become Muslims and great numbers are Christian, the tribe, taken as a whole, is animistic. The religion of the Zing Mumuye is highly developed, controlled by a traditional high priest who presides over the cults of *Vabo* and *Vodusu*.[57] The chief of Zing has been a Muslim for many years. In 1970 his status was raised to the level of district council member, giving him direct entry to the emir. But his religious position as a Muslim has never had any significant bearing on the religion of the people, except for a few who are closest to him. He protects his personal status by this religious independence. The people, in turn, have accepted his right to rule, for he is himself a native of Zing.

The effect here is a separation of church and state. The chief is not the religious leader. He is a political figure only. This is anomalous both to Islam and animism, for the *imam* has no *umma*, and the priest of the people is not their chief. The result is a mutually exclusive situation which averts conflict, since the chief, as a Mumuye, knows the areas where religion has the authority, and he carefully avoids them. The religious situation is, therefore, not threatened, and obviously the religion of the chief is his private matter. This is of little concern to the people.

The situation found at Biu, however, is in sharp contrast to the one at Zing. The chief of the Pabir did not need to establish himself as a Muslim, since the royal Islamization of the Pabir was an internal movement that carried massive groups of the Pabir people along with it. The cultural influences from Borno gradually shaped a ruling dynasty at Biu which, even though it was minimally Muslim, became in time the central authority that now governs.[58] The course of Islam has been erratic among the Pabir. It is difficult to establish when the line

---

[57]*Vabo* is the active god between the priest of the clan and the transcendent creator-provider god *La*; *Vodusu* is a male secret society, mainly for the subjection of women, for dancing, and for feasts.

[58]See Meek, *Tribal Studies*, Vol. I, p. 139.

line between animism and Islam was crossed.[59] It is generally agreed that Ali Pasikur was the first Muslim chief, even though the mythical Yemta-ra Wala, the founder of the Woviri dynasty, has become the "saint" of the tribe. Islamic practice among the chiefs up to thirty years ago was erratic, and their royal rituals have always been saturated with traditional rites. The chief in 1969 did refuse to disrobe and wash in the river for his inauguration, as the "pagan" Pabir chiefs always did. The people excused him on the basis of his "riches and education."[60] It was a significant break, however, with the conservative past. While the Muslim influence is not strong in rural areas, the support for Islam is centered at the emir's palace and has definitely shaped Pabir religion to the side of Islam.

It was the same kind of development which made the Nupe society what it is today—a culture that is ostensibly Islamic and yet "Nupe" at its very heart. The Nupe have a longer history of interaction with Islam than the Pabir. Their movement to Islam began with cultural conditioning through an historical figure, Malam Dendo, and was climaxed by military conquest. Through Dendo, who was the spiritual adviser to Etsu Ma'zau, the way was paved for overthrow of the old dynasty, after which Nupe became a vassal kingdom under Sokoto. Nevertheless, the result was a great wave of support for the royal elite, and the religious change came from the ruling class.

> Even today Islam stands for some such identification with the powers that be, with the social elite, and very implicitly with the culture that grew up in the capital where that power is centered and where that elite reside.[61]

Islamization of both the Nupe and the Pabir developed from the central force of the chief, who was able to carry the consensus of his subjects.   Both social and political circumstances combined fortuitously in opening the way to Islam. These cases do show that an alien system can offer an option to the traditional pattern, and, with the

---

[59]Yemta-ra Wala, the founder of the Woviri dynasty, is said to have been a Muslim. But the account of his rejection of the Kanuri Ngasrgamo in Palmer's Bura Grammar (a Borno emissary) would indicate that if he were a Muslim at all, he had an indifferent knowledge of Muslim practices. Ali Pasikur, the first Muslim king (120 years ago) had sixty wives. See *ibid.*, p. 157.

[60]This answer was not explained. It would appear that enough people who would be involved with the ritual were satisfied with the amount of money given and so did not press the issue.

[61]Nadel, *Nupe Religion*, p. 233.

principles of compatibility and selectivity at work, the new religion can develop quickly.

When authority for the new religion is centered with the chief and the socio-economic factors are right, the religion is in a state of change. This observation was made by Skinner in Mossi society. The Nobere chief was converted to Islam in gratitude to a Muslim cleric who cured his illness. Since the chief's compound was the center of political and social life, it became a demonstration area for Muslim prayers, and even non-Muslim chiefs allowed their own compounds to be used for Muslim prayer. The prayer periods were powerful propaganda for Islam, and the quiet respect allowed for these royal prayers was the context within which Islam developed quite naturally. Pagan wives were given to Muslim royalty, and the Islamic community grew.[62] This phenomenon can take place when the traditional religion has the capacity for innovation. In such circumstances the chief can redirect the course of religion.

THE CHIEF AND THE TRIBAL CONSENSUS

Where an Islamic chief rules a non-Muslim constituency, the situation can be either disruptive or positive, depending on a number of factors. The religious system of the people may be tolerant or resistant. Or it may depend on the nature of the chief's own personal commitment to Islam, whether dedicated or casual. These combinations were played out in the Dalla-Bagoda conflict of early Kano, because the kings themselves varied in the intensity of their Islam, and the people reacted accordingly. Two rather contemporary case studies illustrate the negative effects of a Muslim ruling figure who did not have the support of the people.

The Makurdi Affair

The Tiv were the first to openly oppose colonial policies which had not taken seriously the power of traditional culture. The Tiv form a tribal nation. They were difficult for the British to administer because of their great numbers. In addition, British officers were oriented to a

---

[62]Elliot P. Skinner, "Islam in Mossi Society," *Islam in Tropical Africa*, pp. 359-60.

Hausa Fulani model of control. Indirect rule did not work well where there was no centralized traditional government. A Hausa man, Audu,[63] became the first chief of the Tiv, appointed, of course, by the British. This was an amazing development, considering the antipathy the Tiv have always carried for the Hausa. What reasons the British had in forcing such an unnatural rule is not clear. While organizing the Tiv, Audu had been used as an interpreter by the Tiv elders when speaking to the British. He was from a slave family but had grown up among the Tiv, so he knew both the language and the culture.

Strangely this Audu became very powerful, due primarily to the fact that the colonizers could not speak Tiv or work directly with the Tiv. As a go-between, he spoke the will of the people to the authorities. When a chieftainship for the Tiv was organized at Makurdi, Audu became the ruler of all Tiv-land. When Audu died in 1946, it was obvious that his son was in line for the chieftainship. He was also Hausa-speaking and a Muslim. But the Tiv now had a much improved self image. What happened at Makurdi will always be remembered. Tiv soldiers returning from World War II were the catalyst. They sparked off riots, calling for the ouster of the "Hausa-Muslim strangers." They refused totally the continuation of non-traditional rule, and days of fighting between Tiv and Hausa-speaking people resulted. The results of the Makurdi riots of 1947 resulted finally in moving the Tiv chieftainship away from Makurdi to Gboko and the appointing of a Tiv man as chief.

The direct effect of this history and the influence of Islam among the Tiv is illustrated by the explosive situation which developed during Sir Ahmadu Bello's days as premier of Northern Nigeria.[64] Tiv who supported Ahmadu Bello and his Northern People's Congress were literally under siege by the majority of Tiv. Houses were burned and Tiv men were injured, even killed by other Tiv. It was considered treason to the Tiv to give consent to the Islam-dominated NPC. The

---

[63]It was not available if this was, in fact, a Hausa man--or a northern tribesman who spoke Hausa. The Tiv are very general in their classification of all Hausa-speaking people as being Muslim and rarely bother to differentiate between Hausa-born and others who use Hausa as a trade language.

[64]The politics of 1960-65 were of such a divisive nature that the chiefs who felt disposed to support the Sardauna became subjects of bitter attack. For a time the Tor Tiv himself was N.P.C., but never Islamized. The issue was so strong that riots erupted in 1964, Tiv against Tiv, the issue being whether any Tiv should be attached to the Sardauna politically. This was a time of great destruction of property and loss of life.

present attitude to Islam among the Tiv is so much a part of this political history that the Tiv cannot be understood without it. Once the Tiv began to see the effect a Muslim administration would have on their highly developed cultus, it was categorically rejected. When I asked a Tiv man why Audu was put forward by the Tiv in the first place, his answer was, "We feared the colonizers and misunderstood what we were supposed to do."[65]

Resistance at Guyok

In a somewhat different way the Longuda rejected their chief in 1952. This chief, whose name was Grema, was, however, a Longuda and a member of the Bonkumbebe, traditionally the royal clan. The way in which Grema became a Muslim is directly connected to colonial practice. Many of the British district officers brought Muslim staff with them and, consequently, Islam was the religion among the clusters of aides employed in regional and district offices. Grema was the district officer's messenger for many years. This was a position of status, so it was from this post that he was appointed chief in 1940, with the support of the people. As a Longuda, he was loyal to the traditional rites, but at the same time he was a practicing Muslim. David, with whom I talked, knew Grema and described him as one who "performed all the traditional rites."[66]

As the political picture began to take shape on the side of the NPC, the party of Ahmadu Bello, Grema became more and more open in his Islam and began to press his religion on his council. During the last years before his ouster he attempted to force the Longuda people generally to embrace Islam. The anti-Muslim sentiment is unusually strong among the Longuda, and the people became unified in their opposition to Grema. A direct appeal was made to the district officer residing at Numan for his removal. The political issues were complicated, but those who remember the incident say that they wanted Grema's removal for one reason only—"he wanted the people

---

[65]The speaker for this and the above footnote is Jonathan Ukpekeh of Mkar.
[66]David Windibiziri, at Bukuru, August 14, 1970.

157

to become Muslim."[67] Here was an indigenous leader who attempted to move the traditional consensus off center but was overruled. The chieftainship at Guyok was returned to traditional power.

These illustrations show that when religious change is advocated from the top and a society is not open for change, the role of the chief is a negative, even disruptive one. When the environment is open and the Muslim chief has a congenial relationship over a long period, the outcome can be quite different. The Kilba have demonstrated this. The chief of Kilba, who died in 1957, himself a Muslim, is generally remembered for drawing many into Islam and for establishing a Muslim royal community. The Kilba have shown how the sociological and ethnic factors, combined with a chief who is a moderate, can produce a receptive atmosphere for change.[68]

RELIGIOUS POLITICS FROM 1960 TO 1970

The years between 1960-66 produced a political situation that was so integrated with Islam that a separation would be impossible. This was due directly to the influence of Sir Ahmadu Bello, Sardauna of Sokoto and the premier of Northern Nigeria until his assassination on January 15, 1966. We must look at the effects of Ahmadu Bello's policies for the religion of non-Muslim tribes.

Lloyd sums up the political and economic pressures which led up to the crisis of 1966 in the following way:

> The status of the Fulani aristocracy protected by the British was seriously threatened by the modernization of the 1950s — by increasing industrialization and by the growing power of the Federal and Regional Government. But during this period the N.P.C. leaders realized that preservation of their status lay not in isolation but in control of the Federal Government and of the modern sector of the economy so that the emirates would experience only those changes which their rulers could accommodate.[69]

---

[67]It is recalled that the sentiment against Islam is very high among the Longuda. Some of the strongest statements showing a negative Hausa image were found among the Longuda. See Chapter Two, p. 64.

[68]For Kilba see pp.

[69]Lloyd, *Africa in Social Change*, p. 322.

The rush for control by Ahmadu Bello's Northern People's Congress was expressed through demands that northern peoples have greater share in civil service and in federal administrative posts. This resulted in a strong "northernization" program especially in high-level jobs. The census issue of 1961 illustrates the point. The first census (1961) was never published, because it would have, apparently, assured a majority for the south. A second census (1963) gave the north control while southern factions claimed it had been rigged.[70]

Until his death, Ahmadu Bello saw himself as the one to fulfill the theocratic ideal of his noble family, headed by Uthman dan Fodio.[71] This he stated unequivocally at a politico-religious rally held at Jalingo, Gongola State, on October 16, 1965. His words were (Hausa):

> The father of enlightenment and good in this land was the prophet, Uthman dan Fodio, and the work of salvation for all the people which he so nobly undertook has now been handed to me. I dedicate myself totally to its completion.[72]

This was spoken at one of the many town meetings which the premier had been holding all over Northern Nigeria during the two years before his death. His commitment to the Islamization of all people and the idea of a Muslim state is stated clearly in his autobiography, *My Life*.[73] Long before Nigeria's independence, his politics were widely known. As early as 1943 Ahmadu Bello spoke to issues raised by the West African Students' Union on the subject of constitutional reform. Bello objected to the idea of "people who do not habitually reside in a country" making proposals for its government.[74] He added at that time that the southerners who desire a united Nigeria "should embrace the religion of the prophet."[75]

---

[70]*Ibid.*

[71]Ahmadu Bello had worked out a careful genealogical chart which, beginning with his name, pushed back the history of his Toucolour family to the Prophet Muhammed, from whom he claimed descent through Hadija. These colorful charts hung in public places and were generally accepted as fact.

[72]On the occasion of the dedication of the government hospital at Jalingo, Muri, October 16, 1965.

[73]Sir Ahmadu Bello, *My Life* (Hausa: *Rayuwata*), (Cambridge: The University Press, 1962).

[74]"Macauley Papers," papers of the late Herbert Macauley on deposit in the library of the University of Ibadan.

[75]*Ibid.*, quoted by James S. Coleman, *Nigeria: Background to Nationalism* (Berkeley: University of California Press, 1963), p. 361.

The resentment against Ahmadu Bello in western Nigeria increased as a result of his party's role in the parliamentary emergency which arose there in 1962 and in the violent elections of 1964. Sir Ahmadu's open support of Chief S. L. Akintola for premier of the western region was viewed by anti-northern factions in the West as an attempt by the premier and his party (NPC) to crush Chief Obafemi Owolawo's Action Group.[76] This being done he would turn on the N.C.N.C. (the party of Okpara and the Ibo east), "and thus achieve their (NPC's) long-cherished conquest to the sea."[77] This foregoing statement, published by a lawyer from Benin betrays the suspicion and fear with which people viewed Bello's politics.[78]

Two months before Ahmadu Bello's death the *West African Pilot* carried a political indictment against Ahmadu Bello sponsored by the United Progressive Alliance. Among other statements against the Fulani was the following:

> It is their (Fulani) modern leader Alhaji Ahmadu Bello, who in 1959 described Nigeria (including Western Nigeria) as his grandfather's old empire, over which he would appoint his lieutenants to rule.[79]

This political statement does show how Sir Ahmadu had created an image around himself supported by his Muslim ancestry. Lloyd speaks of the "megalomania of his aspirations to the role of dan Fodio," and made the following observations about the problem Sir Ahmadu's aspirations carried for Islam itself.

> The Muslims of the North, though united by the dire prediction of their own politicians on the fate of Islam should the Southerners ever achieve control of the north, were divided by their sectarian movements, with the vast membership of the Tijaniyya only lukewarm in their support for the orthodox Sardauna.[80]

---

[76]Obarogie Ohonbamu, *The Psychology of the Nigerian Revolution*, p. 147.

[77]*Ibid.*, p. 148.

[78]*Idem.*

[79]*West African Pilot*, November 2, 1965.

[80]Lloyd, *Africa in Social Change*, pp. 322-23. For a good summary of the recent Nigerian Civil War see Lloyd, pp. 321-26. Attention is also called to the "official" book on the war by Sir Rex Niven, *The War of Nigerian Unity* (Ibadan: Evans Brothers, Ltd., 1970).

Following are some observations on the policies of the Sardauna and his Northern People's Congress and the effect their policies had on the shaping of politics from 1960-66.

Endorsement of the Premier's Faith by Tribal Chiefs

The extent to which village heads (chiefs) converted to Islam during the period of the Ahmadu Bello's leadership would be difficult to know for certain. But conversions to Islam were many because it was politically advantageous. During the years 1960-66 eight of the traditional village heads in Muri Division began to do Muslim prayers. Though a number had actively supported the opposition (Action Group) in 1960, by 1964 all were brought into line with the northern party (NPC) through their district heads and emir. The movement to NPC was not quite so straightforward in the Middle Belt areas which were not under emirs. But even so, the resistance to Ahmadu Bello became almost non-existent by 1964.

A tribe which illustrates this political kind of conversion is the Rukuba on the Jos Plateau. The Rukuba, through their chief, became an object of Ahmadu Bello's special interest. It is a tribe which we would classify among the "active resistant." The story there is typical of what happened, especially in many rural areas.

The Rukuba chief had always suffered in prestige because of the dominance of the Birom. The Birom traditionally provided the district head, who also functioned as the chief of Jos. In 1963, the Sardauna offered new status to the Rukuba chief, which included a trip to Mecca and, consequently, the title of "Alhaji." This was especially controversial since the Rukuba chief was known to be a Christian. But he did accept the offer which, in effect, made him a Muslim. The Rukuba people, especially his family, never consented to the idea that their chief was a convert to Islam. The political motives behind his attachment to Ahmadu Bello caused doubts about his conversion. People in general were unimpressed. Only his very closest associates joined with him, and most of them dropped away, even before the chief's death in 1968.[81]

---

[81] Ainadu Zagan (Rukuba), in interview at Jos, August 18, 1970.

The activity of the Sardauna at Rukuba is believed, by many, to have been part of a long-range plan whereby the Rukuba chief would take over the district chieftaincy from the Birom in Jos.[82] The respected chief of Jos, Rwang Pam, was well known as a Christian. It is important to note that when the Islamized Rukuba chief died, his son and logical heir was residing in Lagos, so the new chieftaincy quickly went over to a rival clan.

There is little evidence of Islam in Rukuba today.[83] By 1970 most people in Rukuba felt that the resentment of the Fulani and Hausa was greater than before Ahmadu Bello's time. The effect has been a strengthening of the traditional core of the Rukuba clans. The Rukuba were saying in 1970 that they knew of no conversions to Islam apart from those which may be traced back to the influence of the Sardauna.

A similar report came from the Birom who avowed that no major chief had become a Muslim during the 1960s, but some of the village heads and a number of the clan heads did profess Islam.[84] Of the seven or eight political conversions in 1962-64, there remained only three village chiefs who continued to "do *salla*." The rest have gone back to the old way, and others have become Christians.[85]

Appeals Made Directly to the People

The Rukuba and Birom represent areas where the Fulani have not historically had control. The effect produced by the Sardauna was much more pronounced in districts where an emir resides. The Sardauna's celebrated visit to Jalingo, in Gongola State, was in October of 1965. The visit was typical of the organization and planning which characterized his movements. The occasion was to coincide with the opening of a new government hospital, the newly constructed Council

---

[82]The natural jealousy between the Rukuba and the Birom over the chieftaincy of Jos provided an ideal setting for this: (1) The motivation of the Rukuba to take the chieftaincy away from Jos was high, (2) the traditional chief of Jos was a Christian who repeatedly refused to Islamize, and (3) the regional government would have had the political advantage in working the Islamized Rukuba chief (or his son) into the district headship, had not the events of 1966 transpired.

[83]Ainadu Zagen, also Ishaya Ayok Zagen (Rukuba).

[84]Davou Dalyop at Bukuru, March 6, 1970.

[85]*Idem.*

Hall of the Muri Native Authority, and a modest mosque. Sir Ahmadu officially dedicated these buildings. Those who attended the public ceremonies numbered about 5,550.[86] All twelve districts of what was then Muri Division were officially seated as well as most village heads. The Sardauna's address was in two parts — the first political in nature and the second religious. He directed his religious appeal to the officials and chiefs, challenging them to "take up the cause of Uthman dan Fodio in a peaceful *jihad* which changes hearts of people." He declared that with each day the numbers of Muslims were growing, and the party would soon become "one for all the people."[87]

After calling on the *malamai* (teachers of Islam) to increase their efforts to convert the "unenlightened," he turned his attention to more than 300 converts to Islam, seated in front of him, who had been rounded up ahead of time.[88] He led them in the *Fatiha* and charged them as new Muslims to "embrace the faith in all sincerity." Following this ceremony a check in the amount of 1,000 pounds ($2,250) was presented to the resident emir, the late Muhammadu Tukur. The money was given for the express purpose of "spreading the news of the prophet in the land," as the Sardauna put it. As was his custom in official public meetings, he gave new gowns and prayer beads to each convert. The climax of the day came when the converts followed the Sardauna into the new mosque. Here, together with the other Muslims, the converts participated in the Friday service led by the Sardauna himself.

The following facts on protocol of the day reflect the status of the village heads. All village heads (chiefs) were present and officially seated, but only the Muslim chiefs were seated close to the dais of the Sardauna and the Emir of Muri. The identity of local Muslim chiefs with the political hierarchy was unmistakable, while the non-status of

---

[86]All of the twelve districts were represented by official delegations and dancers as well as a full core of village chiefs. The public celebration was open to all. On this occasion the writer and one other missionary were the only Europeans who were present.

[87]Speculation seems well founded, based on the developments which followed, that Ahmadu Bello felt a numerical majority actually committed to Islam in the northern region (based on the 1964 census) would give justification to rule by a single party (N.P.C.). Much publicity, radio and press, was given to the numbers who joined Islam as he moved from town to town. For most of 1965 the impression was one of massive movement to the side of the Sardauna.

[88]These new converts had been prearranged in the weeks before Ahmadu Bello's arrival, by careful work among his subordinates, working through the district heads.

the *kafiri* ("pagan") chiefs was likewise obvious. Each district head had the responsibility to produce a determined number of converts from his district. The district heads, in turn, solicited their quota from the villages which were mainly non-Muslim. This meant that many non-Muslim village heads were left with the task of recruiting converts to Islam, when they themselves were not Muslims.

The above scheme did not work well in the areas where emirs were not in control. Yet as the premier of all the North, the Sardauna had *carte blanche* entry into all communities, and his attractive offers to the leaders in return for embracing Islam were common. The Sardauna was known for giving gifts in the tradition of African royalty, so it was his usual pattern that when people presented themselves publicly as converts, the men received a gown and the women a headdress.

The quality of these converts would naturally be suspect, especially when they came from tribes where Islam was weak. Of ten converts from the town of Jen, only two are still Muslims. After the Sardauna's death (1966), two returned to the Christian Church that they had left, six stopped doing prayers immediately after the *coup*. The two who continued with Islam now live in the Hausa section of the town.[89]

Among the Kilba a rather high percentage of the Sardauna's converts continued in the Muslim way for some time. Here, correspondingly, is a tribe that has had a congenial attitude to the Fulani, where there is a lot of intermarriage and where, quite independently of politics, the Kilba chief popularized Islam twenty years ago.

It is important whether the tribe can assimilate the convert or not. Where the motivation for religious change has been primarily social or political rather than "religious" and where, in addition, the tribal environment is not hospitable to Islam, the ability of the convert to retain his practice in the tribe is minimal. The spokesman for the Yendang claimed that all those who converted to Islam in 1965 are "now all back in the old way, while some have become Christians."[90] Those who spoke for the Birom said essentially the same. The Pabir

---

[89]Jonah Bubajoda, at Jen, August 15, 1970.
[90]Timon Konvizinti, at Bukuru, March 2, 1970.

164

(Biu), on the other hand, remember the Sardauna's visit as a great boost to the emir's prestige and say that many from the villages who embraced Islam as a result have now settled in the town.[91] The chief of the Kutep is a Muslim,[92] but as a people they were not receptive to Islam. They speak openly of the 1964-65 conversions as being *wonkan Sardauna* (Sardauna's washing), because there is the ritual of washing connected with conversion. The Kutep have not shown anything like a movement to Islam. They also feel their Muslim chief was a political convert, so his Muslim status is not binding on them.[93]

The pattern, therefore, is quite regular. The tribes who produced the most converts were those tribes who had always been congenial towards Islam and whose royalty had influenced the structure in favor of Islam prior to the political period of the sixties.The tribes who had a strong traditional religion prior to the formation of independent Nigerian politics showed little, if any, inclination to change. Those who did convert to Islam within this group did not continue once the Sardauna's politics had passed.

The question is whether religion is the absolute, against which all other issues fall into place, or whether the secular African situation uses religion as one way to success. The overall impression is that the religion is so basic that it will not be distorted or tampered with easily, simply to serve political ends. The heated environment of political conversion was changed with the death of Ahmadu Bello. Watt has asked a question which is still before us: "Whose ends are best served by the transaction, the politician's or the religious?" In a somewhat prophetic way he then suggests the directions possible:

> There seems to be two distinct types of case to what happens to the religion . . . . He (the politician) may increase his power, and he may die while his power is at its height . . . but insofar as religious ideas are propagated by the politician, however, there is a chance that the religion will prosper.[94]

---

[91]Integration into Islam means that people settle into the town. Obviously, village life is unable to accommodate Islam with the same degree of success as urban life, even among the Pabir.

[92]The chief, Ali Ibrahim, was raised a Muslim in the town of Ibi where, like Takum, both the Jukun and the Kutep reside.

[93]Iliya Madaki, at Takum, February 10, 1970.

[94]Watt, *Islam and Society*, p. 179.

The second type of case occurs when, after the politician has been making use of religious ideas, the tide of the religion, instead of rising, recedes . . . . The cleavage between the official religion and that of the common people, though never absolute, has continued to exist.[95]

Either of these alternatives was possible in North Nigeria in 1966. But the changes have been so radical in the past twenty years that we can speak of a new situation.

---

[95]*Ibid.*, p. 180.

CHAPTER SIX

RELIGIOUS CHANGE
SINCE 1965

CHAPTER SIX

RELIGIOUS CHANGE SINCE 1965

The reader must be asking if traditional religions have actually continued to exist in these dynamic forms up to the present period. Or, somewhere around a generation ago, did they not begin to drop away, fast becoming treasures of an inert past? Anyone familiar with the modern history of northern Nigeria knows that in a relatively short time there has, indeed, been a turning away from ancestral religion to both Christianity and Islam. In the past two decades religious change for all of Nigeria was determined overwhelmingly by shifts among the so-called minority tribes of the middle belt. Education, as well as modernity and political change, have made it much easier for traditional peoples to leave the old structures. We want to observe these changes and some of the factors that have brought them about before analyzing the response that Islam has made.

TRADITIONAL RELIGION AND THE MODERN STATE

RAPID GROWTH OF CHRISTIANITY

Many years before the British came to rule, the feudal system of Hausa-Fulani emirs had controlled whole tribes, numbering millions of people. Under the colonization policies of Lord Lugard these traditional structures were kept more or less intact as a part of the "indirect rule" philosophy. Problems for the colonial system began to arise when education in mission schools and conversions to Christianity became agents of change through the decades of the thirties and the forties. From that time, and especially in the past twenty years, the changes have been far-reaching, particularly for Islam. The shift from traditional religion to Christianity in the middle belt area is nothing less than remarkable. This fact is changing the direction the country will take in the next generation.

The nine states of the southeast and southwest have not changed much during the past two decades. Except for Yoruba Islam, this has generally been the Christian area for many years. However, not only does traditional religion underlie much of the religious expression of these southern areas, but the forms of Christianity itself are quite bewildering. Christianity ranges from Roman Catholicism, Anglicanism, and the major Western denominations to a variety of African indigenous churches. Some of the churches of this latter group are an amalgam of both Christian forms and traditional practices, put together in such a way that the product is little more than revitalized African religion.[1]

The formation of states identified more precisely than ever the borders of Islam in the far north, primarily Borno, Kano, and Sokoto States. The new picture has been drawn, primarily, by the five or six states of the old Middle Belt where traditional religionists and young people have chosen between Islam and Christianity. The shift to Christianity had been taking place during the latter half of the colonial era, but Kaduna-based politics did not take it seriously enough. In retrospect, one would have to say that the tactics of the late Ahmadu Bello actually sped up the process of Christianization rather than retarding it.[2] The record shows that an overwhelming majority of the "middle belters" who experienced religious change since 1960 opted for Christianity rather than Islam. In addition, it is widely reported that most of the conversions made under pressure from Ahmadu Bello in the early sixties did not stick.

Earlier, for example, we cited a section of the Birom known as Zawan (p. 68). This village, with its chief, was supposed to have led the way for conversion to Islam among the Birom. Upon revisiting

---

[1]Little has been written on the more extreme movements. For the Aladura churches see J. D. Y. Peel, *Aladura* (London: Oxford University Press, 1968), and for the Cherubim and Seraphim see A. Omoyajowo, *Diversity in Unity* (Lanham, MD: University Press of America, 1984).

[2]See pp. 74-75.

Zawan in 1985, I saw no trace of a Muslim presence. The chief who had Islamized for political reasons no longer practices the prayers, and his children never followed him.[3] Nearly all who went over to Islam from among the Bachema between 1960-1966 have become Christians. It is said among the Bachema, "Even if I fall from a wild horse, my forehead will never touch the ground."[4] This is a colorful way to declare that the Bachema attitude toward Muslim prayer is extremely negative.

To support the statement that officially traditional religion has all but disappeared, the following data must be taken into account. At the beginning of this century 73% of all Nigerian people were traditional animists. By 1950, 34% were still following ancestral religions.[5] But by 1980 this number had been reduced to somewhere between 5% and 8%.[6] In fact, the census of 1963 was the last time the government used the category of "other" as a way to officially count those who were animists. In the 1973 census, people were expected to answer that they were either Muslim or Christian. There was no third category.

For its part, Islam had its initial growth after the great *jihad* (1804) and by 1900 had claimed 25.9% of the total population. Islam now accounts for 45%, and this will change very little until the year 2000.[7]

Christianity gained dramatically in the Middle Belt after independence. A parallel development alongside independence was the gradual reduction of Western missionaries and the handing over of mission institutions and administration of churches to nationals. This brought a sense of ownership and freedom to the minority Christian groups. Along with this feeling of dignity there was widespread acceptance of Christianity among peoples of Plateau, Benue, Gongola, and large parts of Kwara and Kaduna States. As a result, where in 1945 only 20% of the population of the entire country was Christian, (concentrated in the southern part), by mid-1980 this figure has

[3]Conversation with Barnaba Dusu, Jos, October 18, 1985.

[4]John Ambe, Director, Nigerian Merchants' Bank.

[5]*Nigeria: A Country Study*, Ed., H. D. Nelson, Foreign Area Studies (Lanham, MD: American University Press, 1971), p. 123.

[6]*World Christian Encyclopedia* , Ed., David B. Barrett (London: Oxford University Press, 1982), p. 527.

[7]*Ibid*, see Table 1 Religious Adherence in Nigeria.

climbed to 49%.[8]   As we have already noted, most of this new Christian strength has come from conversions among middle belt traditionalists, mainly young people. This presents a new situation for Islam among the peoples studied in this book. The following graph shows that Christians are numerically equal with Islam and will be well ahead of Islam by the end of the century.

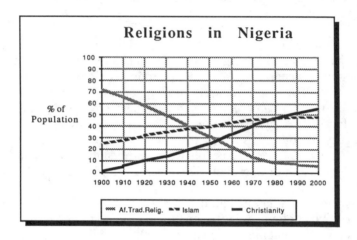

This overall picture of the numerical strength of the two religions must be adjusted through an understanding of the variations, even contradictions, within both systems. Likewise, both have been shaped by modern cultural, economic, and political forces. In the past twenty years these changes have been swift and have altered the old structures radically.

AMBIGUOUS STATE OF TRADITIONAL RELIGION

Of course, nothing so pervasive as the cultural religion of a people could ever disappear in a single generation. We showed in the early part of this study how tenacious the traditional system is. The assumptions of the "tribal world view" are in place long after many of the traditional formulas have been set aside. But it may be that the new forms of the old religion will have the last word after all. The

---

[8]*World Christian Encyclopedia*, p. 527, Table 1.

ancestors have not been silenced by the politicization of religion. They have simply taken on a more indirect style and speak in more sophisticated cultural forms.

Returning to many of the same places referred to earlier produced an interesting, almost conflicting range of data. The Jos Plateau is a fair representation of the peoples covered in this study. Responses among these groups show the unclear situation of traditional religion. Dr. Musa Gotom states:

> African religion has declined considerably and is still on the decline. One would say African religion persists, however, as a world view and, as such, is still active in both Muslims and Christians without their realizing it.[9]

Gotom goes on to say that the influence of African religion now comes primarily through traditional healers and "medicine men," who still thrive and who retain many of the old rites in their healing practices. "Those who consult these healers do encounter the spirit of traditional religion."[10] At least half of the others who were interviewed stated categorically that in the past fifteen years there has been a waning of the rituals of old religion.

On the other hand, Professors Lombin and Gana of Ahmadu Bello University are convinced that while many of the practices have not been taken up by the younger people, still:

> "Tsafi" (animism) holds strong influence in the issues of sickness and foretelling the future. Very educated Nigerians pay regular visits to the priests of African religious shrines to obtain material objects and concoctions. It is simply amazing the way intelligent Africans visit fortune tellers. It is ridiculous the extent to which people will go to assure fertility. Drivers consult priests for charms and medicines that would guarantee protection on the road. Also, in the area of seeking advancement at work and in business ventures consultations with diviners are common. There are stories of horrible sacrifices made in order to get rich quickly.[11]

A. M. Nyam, a commissioner for health, is convinced that little has changed in the traditional practice of seeking medical cures. He sees the pressure of inflation since the oil boom and the shortage of basic

---

[9]Musa Gotom, General Secretary, Church of Christ in Nigeria, May 1985, Jos.
[10]*Ibid.*
[11]G. Lombin and Gana, Ahmadu Bello University, unpublished paper, 1985.

medicines as contributing to the situation. Because of these problems people are visiting traditional healers as never before. Nyam states:

> At the recently concluded meeting of the National Council of Health, traditional healers were formally recognized. The net result is that the Secretary to the Military Council is now advised to promulgate a decree which formally recognizes them and regulates their activities alongside their "orthodox" medical counterparts.[12]

The above decision was made by professional medical personnel upon admission of the fact that "70% of our people do recognize and patronize traditional healers."[13]

This is the kind of mixed reporting that one encounters everywhere. The first impression is that there is no official recognition of the ancient forms. Yet in many ways tribal belief and practice is as visible as it has ever been. The most popular live television programs are cultural dances and games put on by the various ethnic groups. In colorful and ecstatic performances, the songs, dances, and drama of traditional life leave little question as to the attraction and lively place they hold for modern life.

REVIVAL OF CULTURE

The inseparable relationship between the religion and culture was one of the features of FESTAC (Festival of African Culture) which was held in Lagos in 1977. This was an event that gave prominence to all aspects of tradition. There was a long preparation period during which time all groups were asked to revive the best and most colorful aspects of their respective cultures. FESTAC left nothing uncovered. It was much more than a fair. It had a competitive spirit and successfully generated enthusiasm for the ancient forms as nothing before. Art of every variety, indigenous costumes, songs, and drama from every corner of the country were on display. The celebration of the past was given publicity months before and during the year of FESTAC. The impact this had on the revival of religion, at least temporarily, was obvious. In the context of a reawakened culture the specifically religious was again alive and seen as valuable. Charms,

---

[12]A. M. Nyam, Commissioner for Health, Plateau State, April 1985.
[13]*Ibid.*

objects of worship, and rituals were legitimized and celebrated. The Catholic Bishop of Jos states categorically,

> With the staging of FESTAC '77 there was an upsurge of African Traditional Religion. Those who had found some tenets of Christianity unpleasant opted for the religion of their ancestors in the name of cultural revival.[14]

The manager of the Albishir Bookshops said that FESTAC was seen by many "as a return to the old."

> The juju worshippers welcomed it so much that some said Nigeria is a country where black magic still rules. There were various calls for a return to tradition, and it was obvious that many who hold to Christianity and Islam have, in fact, not given up their traditional practices.[15]

The nationwide participation in the Festival provided tangible evidence that, lying beneath the surface, there is still a strong attachment to the substratum of African life. Granted, the novelty of FESTAC ran its course and in a short time the general euphoria that accompanied the return to tradition died down. Sule Ibrahim, speaking from the side of the Muslim, said flatly that FESTAC, "brought about such a rise in the consciousness of African religion that it might be called a revival." Its effect eight years later can be seen through a continued fear of witchcraft and the widespread consulting of oracles and seers for projecting into the future.[16]

The old rituals of power, both the destructive and beneficial kind, have become more institutionalized in the past decade. They now take up residence in institutions that before would not have readily been seen as functional "paganism." For example, quite recently there were widespread rumors that Masonic societies were practicing black magic. In 1983 cases of kidnapping children for secret ceremonies were reported. This was known only to the insiders of the society. While I was holding classes in Kaduna in March of that year the Masonic building was burned to the ground by a group who were convinced that this new form of black magic must be put down.

---

[14]Rev. Dr. G. G. Ganaka, Roman Catholic Bishop, Diocese of Jos, April 1985.

[15]Mr. Mang, Manager, Albishir Bookshops, Jos.

[16]E.g., the Ogboni and Reformed Ogboni Cult, widespread among the Yoruba.

In a more discreet way some extremely tribalistic churches are also meeting the need to keep the old traditions alive. Referred to in various ways as "independent churches," "indigenous churches," or "prophet-healing churches," these movements have proliferated as part of the phenomenal growth of Christianity. It stands to reason that independence from colonial control and the need for continuity with the past will find expression in churches. Here, in some of their most intense forms, the old rituals for healing, exorcism, and personal power can be played out in a new format.[17] However, the so-called independent churches represent a wide range of belief and practice, and it would be grossly unfair to characterize them generally as new manifestations of the old religions. Yet there is no question that most of these churches are much closer to primary religious forms than any of the "mission-type churches."

In Nigeria the independent African movements are best known by the Aladura churches, representing many separate groups with a wide range of worship styles. The controversy these churches raise is around the question of what really constitutes a Christian Church. The point is that some of the more radical groups appear closer to the practice of magic, divination, and ancestor veneration than they are to universal Christian norms. Nearly all are centered on a charismatic leader who is prophet and healer, filling a role not unlike the traditional priest. The more syncretistic of these indigenous churches reveal that primary religions that have faded in the modern order can survive in new, though greatly modified, forms as churches.

SECULARIZATION

The past twenty years have seen an increasingly large number of people who no longer wish to identify themselves with any religion. This group, primarily among the educated, would say that they are following a secularist-humanist philosophy in the modern African context. This secularization process has come with the expansion of education, particularly at the graduate level, and the inevitable

---

[17]Bengt Sundkler, in his first edition of *Bantu Prophets in South Africa*, spoke of these "nativistic" churches as "the bridge over which Africans are brought back to that traditional religion from which they had once emerged" (London: Oxford University Press, 1948), p. 297.

westernization that attaches to it. Also, economic changes since 1960 have had a tremendous impact. With the oil boom, beginning in the middle sixties, the country converted from its diversified, quite simple agrarian economy to a single commodity economy. There was a need to move ahead again after the debilitation of the Civil War, and easy oil money provided the new basis of wealth. Money was available, and accumulating money became a national preoccupation. The effect of an inflated economy, the free flow of money, and the availability of luxury goods all contributed to a mood of materialism.

The "national cake" became the center of attention for people at all levels. Nigeria's ancient strength had come from strong traditional structures that had produced solid ethics and social integrity. With the erosion of these controls and with the new religion of materialism, the floodgates of excess were thrown open. Both Muslims and Christians were victims. The economy pandered to the demands of the elite. At state levels massive building projects were begun that would enhance the image of the state. Quick oil money brought about the hoarding of cash and astronomical inflation. Worst of all, bribe and various forms of corruption became widespread. Exploitation touched all levels—the private sector, law enforcement, and even the courts. Traditional religion found new ways to survive. While in many ways it "went underground," it reappeared as a part of detribalized materialism.

INFLUENCE OF THE MILITARY REGIMES

Since the fall of the First Republic, which took place on January 15, 1966, and up to the time of this writing, there have been six military heads of state covering a period of sixteen years. The period of civilian rule was brief by comparison (August 1979 to December 1983). Hence, the policies pursued by the military are extremely important in the shaping of religion in the past two decades.

Yakubu Gowon

General Yakubu Gowon began his administration with the quality of person and a level of dedication that gave hope to all segments of the

177

nation. The prudence he showed in dealing with the "Biafra problem" following the Civil War will never be forgotten. Writing in 1971, Kirk-Greene said of Gowon, "The transparent quality of his leadership, its adroitness and its patent humanity have added a new dimension to the makeup of the typology of African heads of state."[18]

Words used to describe Gowon during his early years were sincerity, magnanimity, and consensus. Yet the end of Gowon's political career is as regrettable as any in modern Africa. His postponement of the date for civil rule was announced but not explained. There were serious labor disorders, painful inequities in pay and salaries,[19] the unexplained shortage of petrol, and a scandalous backup of cement shipments. Gowon's governors were very unpopular, and he seemed unable to do anything about it. All of this contributed to his downfall in a bloodless coup on July 29, 1975.

When asked about the effect of the Gowon regime on Christianity, nearly all Christians showed resentment for his quite relentless takeover of mission schools and hospitals. Though Gowon is, himself, a Christian, Christians generally felt that he had deprived them of the most effective means they had for controlling the minds of young people and keeping their leaders at the forefront of Christian expression. Many African church bodies had recently been given proprietorship of these influential institutions by mission organizations which had controlled them for so many years. It was felt everywhere that with the demise of Gowon, a governmental system that was biased heavily toward the promotion of Islamic principles would dominate. These fears were especially true among the churches located in the middle belt.

While Christians held Gowon to be one of their own, they were mystified by the heavy control of a northern power base located at Kaduna and Sokoto. Yet while the appearance may have been otherwise, the fact is that the end of the Gowon regime was the result of intra-personality and tribal tensions. Those who unseated Gowon were, from a religious point of view, closest to him. Nine years to the day after taking control, Yakubu Gowon fled the country. Ironically,

---

[18]A. H. M. Kirk-Greene, *Crisis and Conflict in Nigeria*, Vol. II (London: Oxford University Press, 1971), p. 474.

[19]E.g., the Udoji and Morgan Commissions

while he had attempted to steer a middle course between Islam and Christianity, Christians generally felt he had put them to a serious disadvantage.

Murtalla   Mohammed

It was the Islamic community that would benefit the most from Gowon's overthrow on July 29, 1975, when Brigadier Murtalla Mohammed took over. The increasingly diffident style and almost royal demeanor of Gowon in his later years was quickly put to an end. The new leader was direct and straightforward. The country knew where he stood within hours after his takeover. In his words, "The nation was being plunged inexorably into chaos. It was obvious that matters could not and should not be allowed to continue this way."[20]

Murtalla Mohammed instantly dismissed twelve governors who had long since lost favor with the people. The replacements made by Murtalla were Muslim in all of the middle belt and northern states. Murtalla proceeded, without delay, to retire police officers, federal employees, diplomatic heads, university administrators, and ordinary staff, including clerks and cooks. This created a vacuum for replacements which he then filled according to his own choice. Christians again recognized that massive changes were taking place in the six months that Murtalla lived. They saw his appointment of the Muslim governors in Christian majority states and became alarmed at the establishment of *shari'a* courts in the ten northern states. Once again came the feeling that the old assumptions about the North were still there, that the North was traditionally Muslim, and that no change in that notion would be considered.[21]

Subsidies for Muslim pilgrims were not questioned by Murtalla, while almost every other budget item was under the knife, including FESTAC. FESTAC was even postponed in order to take a closer look at its extravagant costs. Christians watched while Murtalla built a mosque at the State House Dodan Barracks but made no provision for a Christian place of worship.[22]

---

[20]Broadcast by Murtalla Muhammed as new head of state, 30 July, 1975.

[21]V. K. Dangin, Permanent Secretary, Plateau State

[22]Rev. Dr. G. G. Ganaka, Roman Catholic Bishop, Diocese of Jos.

Murtalla Ramat Mohammed quickly became a legend. His was energetic, creative leadership that would be memorialized in Nigeria's history. On an awful morning, February 13, 1976, Murtalla was killed by a sergeant from the middle belt. This event brought to front and center once again the fact that deep-seated tribalism was still at large in the country. When ethnic tensions are present religious implications are inevitable. The assassination of Murtalla by non-Muslim factions of the army was bound to touch religious feelings. One hundred twenty-five people were arrested for their part in the plot to kill Murtalla. The majority of these were indigenes of Gowon's area, many from his own ethnic group including Lt. Col. Dimka who strategized the tragic affair.

Olusegun Obasanjo

The Obasanjo regime (1976-79) is remembered for the preparations he made which would lead to civilian government. Particularly important was the convening of the Constituent Assembly (1978).

It took nearly six months to forge a plan to govern the nation. The *shari'a* issue, discussed elsewhere in this chapter, underlined the mood of the nation as it drew sides between Muslim and non-Muslim factions. Obasanjo, while himself a Christian, was not unaware of the need to guide a middle course so as to preserve the atmosphere for a peaceful transition to civilian government. Again, Christians felt that he was not paying attention to them as he should. They also felt he was controlled by Muslim members of his own council, especially Maj. Gen. Shehu Yar Adu'a, the Chief of Staff at Supreme Headquarters.

ISLAM FACES THE NEW SITUATION

It was plain that an irreversible trend was already under way by 1956. In that year R. S. Hudson of the Colonial Office (U.K.) was commissioned by the government of the northern region of Nigeria to draw up a plan that could have led to the power of government being handed over to the former provinces. While the plan was never adopted, some of the observations that Hudson made in 1956 were almost prophetic. Speaking of the Lugard administrative structure whereby emirs ruled over scattered non-Muslim clans, he wrote, "A peculiar structure has emerged which from afar and at first sight appears eminently suitable but on closer examination reveals an ominous number of cracks and weaknesses."[23]

As long as thirty years ago the Middle Belt of Nigeria signaled a need for change and sensitivity which did not come with the early policies of independence. Hudson commented on the anomaly of the so-called Middle Belt, probably not knowing the full significance of what he observed.

> In these areas we find agglomerations of tribes pushed into the hills by successive waves of invasion, some of whom retain their independence, others of whom owe nominal allegiance to the local emir but who, in many cases, have won the right to select their own leaders from among themselves.[24]

Hudson goes on to mention that while these groups had been culturally backward, they were now making full use of Western education and had their own leaders who were being heard in the region.

The Muri Emirate of Old Adamawa Province is a classic example of the way in which a Muslim family of kings and their councils held sway over hundreds of square miles of land. These were almost totally animistic peoples comprising over twenty-five language groups. It was my privilege to arrive in Muri Division of Adamawa Province in 1956, and I have been in close touch with this area ever since. The old town of Muri was never accessible by an all-season road. Yet it became a symbol of the old system. Its chief was a figurehead who after 1960 had minimal influence. Funds were not available to repair the royal compound, and by 1960 the town was cut off from market and transport. Only a few people continued to live on in old Muri. Change had done its irrevocable work.

There are at least five indicators of the new situation in which Islam now finds itself. These same factors also have had a direct bearing on

---

[23]*Provincial Authorities*, Report by the Commissioner, Mr. R. S. Hudson, C. M. G., Kaduna, Government Printer, n.d.

[24]*Ibid.*, p. 5.

the rise of strong new Christian communities. These developments also reveal ways in which Islam has adjusted to face a changed environment.

THE DEATH OF AHMADU BELLO

As this chapter is being written, Nigeria is remembering "the Sardauna" on the twentieth anniversary of his death. The *New Nigerian* carried several articles to honor this unusual personage. One admirer who reviewed his life two decades later described him as "a veritable phoenix."[25] On January 19, 1985, Adamu Adamu wrote:

> While yet dead he exercises greater influence over the lives and actions of a greater number of people than those most ascerbic in criticising him. He was at once an idol to those who love and adore him and a devil and the "cause" of the problems of those who despise his very being and ideal.[26]

The assassination of this direct descendant of Uthman dan Fodio on January 15, 1966 had a demoralizing effect on both the psyche and prestige of the Muslim community. The long-range effect of having lost this powerful center of the Islamic dream was not immediately understood. In the early sixties 75% of the people of Nigeria were living in the Northern Region. The dream was that if the Northern Provinces could be declared a Muslim domain, Islam would be *de facto* the religion of the nation.[27]

It is difficult for those outside of the House of Islam to grasp the rationale that motivated Ahmadu Bello along this course. Considering the bitterness of the military faction that assassinated him, it seems incredible to the non-Muslim that Sir Ahmadu could ever have accomplished his dream of "dipping the Qur'an in to the sea." This is not to mention thousands of committed Christians and their leaders who would never capitulate to Islam. There were well documented cases of political conversions, Christian chiefs and ministers among them, in which Ahmadu Bello was the key agent. But, in retrospect,

---

[25]Adamu Adamu, "Sardauna: The Power of a Ghost," *New Nigerian*, January 19, 1986, p. 3.

[26]See Ibrahim Tabir's review of the book by John Paden, *Admadu Bello, Sardauna of Sokoto*, in *New Nigerian*, January 20, 1986, p. 5.

[27]Manessa, T. B. Daniel, former senator, Gongola State.

these were relatively few. The almost completely pragmatic nature of these conversions may have led the premier to believe that Christians, in time and with the right incentives, could be proselytized. So superficial were these conversions, however, that one responsible person from the Jarawa noted how these converts lost all incentive to continue as Muslims after Ahmadu Bello's death.

> One case in point was that of a traditional chief who became a Muslim to protect his stool. When he heard of the Sardauna's death he immediately threw away his prayer beads and grabbed a calabash full of "burkutu" (strong alcoholic drink). He is said to be, up to date, a traditionalist together with his subordinates who converted to Islam with him.[28]

With the death of the Sardauna the Christians felt that God had somehow used the tribalistic factors of the army[29] to rid them of a fearful element. The Sardauna was feared because he was using the classic model of an Islamic state to align Christians with his party against their will. The Christians now felt they could start anew with a sense of the power of their true numbers and with their own leaders. Unfortunately, any clarification of the Christian role in society and government was diffused by the Civil War, which followed so quickly after the death of the Sardauna.

The long-range effects of the death of the Sardauna on the political aspects of Islam were slowly revealed as Muslim leaders regrouped themselves for a restaging of their now leaderless forces. There would never be another Ahmadu Bello. What he did for the Muslim cause is reviewed critically by Wilson Sabiya, a Christian from the Kilba people. Sabiya shows that the Northern Establishment made Kaduna (capital of Kaduna State) the base for federal politics. For the northern "power brokers" there had developed two states—Lagos and Kaduna. In Sabiya's view,

> We should talk of one Nigeria only as long as the (power base at Kaduna) rules the country. Nigeria is the Kingdom of the Northern Establishment. Nigeria as one nation and destiny is, therefore, acceptable to them because Nigeria belongs to them.[30]

---

[28]A. M. Nyam, *op. cit.*

[29]Ben Gbulie's book, *Nigeria's Five Majors* (Onitsha: African Educational Publishers, Ltd., 1981). Reveals the tribal bias with which an Ibo officer interpreted the 1966 coup.

[30]Wilson Sabiya, *The Politics of Zoning* (Jos: City Press, n.d.), p. 6.

This Kaduna power base was a reality during the height of Ahmadu Bello's reign. It would never be quite the same again. No one has been able to present the historic posture of a conquering Islam the way the Sardauna did. The party that succeeded Ahmadu Bello's NPC was the National Party of Nigeria. The NPN was launched by Aliyu Makama Bida with help from Joseph Tarka of the Tiv tribe. In a real sense the NPN candidate was seen as the torchbearer for Ahmadu Bello. Yet Shehu Shagari, who won the elections in 1979 and again in 1983, never fulfilled the ideals of the Sardauna. He was a disappointment to the Kaduna establishment because he did not advance the cause of Islam in a definitive way.[31]

Without a strong power center and a charismatic personality to fill the vacuum created by Ahmadu Bello's death, various new voices came forward to undermine Muslim solidarity. These movements took radical fundamentalistic forms (e.g., *Izala*), which will be described below. Under the pretext of cleansing Nigerian Islam of its sectarian Sufi history (*tarikas*), a vicious rift opened up in the Islamic *umma* exposing its disunity as never before. The loss of the Sardauna was, indeed, a major setback for Islam as it moved into the realities of the seventies.

THE FORMATION OF STATES

In the sequence of events which altered the historical image of Islam, May 27, 1967 is a date of special importance. On that day Lt. Col. Yakubu Gowon abolished the four regions and replaced them by twelve new states. The implications of this move for both Christianity and Islam may not have been a conscious factor in the decision. But the future of Islam was redirected by this new governing structure and even more by the redivision into nineteen states in 1976. Kirk-Greene says that the formation of states, "brought to an end a way of administrative, political and fiscal life that had endured since 1900, had received confirmation in 1914 and had, despite the political tremors of the 1950s, remained apparently sacrosanct."[32]

---

[31]V. K. Dangin, *op. cit.*

[32]A. H. M. Kirk-Greene and Douglas Rimmer, *Nigeria Since 1970* (New York: Africana Publishing Co., 1981), p. 27.

184

The first arrangement of states followed in rough fashion the provincial boundaries of the old North. For example, the original North East State was a massive land space meant to accommodate ethnic groups that had already shown they could not be administered easily. This awkwardness was caused, in part, from the Muslim orientation of the northern part of the state where there was a growing Christian community. This Christian strength centered around Numan and among the Margi and Bura peoples to the west of Mubi. Numerous minority tribes added to the problem.

In the same way, it was not long before the original Benue-Plateau State showed internal stress. This was not only because of its geography but because the state attempted to cater to the interests of numerous ethnic groups on the Plateau, together with the large Tiv tribe. The Tiv are such a large homogeneous unit that the partitioning of the Benue Plateau State was inevitable. The impact that new states would have on both Islam and Christianity seemed implicit in the principles that underlaid a 1967 declaration. It was promised that local situations would have bearing on how additional states would be formed. "Among the factors to be taken into account in the creation of any new state would be administrative convenience, local wishes, and 'the facts of history.'"[33]

When the new structure of nineteen states came into effect in 1976, the ethnically true Muslim states were even further defined (Kano, Borno, Sokoto, and much of Kaduna). This left the "mixed" states of the Middle Belt to reorganize themselves with a more accurate Christian-Muslim representation based upon "the facts of history." These new states, which were formed out of a restructuring of the original twelve, left an impressive message concerning the relative strength of Islam both geographically and numerically. The monolithic hold of Islam on the north was broken and the Kaduna base, shaken by the Sardauna's death and the Civil War, was further decentralized. The identification of the true strengths of both Islam and Christianity now became possible. Professor G. Lombin of Ahmadu Bello University made the following observation:

> The huge Muslim populations of Kano, Sokoto and northern Kaduna had been used to intimidate minority Christian groups of the Middle Belt.

---

[33]*Ibid.*

185

With the creation of States a solid independent base was formed for Christians in the North, especially in Benue, Kwara, Plateau and Gongola States.[34]

On the other hand, the predominately Muslim states have become more closed to Christianity. In these states, Islam is taught in the schools as a natural part of the curriculum of history and culture. Arabic studies is the norm for the state universities. Newspapers and television programs carry an Islamic bias.[35] In the "mixed" states where Christianity dominates (e.g., Benue and Plateau) the "differentiation between the two religions has become clearer. It is impossible now to generate the impression that the middle belt is a Muslim-controlled area."[36] J. P. Mambila, commenting on the effect of the formation of states, said:

> While the far northern states have become more closed, in the mixed states there is flexibility for dialogue and a fair hearing on both sides. For instance, the Military Governor of Plateau State set up a joint committee of Christians and Muslims for mutual consultations and a similar committee was set up in Gongola State.[37]

In summary, the Muslim strongholds are more accurately defined by the state boundaries. It is no longer possible to diffuse the boundaries of Islam so as to give the wrong impression that all northerners are Muslim. And while the Islamic states have intensified their hold *vis-a-vis* Christians, the Christians, conversely, have utilized the freedoms they feel where the population is dominated by Christians.

THE SHARI'A ISSUE

While attending O.A.U. talks in Kampala in July, 1975, General Yakubu Gowon was ousted from office in a bloodless coup. Brig. Murtalla Mohammed became the new head of state. One of the ambiguous issues left by the Gowon government was the question of

---

[34]Professors Lombin and Gana.

[35]V. K. Dangin, *ibid.*

[36]George Bako, Director General, Federal Radio Corporation.

[37]J. D. Mambila, General Secretary, Fellowship of Churches of Christ in Nigeria, April 1985, Jos.

when the military would hand over to civil rule. Gowon had made a promise in 1970 that civilian rule would commence in January, 1976. However, four years later he announced that this would not be possible but did not give a new date. Therefore, when Murtalla Mohammed began his ill-fated rule of six months, he lost no time in setting 1979 as the target date for return to civil rule.

It was necessary to summon an assembly for the adoption of a constitution. This took place in a closed session beginning October 7, 1977. Membership, clearly enough, was based on the estimated population of the various states. This was an estimate at best, since the census of 1973 was completely unreliable at the time it was done and was even less useful six years later. This meant that the proportionate representation from the Christian and Muslim factions was such that any power struggle between the two groups could reveal much about who would dominate the country.

What the Constituent Assembly accomplished was commendable from many sides. The members were able to reject two possible models of government and then adopt a Nigerian variety of the American system.[38] However, one of the most critical and polarizing debates was a religious one that very nearly brought down the Assembly. It had been recommended by the Constitutional Drafting Committee that a Federal Shari'a Court of Appeal be established. By this arrangement court cases could be conducted under Islamic law. No issue that came before the Assembly raised the deep feelings of the two worlds, Islamic and Christian, like this proposition.

It is important for the reader to understand that discussion on *shari'a* was not a simple matter of determining right or wrong acts that are punishable or not punishable in a court of law. *Shari'a* is the sum total of the Muslim way of life. Literally, it is "the trodden path" leading to peace and submission. The *shari'a* is both the Qur'an and tradition. It touches every aspect of belief and life. *Shari'a*, therefore, is the core of Islam, and strict obedience to *shari'a* is the essence of Islam.

The opponents of the pro-*shari'a* group agreed that the whole principle of elevating Islamic law to federal status was divisive and discriminatory. It was tantamount to institutionalizing two separate

---

[38]For discussion see Kirk-Greene, *ibid.*, p. 20.

systems of law in a time when the nation needed every possible symbol of unity.[39]

The supreme test came when the pro-*shari'a* members of the Assembly staged a walk-out on April 5, 1979 with the intention of boycotting all further proceedings. The abruptness and finality of their action was not missed by the non-Muslim sectors of the country. It happened, however, that those who bolted the Assembly did not comprise half of the total number. Eighty-eight members withdrew, leaving a working majority of 142. This number continued their work, though an editorial of the *New Nigerian* in August 2, 1978 stated that:

> Every decision taken during that period (while the pro *shari'a* group was absent) was illegal, undemocratic and in total violation of the Constituent Assembly decree.[40]

The Head of State, General Obasanjo, interceded with the group to return, which they did two weeks later. They went on record, however, that they would "reopen the issue whenever they thought the moment appropriate."[41]

The fact is, that the *shari'a* issue lost on the first round. The numerical strength of the pro-*shari'a* group could not, in the final count, have their way. Beyond this, the opponents of the argument showed a resolve and determination to proceed with the business of government with or without those who had walked out on the deliberations. This, in the end, was a rallying point for Christians. The Catholic Bishop of the Diocese of Jos states, "The *shari'a* demand sought to galvanize the Muslims on one hand but it was the basis of a great volume of protest on the part of the Christians."[42]

S. G. Mufuyai, former Federal Minister of Civil Aviation, said that the *shari'a* issue did not change the status of Islam in the country. What it did, rather, was to remove the false impression that Islam

---

[39]Professors Lombin and Gana.

[40]Mohammed Rimi, *New Nigerian*, August 2, 1978·

[41]Kirk-Greene, *ibid.*, p. 21. The "Shari'a Debate" is by no means a dead issue. It has recently been argued against by the Christian Association of Nigeria. See *New Nigerian,* January 16, 1986.

[42]Rev. Dr. G. G. Ganaka, Roman Catholic Bishop, Diocese of Jos.

dominates at all levels in Nigeria. Christianity was seen for what it is.[43]

Professors Lombin and Gana comment further that it became clear now that non-Muslims combined with Christians are, in fact, a clear majority. They also noted that the ordinary Muslims (*talakawa*) did not back the *shari'a* issue because of the repressive tendencies of the traditional *alkali* courts. Likewise, educated Muslim youth were uncommitted because of the tragic results of its operation in such countries as Sudan and Iran.

> It is important to emphasize that through the defeat of the shari'a issue the myth of an impregnable Muslim majority has been broken. Had shari'a been introduced into the legal structure of this country in the manner advanced by its advocates, requests for further and fundamental changes with far-reaching socio-political consequences would have followed. The inevitable result would have been a serious religious polarization, the end of which would have been a disaster for the country.[44]

It seemed that the supporters of *shari'a* law did not see that traditional Islamic jurisprudence is based on a world view of another time and place and would be out of touch with modern principles of human rights. An important feature of the discussion showed that Muslims were unable to grasp the threat that *shari'a* law posed for the now powerful non-Muslim sector of the population. It was incredible the way the debate was pressed without acknowledging that Christians would again be relegated to a second-class status, which they abhorred. Attempts to show Christians how they would have status under *shari'a* law only added to the problem. It was obvious that the Muslim cause was being set back and that the "new situation" in Nigeria was more complex for Islam than it had ever been before.

> In the outcome many Muslims did see what a divisive element the shari'a debate had become. When they saw what (it) would also mean for themselves, the development of society as well as the hatred it would arouse, (some Muslims) voted against the idea of a Federal Shari'a Court of Appeal.[45]

---

[43]S. G. Mufuyai, Civil Aviation Minister, Nigeria Federal Government.

[44]Lombin and Gana.

[45]Private paper, "The Hausa Polity, Islam and Modern Political Operations," Jeremy Hinds, Bukuru, Nigeria.

The *shari'a* debate is not over. The *New Nigerian* has recently invited readers to contribute points of view once again. The opponents of *"shari'a* court" are more vocal and better prepared for the debate than they were eight years ago.[46]

THE FUNDAMENTALIST BACKLASH

Events that took place in major cities of the North in 1980-81 amazed the world at large and exposed the inner tensions of Nigerian Islam as never before. During riots precipitated by followers of a radical group called Maitatsini hundreds of fellow Muslims were killed by right-wing fanatics who claimed they were restoring true Islam to Nigeria. Such killings among Muslims, openly and in cold blood, had never taken place in Nigeria before. They were as heartless as anything between Iraq and Iran and seemed incongruous to observers both inside and outside the country. Nigeria was making attempts to unite the forces of Islam, but now a Muslim head of state had to dispatch federal troops to put down the disturbances.

The movement centered around Mohammed Marwa who bore the title Mai Tafsiri, meaning, "One who explains the Qur'an." Hausa speakers corrupted the term *tafsiri* and it became *"tatsini"* which, in this modified form, carried the force of "one who can put a curse on people." Maitatsini was not a Nigerian but came from Marwa in the Cameroun. There is an old tradition associated with Marwa which goes back to the nineteenth century. It is from here that Rabih, a representative of the Mahdi associated with the Sudan, plundered and destroyed, without mercy, whole areas around Lake Chad and in the Kanuri Empire. That bloody period is remembered as a mixture of fierce traditional religion merged with militant sectarian Islam and is well documented.[47]

It is not difficult to compare the rise of Maitatsini in Chad with an earlier period when the army tried to revive religion there as a part of a national movement. But the deeper question is, Why did this

[46]See "Shari'a or Common Court" by Makwugo Okaye in *New Nigerian*, January 20, 1986, and "No Shari'a Courts, Please" by John Albi, *New Nigerian*, January 16, 1986.

[47]E.g., W. K. R. Hallam, *The Life and Times of Rubih Fadl Allah*, Ufracomb (U.K.: Stockwill, 1977).

movement, based as it was outside of Nigeria, set off such a conflagration in major Islamic cities of northern Nigeria?

Nigerian Islam is classic for its West African brotherhoods. The major brotherhoods are very large and have a long history. The Qadariyya are associated with Uthman dan Fodio and those who attach to his tradition, including the late Ahmadu Bello. The Tijaniyya, popularized in the nineteenth century by Al Hajj Umar Tal of Senegal, has been growing steadily. These are known as *tarikas*, which means "ways" in the Sufi tradition. Not too long after the Constituent Assembly certain "reformers" described themselves as against all *tarikas*. They took the objective of destroying what they claimed to be distortions caused by Qadariyya and Tijaniyya practices.

The uprising cannot be understood apart from revisionist groups that aligned themselves against the Nigerian Islamic establishment. In their campaign to spread this "new" and "pure" form of Islam

> They recruited a large number of violent preachers in all parts of the Northern States who went about condemning all Islamic sects, criticizing the tradition and method of worship adopted by the followers of those sects and the worst of it was the condemnation of their leaders.[48]

The most radical organization became known as the Izala Movement. The main objective of this organization was to fight the *tarikas* with a vengeance and to treat their followers as infidels. Some felt that this fanatical movement was related to the *shari'a* crisis because it was felt that the Islamic establishment had failed the country by losing the *shari'a* issue. The Izala Movement held out hope to all levels of Muslim rulers that they would be returned to power if their cause prevailed. One less informed group of Muslims known as the Gardawa knew very little about Islamic law even though they were literate in the Qur'an. This group, together with an aggregation of quite illiterate Muslims, were used to harass, intimidate, and persecute, by every means, the "*tarika* Muslims." It seems that what lay behind the dark exercise was the hope, even promise, of a Muslim state in which all who participated in the Izala disturbances would have prestige and position.

---

[48]Dr. Sadiq Labo, "Memoranda on Kano Religious Riot 1980-81," Zaria, unpublished.

This then brings us back to the crisis of the Maitatsini uprisings. It is against the background just given that an outsider could rally his forces.

> The Kano disturbance, led by Mohammad Marwa Maitatsini, was a pure action of the *Izala* movement. The fanatics involved in it were only Gardawa. . . . Although the Kano riot was led by an alien, the majority of the fanatics were Nigerians.[49]

The result of this sad time in Nigeria was that the government had to restore peace and order through armed intervention. In the end, all open-air preaching was banned for both Muslims and Christians. This action has been an irritation to Christian churches, that feel they have the right to evangelize in public preaching services but are detained from doing so because of trouble caused by divided and antagonistic Islamic groups. These disturbances left the Muslim love for unity and brotherhood badly marred. Fragmentation and divisiveness that has been the political weakness of Christianity in Nigeria has now raided the Muslim camp. Further, these events demonstrated a hostile irreverence on the part of some Muslims for others in their own ranks. These splits have not gone unobserved by those who are outside "the house of Islam." As J. P. Mambila of the Bura people reports:

> The uprising of Mai Tatsini and the conflicts between various Muslim groups have caused great concern and confusion even among the Muslims themselves. This has convinced non-Muslims that Islam is not a peaceful religion and has reduced Islam's effectiveness as an agent of change.[50]

The sectarian activities of Islam, including the Maitatsini disturbances, means that, "Islam will not be as acceptable as it was two decades ago."[51]

GOVERNMENT SUBSIDIES FOR *HAJJ*

One of the most controversial moves made by the military government following the Civil War was the establishment of a Pilgrim Board for the subsidizing of journeys to Mecca during the

---

[49]*Ibid.*

[50]J. P. Mambila, General Secretary, T.E.K.A.N., Jos.

[51]Manessa T. B. Daniel, former senator, Gongola State.

holy month of Ramadan. The fact that federal funds could be used to provide travel to Muslims demonstrated how powerful the forces were at the highest levels of government. There was a special irony to the formation of the Pilgrim Board since it proceeded unabated during the regime of Yakubu Gowon, a Christian who had origins in the Middle Belt. These operations became notorious for the favors granted to special persons and for the attractive political arrangements sometimes made to non-Muslims to convert and make the journey. Carried on through the administrations of General Murtalla Mohammed and General Olesegun Obasanjo, the Hajj Operations were treated as normal government responsibilities of the Ministry of Social Welfare and External Affairs. The sending of even whole delegations at government expense produced the erroneous impression that Islam was the state religion of Nigeria.

Christians were incensed at what they saw as a misuse of the nation's wealth, especially in light of the numerical strength of Christianity. Yet while there were as many Christians as Muslims by 1975, Christians were unable to speak with one voice. This was due to the crippling divisions between Roman Catholics, various Protestant denominations, and the plethora of indigenous churches and splinter sects. Nevertheless, Christians finally countered this one-sided expenditure and demanded that the same opportunity be given to them. In the states of the Middle Belt, Christian Pilgrim Boards were set up so that Christians who qualify could be subsidized for visiting both Rome (Catholics) and Palestine (Protestants).

THE KADUNA MAFIA

During the Civil War Christians organized the Northern Christian Association of Nigeria. Some northern denominations had long been cooperating in the Christian Council of Nigeria. Moreover, the Nigeria Evangelical Fellowship and the Christian Association of Nigeria had been formed in the 70s. All was to foster the cause of Christian unity. Yet the overall impact of these organizations was spotty and the feeling of second class treatment of Christians by the government continued. Key appointments to commercial and civil service posts seemed to be consistently handed to Muslims. The suspicion was that a very influential group of Muslims living in or near

Kaduna was committed to keeping the dream of the the late Premier of Northern Nigeria alive. Referred to, almost mysteriously, as "the Kaduna Mafia," this inner circle seemed to wield amazing influence beginning with the Gowon regime. The "mafia" is an enigmatic group. When questions arose as to why certain pro-Muslim directions were taken at the federal level, the "Kaduna mafia" was often cited as the hand that moves the head. The popular name for this pressure group is misplaced because

> The Kaduna Mafia, as it is known, doesn't have the criminal image like the mafioso of Italy, America and Israel, whose principal commodities are lust, greed and blood. Rather, what we have is a group of northern barons based in Kaduna whose main reason is to ensure that the North maintains a leading position at all times in matters related to Nigerian politics.[52]

Michael Awoyinfa, writing in *The Concord*, stated that until recently little was known as to who and what the organization really is. One reporter sent to do a story on the "mafia" said, "It was like chasing a chimera. How do you write about a faceless organization without any known address?"[53] Awoyinfa says that now the identity of the "mafia" is beginning to clear up. It came into existence

> . . . in the wake of the first coup (1966) when the Sardauna of Sokoto . . . was killed along with other regional premiers and Aguiyi Ironsi became Nigeria's first military leader.[54]

The article goes on to say that "the pioneering members of Kaduna Mafia are said to be people whom the Sardauna favoured with appointments as permanent secretaries and others who got contracts from him."[55]

The religious side of the *raison d'etre* of the Kaduna Mafia is mentioned by Professor B. Dudley in his book, *Nigerian Government and Politics*. According to Professor Dudley, the "mafia" became concerned about what they saw as a "southern influence" around

---

[52]Michael Awoyinfa, "The Kaduna Mafia," *Sunday Concord*, September 22, 1985, p. 7.

[53]*Ibid.*

[54]*Ibid.*

[55]*Ibid.*, p. 8.

was also *Christian*. There was a religious dimension to the opposition.[56]

It is not surprising, therefore, that Christian commentaries on the political trends of the late Gowon administration, and clearly that of Murtalla Mohammmed and Obasanjo, carry convictions about the real presence of the Kaduna Mafia. Christians, however, did not seem to be aware of this power center in the military regimes before 1979.

While Christian leaders believe the mafia is a Muslim political organization, the editor-in chief of *Amana,* a Nigerian journal, does not hide its religious nature and leaves the impression that it includes both Muslims and Christians.

> You have to behave as a religious person to qualify as a member. You must be talking and behaving as if what matters to you most is the protection of life. Whether you are a Muslim or a Christian member of the mafia, you have to behave like that. Most of it is pretension.[57]

Christians would deny that they have any representation in the "mafia." At the most they would say that the "few Christians connected with it never know the inner workings of the organization and would not take a stand against its Muslim bias." It is felt that the "mafia" did not agree on the NPN's backing of Shehu Shagari in 1979 or in 1983. Shagari, while associated with the the first civilian government of Abubakr Tafawa Balewa, was seen as soft on the "south" and as one who gave too much power to the Vice President Alex Ekweme. Ekweme was an Ibo who allowed too many non-Muslims to hold key positions and, in general, did not support the Muslim cause in a radical way. It is therefore not surprising that the Mafia strongly supported the military takeover from Shagari in December 1983.

As was noted in the Introduction, this book was written in two time periods and with two purposes in mind. The first part of the study demonstrates the impact that African Islam had on the ancestral religions and how the two systems were accommodated or raised conflict. These latter two chapters provide an opportunity to evaluate

---

[56]*Ibid.*

[57]Alhaji Hamza Aminu in "The Kaduna Mafia," *ibid.,* p.7.

the direction both Islam and traditional religion have been moving in recent years. It would be irresponsible to lock the study into a time period that is already past. Religious changes since 1965 have been momentous. They have marked out a direction that is important for the whole country and are tied, irrevocably, to the history we have described.

We have reviewed some of the reasons for current trends in religion. It remains now to go back to some of the earlier descriptions of "tribal" responses to Islam and take note of the recent changes now taking place within some of these same groups.

CHAPTER SEVEN

ETHNIC EXPERIENCE AND RELIGION TODAY

CHAPTER SEVEN

ETHNIC EXPERIENCE AND RELIGION TODAY

We have shown that three factors must be accounted for if we are to understand contemporary religion in northern Nigeria. First, progress toward modernity has weakened the hold of traditional religion in the past two decades. As a system it no longer governs directly the ritual life of the people, but it retains strong influence at the world view level. Second, Islam has been forced to reassess both its strength and its structure, especially in light of Christianity. As changes took place it experienced stress and the need for reorganization. Third, Christianity began gaining ground in the Middle Belt fifty years ago, but quite recently it has shown a dynamism that appeals to minority groups. This brings it into tension with a much older Islam.

We shall finally observe changes, some quite surprising, that will show the types of religious response of the tribes in light of the previous chapter. Without doubt, the major external forces that have effected change have been economic needs and political status. The rapid growth of Christianity is related directly to education and a heightened sense of self awareness that accompanies the spread of churches. Lying at the center of religious change is a strong conviction of what is best for the whole community. Individual decisions to follow Islam or Christianity depend in a very critical way on the consensus or direction the tribe as a whole has chosen. The context of change continues to be a combination of the many factors we have been analyzing.

There is a sense of freedom and experimentation by non-Muslim people not previously shown. The ethnic groups we have studied seem much more innovative, less bound to follow a historical pattern. With advanced education the strict attachment of religion to a prescribed political-social stance is being overcome. For example, the way the Tiv people embraced the Muslim political party in 1978 is a striking study. It must be reviewed to show that when internal needs are being met, deep religious prejudices can be set aside. Having analyzed the case of the Tiv, we shall turn again to review ways in which the various tribal groups have adjusted to the new situation described in the preceding chapter.

THE SPLIT OF RELIGION FROM POLITICS

TARKA AND THE TIV

Earlier we spent considerable time to show the anti-Muslim attitudes of the Tiv. The unrest among the Tiv after the Second World War has not been forgotten. Traditionally, it was no less than traitorous to the Tiv culture to sympathize with Muslim politics. The last of the very serious troubles in Tivland came in 1962, when some of their leaders joined the party of Ahmadu Bello (NPC). During that crisis family members were known to inflict bodily harm on their own brothers who had publicly declared themselves for NPC. Scores of houses, sometimes whole villages, were set on fire if the residents were suspected of capitulating to northern politics.

The Tiv were, in a sense, a people who had no government looking after them. Their uncompromising ethnic pride had cut them off from federal amenities for many years. Geographically, they were located in such a way that their identity as "northerners" was ambiguous. The Tiv felt they were running behind almost everyone. While modern highways were being constructed all around them, the Tiv had some of the worst roads well into the seventies. They felt deprived of higher schools and technical colleges. They also felt they had been virtually ignored in the places of political power.

Then in the 1978 election an outstanding turnaround took place. The Tiv voted almost unanimously for the National Party of Nigeria

200

(NPN), the new version of Ahmadu Bello's NPC. The strength that Tiv backing brought to Shehu Shagari in the Second Republic did not go unrewarded. Not only did remarkable improvements for the Tiv people people continue, but Shagari chose the heart of Tivland, Gboko, to inaugurate his campaign for reelection in 1983. These unusual developments highlight two phenomena: (1) a natural leader within the tribe can effect critical change for the people as a whole, and (2) a whole society can make pragmatic political changes while refusing any change in religion. The shift of an adamant non-Islamic people to a party that has always been associated with Islam was mainly through the influence of one man, Joseph S. Tarka.

The honor that the Tiv people hold for J. S. Tarka is symbolized by his grave at Gboko. After he died in 1980, his grave literally became a Tiv national monument. The surroundings of the grave are decorated in green and white, Nigeria's national colors. For the payment of a few coins Tarka's casket can be mechanically raised from the crypt for viewing. For some twenty years Tarka had built his reputation as the first Tiv politician to successfully take the plight of the Tiv to the highest levels. With his wealth and personal style, he received appointments to federal posts,[1] so that his influence did bring the Tiv to the attention of the country. His role was bigger than the Tiv alone. He finally emerged as a figure who represented many of the minority tribes of the Middle Belt. The plight of the Tiv was shared by other groups who felt hopelessly defranchised because of their minority status.

> The bitter experience of the Tiv during the NPC regime in the sixties gave Tarka second thoughts about being in opposition to the Muslim northern majority. His approach was to show the Tiv people by his own example that they would be better off to support the Muslim-backed system. In this way they would begin to see some benefits.[2]

He was so useful as a representative of the non-Muslim minority peoples that it was hoped he might even be nominated for president. This was rumored as a real possibility, as Tarka became more and more involved with the "North" during the military regimes before 1979. It seems clear that Tarka felt he did have a chance for the high

---

[1]Federal Minister of Transport

[2]Rev. J. P. Mambila, General Secretary, Fellowship of Churches of Christ in Nigeria, Jos, private paper June 1986.

office but, in retrospect, the religious Muslim underpinnings of the NPN was the main reason why this eluded him.

> Eager to incorporate Tarka into the system, the northern leaders used their opportunity very well, so that by the time of the Second Republic (1979) Tarka was incorporated but still peripheral to the philosophical core of the northern system.[4]

This last observation by a professor at Ahmadu Bello University is crucial to Tarka's later history. Tarka had been a prominent player in an organization of Middle Belt minorities who stood against the Hausa-Fulani status quo. He was, therefore, an ideal person for the NPN to use to bring these unmanageable minority factions together. He helped bring together the organization needed to elect Shehu Shagari. Tarka was a gifted and natural leader. In a time when the Tiv needed him, he functioned as a king. As Joseph Tarka kept his promises to his own people, other minority groups benefited as well.

However, for Tarka's part, his personal hopes for leading the country as president showed an unreal assessment of the Islamic institutions he was dealing with. Neither Tarka nor the Tiv people became Muslim during this period of capitulation, and they are as resistant to Islam today as they have ever been.[5] A former senator reported:

> Tarka seemed not to have known the real intrigue that centered on him. Tarka believed very strongly that Kano State was solidly behind him. "He made Kano City his second home. . . . He thought he was going to have it easy, but little did he know that this was only a 'bridge of thread' that had been prepared for him."[6]

It would have been the highest kind of honor for the Tiv, had they been able to lead a Middle Belt movement with Tarka as the national leader, but,

> . . . there was no way that the deeply Islamic leaders of the North would strongly support a Christian candidate. The only political weapon the NPN had to use was religion. To have supported a Christian candidate on the platform of NPN would have removed the weapon [religion] from the start.[7]

---

[4]Professors Lombin and Gana, Ahmadu Bello University, private paper, May 1985.

[5]The exceptions are Tiv who have married outside the tribe and live away from the Tiv area, and a few living in Makurdi City.

[6]Manessa T. B. Daniel, former senator, Gongola State.

[7]Lombin and Gana, *ibid.*

The point that needs to be made here is that by this surprising turnaround the Tiv responded in a way that reinforced their active resistant typology.

In this whole political reversal the Tiv have shown again how one from within the group can take on a heroic image for all the people. Tarka's personal success was a success for all, and by his own power he was able to redirect the political orientation of more than four million people. As an active-resistant community, the Tiv acted pragmatically and secured for themselves the benefits that would not have come in any other way. They could trust their own "hero" to lead them, and as the elders of the Tiv decided to follow Tarka, the entire homogeneous society followed.

A few of the Tiv did decide to become Muslims during this period, according to one spokesman. The answer these Tiv converts to Islam give is, "Religion is different from tribe, so we can do what we like." It is reported that one Tiv man named Riman Aleade has been preaching the Muslim religion on Benue State radio.[8] Yet a Christian Tiv pastor would not agree with the report about Riman Aleade. He insisted that there are no more Tiv Muslims today than there were before this political turnabout took place.[9] The pastor and his Tiv friend, Fideles Ajebe, claimed that in all the city of Makurdi, the capital of Benue State, they knew of only three Tiv who had converted to Islam. Now, fifteen years after the earlier study, Christianity has grown appreciably among the Tiv, and the resistance to the Muslim religion seems as strong as ever.

PRESENT TRENDS

ACTIVE-RESISTANT GROUP

Returning to observations made early in this study, the main features of the active-resistant group are a very high degree of self-consciousness, a strong agreement on the elements that keep the tribe together, and a long-standing bias against Islam. It is difficult to

---

[8]Paul Unangu at Theological College of Northern Nigeria, Bukuru, October 1985.

[9]Rev. Terzungwe Saamo, Jos, October 1985.

hypothesize what might have happened among the Tiv had Tarka converted to Islam at any point. The fact that he didn't, supports our earlier observation that the closed traditional groups have such a high degree of self awareness that keeping the tribe intact supersedes any other consideration. There is no evidence that any group who resisted Islam in an earlier period has now capitulated to Islam. Other examples of this continued resistance are the Kutep, the Taroh, and the Longuda.

Kutep

It would appear that two developments are taking place side by side among the Kutep. One is the intensification of the Kutep consciousness while, at the same time, conversion to Christianity continues apace. The Kutep seem to have accommodated the institutions of tribal culture to the growing consensus for Christianity in a harmonious way. Throughout all the developments of the past twenty years, the Muslim chief (*Ukwe*), who resides at Takum, has not gained in power and certainly cannot influence anyone to become a Muslim.[10] A well known Kutep physician who resides in Jos claims that it is only "a quirk of history" that the *Ukwe* of Takum is a Muslim.[11] Even though he was promoted to the level of first class chief after independence, this did not add to his influence in the area of religious power.

The obvious factor among the Kutep is the continued respect given the *Kukwe*,[12] who is the symbol of the whole tribe. Even though education is much more widespread and a new generation is growing up since our earlier observations, there is still great enthusiasm for what it means to be "Kutep." The rich traditions are being taught to the younger generation. Many of the rituals have been set aside, but the basic cultus centering on the ancestor figure (*Kukwe*) is, in reality, more powerful than the chief.[13]

As in the earlier period it is still true that intense self awareness and a strong cultic center will inhibit a turning to Islam. As in the case of

---

[10]Dr. Nuhu Andeyaba, physician in private practice, Jos, October 1985.

[11]*Ibid.*

[12]See page 16.

[13]The Kutep illustrate a group that has retained the core of the tribal myth and have passed it on with high level of meaning to the young people.

the Tiv, Christianity is better combined with the basic structure of the primary religion, philosophically at least, than Islam. Even though both the Kutep and the Tiv embrace conservative forms of Christianity, the areas of conflict are being reconciled, and any political alignment with Muslim-oriented persons or groups has negligible or no religious significance.

Taroh

The Taroh (Yergam) went through a period when it might have seemed to those looking on that a turning to Islam was in the making. Not only did the late chief Ponzhi Taroh embrace Islam, but the Taroh people reversed their 1962 stand against the NPC and voted heavily for NPN in 1979. Here again, rather than following their chief, whose motives were political, more became Christians than ever. The Taroh were clear about drawing the lines between religion and motives for switching to the "Muslim party."[14]

> The shift for NPN was not genuine, but it was recognition that the NPN was in power at the center. Again it is clear that the shift could never be interpreted as sympathy for Islam. In fact, the principal actors were and remain the most ardent Christians.[15]

Hence, by a political shift on the part of many Taroh people the image of the NPN as a purely Hausa-Fulani creation was broken up.[16] High profile participation of the non-Muslim minority groups in the destiny of the Second Republic accomplished two things. The first was that Christian Middle Belt leaders would continue to shape the military governments even after the fall of Shagari and, secondly, the unquestioned control of those attached to the Kaduna establishment[17] would be challenged as never before. As for the Taroh, their absolute resistance of the NPC in 1962 was based on the fear that they would lose both their local culture and their preference for Christianity. Twenty years later this was no longer an issue. As a minority group they felt threatened by the system in the early years. For decades they

---

[14]V. K. Dangin, Permanent Secretary, Plateau State.

[15]Lombin and Gana, *ibid.*

[16]The NPN had a more general appeal than the old NPC. The NPN was formed in great measure by an alliance between Makaman Bida, a Muslim, and J. S. Tarka in 1978, the Tiv leader.

[17]See the discussion on Kaduna mafia, pp. 193ff.

knew no other way but to fear a hierarchy that had been placed over them with the blessing of colonial lords. But now they perceived that a shift had come. The role of the minority tribes of the Middle Belt is no longer one of intimidated acceptance but of initiative and change.

There has been little change in other groups that were classified in the beginning as highly resistant to Islam. The Birom were adamant against Islam from the very first to the point that land on which the Hausa traders took residence was ritually separated from any further use by the Birom.[18] In Chapter Six we referred to the fact that the Birom experiment at Zawan completely failed, once the incentives to promote Islam were removed by the Sardauna's death.[19] For a time the Muslim center continued, but the attitude of the surrounding Birom villages was so negative that it had no prestige.

The Longuda are unquestionably resistant to Islam up to today. Manessa T. B. Daniel has calculated that out of the forty Longuda villages not more than ten families are Muslim. Again, the motivation to Islamize was primarily for political appointments. However, a few others, says Daniel, converted because "they wanted to marry either Hausa or Fulani women." However, rather than converting to Christianity, the women succeeded in converting the men to Islam.[20] It is noted by a number of Christians that Muslim men have taken Christian girls into marriage. This has happened frequently enough that it has become a matter of serious concern to the Christians. In many cases these are secondary school girls who do not have deep convictions and are attracted to the promises of money and material things which Christian young men are usually not able to give.

OPEN-TRADITIONAL GROUP

Fifteen years ago the group we called "open traditional" had a definite bias toward the traditional system, and those who became Muslims did so quite superficially. While by far the greatest numbers of the tribal members of this group would be non-Muslim there was,

---

[18]See Birom discussion, p. 62.

[19]Barnabas Dusu, Commissioner for Boundary Disputes, Plateau State Jos, October 1985.

[20]Manessa T. B. Daniel, *ibid.*

nevertheless, a tolerance for Islam, and those who opted to convert to Islam continued to function in the community.

Jukun

Accommodation by the Jukun to a contextual form of Islam has been cited earlier. There has been a series of changes in the *Aku Uka* (divine king of the Jukun) since 1978, so the question arises whether the Jukun Muslim has had a wider role in society or not.[21] When asked to compare the influence of the Muslim in Jukun affairs during the past ten years with an earlier period, David Ashu replied that the change has been minimal. He acknowledges, "Many customs and traditions of the Jukun have been dropped resulting from westernization and the influence of Christianity." The Christian impact has affected the kingship. Ashu felt that the details surrounding the installation of the several kings since 1960 are very important. This is because these symbolic events indicate more than anything else where the religious consensus lies.

> The *Akus* (kings) who followed Atoshi Agbumamu, . . . [up to] the present Shekarau Augya Kewyo II (1976-) all were sworn into their offices with the Bible. This single factor would, naturally, lead the Jukun to choose Christianity, since the *Akus* have been identifying themselves as Christians.[22]

Further, the traditional counselors next to the king are non-Muslims. "No Muslim has ever been considered for the office of Abo Acio (prime minister) or the various offices of District Heads." During the election of the District Heads, influential Muslims may at times attempt to influence the choice of a candidate, but the final say remains with the *Aku* and his traditional counselors.

As a result of this still powerful personage identifying himself with Christianity, most who leave traditional religion will opt for Christianity. However, rarely do the children of Muslim parents leave Islam. There is no negative result in the society for choosing Islam among this open-traditional group as would be true of the resistant

---

[21]David Ashu, Personnel Manager, Nassaradin Group, Jos, October 1986.
[22]*Ibid.*

category. The history of Islam among the Jukun has an honored tradition and continues at the periphery as before.

Mwaghavul (Sura)

Since the earlier data there is a much higher tendency to secularization among the Mwaghavul who will take a neutral position between Islam and Christianity. It is also very difficult to find a practicing traditionalist. As Aristarchus Damap commented, "There are just a few old men who still believe in the rituals."[23] But, as in the earlier period, there are no pressures from parents for their children to be one or the other. It is interesting that in this quite free environment special mention was made of the growth of the numbers who disavow any religious attachment.

Bura

Due to changes that have been taking place since our last reporting (p.32), the Bura now belong to this more conservative category rather than in the open or highly Islamized group. This shift is as much a sociological one as it is religious. The Bura, from history, have not had a clear separation from the ruling class known as the Pabir. Naturally, the prestige associated with belonging to the royal Pabir families had been enviable. The Pabir exploited this status over the Bura, giving them the feeling of being quite inferior. For many generations the closest a Bura could be to becoming a Pabir was to adopt the Muslim religion of the Pabir.[24]

The history of the two groups (Pabir and Bura) is so intermingled that the colonial administrators considered them to be one large homogeneous unit, the distinction being that the Pabir are the royal families that lived in and around what is today the city of Biu. In the years since the Civil War the Bura have emphasized their distinction as a people and have actively pressed social differentiation from the Pabir. This, of course, is bound to include the religious preference as the Bura become increasingly Christian. However, it is not unusual

---

[23]Rev. Aristarchus Y. Damap, Pastor, COCIN, Jos, October 1986.

[24]Dr. Mamadu Mshebila, Principal, Theological College of Northern Nigeria, Bukuru, October 1986.

for Bura parents to allow their daughters to marry a Muslim Pabir. It is considered prestigious and materially beneficial to do so. Bura do not adamantly oppose if close relatives are or become Muslim. But the important change is that, taken as a whole, Bura prefer Christianity to Islam.[25] Here again, the underlying motive has very much to do with rising self consciousness as a people.

Conversely, it is the unusual case if a Pabir is a Christian. The Pabir carry their tradition as a royal people and a Muslim people with great pride.[26] The Pabir would say that Christianity is the religion of the common people, Bura. In the past the Bura would want to be identified with the Pabir, but since the widespread education of the Bura and the fact that they now have their own leaders, they not only desire their own identify but are promoting it with vigor.[27] The Bura are more critical of Islam and resistant to the Pabir who tend to paternalize them and still feel they have the right to rule them.

Bachema

We have noted the shift of the Bura to a more closed attitude to Islam. In much the same way the Bachema, who are centered around Numan, also appear to be more intensely aligned against Islam than before the Civil War. Although we categorized them earlier as an "open-traditional group," developments since 1970 now place them in what we call the active-resistant classification. This could represent a misinterpretation of the Bachema in the first place, but there is little argument now about the closed attitude of the Bachema.

John Ambe says that the Bachema person who becomes a Muslim cannot live freely among the tribal group. If a Bachema man does become a Muslim, Ambe says,

> . . . he is ostracized completely from his kith and kin and has to live with other Muslims. A Bachema never becomes a Muslim because he believes in Islam but because of political expediency.[28]

---

[25]Musa Ndhi, T.C.N.N., Bukuru, October 1986.

[26]Their ethnic roots trace to the Beri Beri (Kanuri) and Shuwa Arabs who migrated to ancient Kanem.

[27]Mamadu Mshelbila, *ibid.*

[28]John Ambe, Director, Nigeria Merchant Bank, private paper, June 1985.

The day of easy money is over in Nigeria, so Dick Mbodwam[28] asks simply, "What advantage would it hold for a Bachema to become a Muslim?" The chief of the Bachema is also an ordained pastor in the Lutheran Church. He has stated publicly that the Bachema do not approve of Muslim men who attempt to marry Christian girls. In addition, when the "Maitatsini" rioters struck in Yola,[29] the chief of Bachema called in leaders of the movement and warned them not to cause any similar kind of disturbance in his area.

While this stiff opposition to Islam goes on, the annual festival at Fare is less and less important.[30] Those who attend now are mostly the old men who still align themselves with the ancient religion. About half of the Bachema did vote with the NPN in 1978 and again in 1983. One reason given for this was that the Bachema are their own people, and they felt that voting for a party other than the "party of the north" would open them to domination by Yoruba politicians. [31]

OPEN GROUP

Pabir

Reference has already been made to the significant separation of the Bura from the Pabir that has been taking place in the past two decades. Not only does this mean greater differentiation for the Bura as an ethnic unit, but it reinforces the Islamic image of the Pabir. The Pabir have taken their history as Muslims seriously. The Kanuri, from whom the Pabir trace their ancestry, have their roots, in turn, with the Shuwa Arabs, a proud Muslim heritage. The prestige that has centered on the extended family of the chief of Biu continues to provide a dynamic context for the institutions of Islam. Continued development through the politics of the Second Republic puts the Pabir firmly into the community of the Islamic peoples of northern Nigeria.

---

[28]Dick Mbodwam, Manager, Radio Muryar Bishara, Jos, October 1985.
[29]1984
[30]For discussion on Fare see p.17.
[31]Japheeth Anneas, T.C.N.N., Bukuru, October 1986.

The social and political factors have been such that a strengthening of identity with Islam has been the natural cause for the Pabir to follow. The Pabir are not situated in the far north, yet they fit the categories of the highly Islamic Borno State. One indication of the strength of Islam among the Pabir is that the young people still adopt it without question. A consequence of this is the attitude that Christianity is for the common people.[33] In this way the Pabir intensify their identity vis-a-vis the Bura. This, in turn, is a factor in the rapid Christianization of the Bura, who are pursuing ways to establish their separate image. Dr. Mamadu Mshelbila, Principal of the Theological College of Northern Nigeria, is one of the few Pabir who is also a Christian.[34] He openly admits that because he is a Christian, he is given little notice by his own Pabir people.

Nupe

There has been little change in the quality or style of Nupe Islam. The high degree of accommodation which characterizes Nupe Islam has already been described. Islam has been able to adapt to the strong Nupe cultus so that Islam is highly visible while the underlay remains Nupe.[35] However, current Nupe Islam shows that tribal interests will continue to dominate when the Nupe people as a whole feel threatened. Loyalty to a Muslim block of northern politicians during elections of 1978 meant very little to the Nupe. They had dutifully supported the NPC in the sixties. George Bako states that during the Civil War about 50% of the Nupe were Muslims, with most of the other half still holding to traditional religion. Islam seemed to offer a guarantee of position and economic security which was not available in Christianity.

With the elections of 1978 Nupe interests came to the fore, and there was a massive movement away from the NPN to the Nigerian Peoples' Party. This was because the Nupe put their own sense of well being above an expected loyalty to a Muslim tradition. The Nupe saw little or no visible change coming out of their alignment with the old NPC and throughout the various regimes of military government. They felt

---

[33]The word "Bura" itself is a deprecating term meaning "small ants."

[34]As is Rev. Mai Sule Biu, Chairman of the Fellowship of the Churches of Christ in Nigeria.

[35]See reference to pp.74-75.

they had been denied power in Kwara State even though they represent the largest ethnic group in the state. Most significant, the traditional rulers were entrenched in the system which bound the Nupe to northern Islam, while the people wanted, more than ever, to decide their own future. The NPP made a direct appeal to the masses, and this brought immediate response from the Nupe.[36] Even *imams* and *malams* were known to leave "the party" to support Christian candidates. While it is emphasized that the change was political rather than religious, Christians among the Nupe did gain in prestige, and their social image was raised considerably.

The similarity of the Nupe switch away from the Muslim party with the switch of the Tiv to the Muslim party demonstrates the same principle. The tough pragmatism of ethnic self interest is what really motivates change. Religious identity is not the first consideration where the demand for concrete changes in the quality of life is being made. As visible as Islam has been among the Nupe, they dared to break with the norm. Likewise, it was not easy for the Tiv to capitulate to a system which they bitterly resisted, but when they became convinced that this would be in their interest, the switch made sense.

RELIGIOUS CHANGE AND THE SITUATION TODAY

We are bringing this account to a close at a most strategic time. Both the religions of Islam and Christianity have developed out of traditional beginnings. In this way they have a commonality that is being played out in important ways in the country. The religious change that took place in the far North of Nigeria five to six hundred years ago resulted in a truly Islamized society. There is no question about the orthodox roots of Borno and Sokoto Islam in spite of the internal conflicts that have arisen in recent years.

Traditional religion, as we have shown, has faded as an official identity for modern Nigerians. It would be irresponsible if we were to portray the ancestral religions as having the same power as in bygone days. This is not to say that traditional religions have disappeared.

---

[36]George Bako, Director, General Federal Radio Corp., Lagos, October 1985.

They still dominate the lives of thousands of older people, forming the world view of both young and old. Traditional religion lives on in both Christianity and Islam, giving authenticity and coloring the forms more than is generally admitted.[37]

Any relevant expression of religion will reflect the matrix in which it was formed. Many Christian movements seem heretical to the more historic Western churches because they reinterpret Christianity in traditional forms. In the same way there are practices in Nigerian Islam that would be questioned by Sunni Muslims of the Arab world. All of this is because traditional religion is at the heart of who the African is. Secondary systems, while determining the forms that are seen, are still governed at their center by the traditional assumptions.

Nowhere is this three-way clash between traditional religion, Islam, and Christianity more significant than in the middle belt region of northern Nigeria. This area is the catalyst that determines the religious direction the country will take in the next generation.[38]

False Division between North and South

Throughout the book we have been emphasizing again and again that the middle belt of Nigeria is a real entity of its own. The history of the problem of the middle belt during the last years of colonialism is well known. It was primarily a non-Muslim area over which Muslims ruled with the sanctions of the British. It has already been pointed out that in light of the formation of states and the rapid growth of Christianity, the middle belt people need to be seen for what they are.

It has been the habit developed through some six or seven generations to speak of the "North" as the entire area of the former Northern Region, including all the people who live in this vast area. This way of speaking had a political basis through the First Republic. We have shown that from the beginning this entire region was considered as Muslim, even though massive areas were inhabited by

---

[37]See discussion by Noel Q. King in *African Cosmos*, Belmont, CA: Wadsworth Pub. Co., 1986, pp. 112 ff.

[38]The far north is a stable Muslim area and the south is historically Christian; it is here in the middle belt where massive conversion growth is taking place.

traditional religionists. In the past fifty years, and especially in the last two decades, Christianity has had its greatest growth here in this middle belt area.

The "South," as it is generally referred to, was the former Western and Eastern Region. The people who live here were the first to become Christians as missionaries arrived along the coast in the nineteenth century. So the designations were fixed. For nearly one hundred years the "South" has been called Christian and the "North" Muslim. While almost any generalization can be proved wrong in West Africa, this particular labeling was especially inaccurate.

THE CHRISTIANIZING OF THE MIDDLE BELT

Certain of the middle belt states hold the key to religious changes in Nigeria today. These states are Plateau, Benue, Gongola, Kaduna, Niger, and Kwara. These are not "northern states" if "northern" is taken to mean simply "Islamic." While there may be a majority of Muslims in a state such as Kaduna, yet these five or six states all have shown a dramatic shift to Christianity. Those who have converted to Christianity are from among the peoples such as we have been studying. Again, if any generalizations are acceptable, it would be much more accurate to speak of the "Christian South," the "Muslim North," and the "mixed middle belt."

Those who are assessing this situation of change must not ignore what has happened. Massive numbers in the states of the old Middle Belt are, in fact, turning to Christianity, and there is no sign that this trend will change in the next decade. The loose, inaccurate use of the terms "Muslim North" and "Christian South," as though there is no other category, can only result in further defensive attitudes. The people in these central areas no longer accept themselves as an aggregate of minorities. Even the historic "Christian South" does not seem to take the Christianization of the middle belt seriously enough.

A habit has developed through the years to speak of this ubiquitous "North" in a generic way by referring to the diverse tribes as "Hausa" people. This is done to some extent by Nigerians but mostly by journalists and the news media who live and work outside of Nigeria.

Such inaccuracies further complicate openness and objectivity about the middle belt communities. The Muslims in Borno, Kano, and Sokoto states find it difficult to admit to the radical shift to Christianity which is taking place. Evidence of this continued misrepresentation of the actual situation in Nigeria was made recently by an officer in the Islamic Students Association. Abubakr Ali-Agan of Bayero College in Kano stated, "We believe Muslims are a 70% majority in Nigeria. . . . They (Christians) want to prevent us from practicing the pure form of Islam."[39] No count of Muslims could come close to 70% except by working with the antiquated notion that these middle belt peoples are collectively classified as Muslims. Such claims are now being tested in ways not known before.

THE CRISIS: IS NIGERIA MUSLIM OR CHRISTIAN?

It bears repeating that this is a critical time for religion in Nigeria. The lines are sharply drawn between Islam and Christianity. The question is whether Nigeria is to be identified as a Muslim nation in 1986 and beyond, or will Christians claim their strength and challenge the image of a Muslim state that developed during colonialism?

Currently there is hot debate between Muslim and Christian sectors of the country arising from an alleged move by certain Nigerian officials to join the country to the Organization of the Islamic Conference. The Islamic Conference is made up of 45 members. Nigeria would be the forty-sixth nation to join. The assumption for membership is that the country has a majority population of Muslims. The charter of the Conference states that its purpose is to "promote solidarity," and to "consolidate cooperation . . . in the economic, social, cultural, scientific and other vital fields."[40]

In light of what has been written in the preceding chapter, it stands to reason that if such a move is allowed by the Nigerian government, there will be polarization as never before. An article in *The New York Times* for February 21, 1986 bears the title: *"A Burst of*

---

[39] Article in *Los Angeles Times*, "Nigeria Divided Over Closer Islamic Ties," by Charles T. Powers, Feb. 15, 1986.

[40] *Ibid.*.

Moslem Fervor in Nigeria, The North Stirs and the South Frets. "[41] It reported in an ominous way what this could mean for the whole country should a national alignment with Islam be pressed. The tone of the article would certainly arouse the deep feelings of thousands of Christians who, twenty years ago, would have made no response. Edward Gargan writes from Kano:

> Here in the northern heartland of Nigeria, agitated demands for the gradual Islamization of the country are impassioned and growing louder. Calls to impose Islamic shari'a courts in the largely Christian and animist south have been increasing.[42]

The article carries the same misunderstanding about the "north" which continues to ignore the massive influence of Christianity. Gargan works with the old concept of a political Northern Nigeria when he says,

> Islam binds this section of the country together, crossing ethnic and linguistic boundaries, defining the soul of the north. But across the south, from the eastern Ibo to the preserve of the Yorubas around Lagos, Islam is seen as a shadow spilling across Nigeria's shaky secularism.[43]

To lump the diverse tribal groups of the middle belt states with the solidly Islamic "north" is the error that can no longer be allowed. It simply does not square with reality. It needs to be repeated that thousands of Christians in central Nigeria who are still being classed as Muslim northerners feel a resentment about this as never before. Already, a group that calls itself the Association of Concerned Christians in the Northern States have met to vigorously oppose the alignment with the Organization of Islamic Conference. In very strong language the "Extraordinary Seminar" speaks of a "betrayal of our commonwealth" and says that the action was not only "unconstitutional" but also "clandestine and surreptitious."[44]

The *Los Angeles Times* article reports Muslims to be nearly one-half of the nation's population. This is accurate enough. However, when it says that Christians are only one third and that all the rest are

---

[41]*New York Times* article by Edward A. Gargan, February 21, 1986.

[42]*Ibid.*

[43]*Ibid.*

[44]The widely distributed *Communique: Extraordinary Seminar on Nigeria and the O. I. C.*, Jos, February 15, 1986.

"animists," the report is clearly out of touch with the real situation. Even those whose daily routine is still "animist" would say that they are either Christian or Muslim, if asked. In any showdown between the religions, nationwide, Christianity would have as many on its side as Islam does.

The attention is still on the "south" when looking for the Christian reaction to these developments. But it is the Christians living in close proximity to the Muslims of Kano, Kaduna, and Maidugari who will have the sharpest reactions.

Christians in Nigeria are working to put their wide ranging forms of churches into some order. The organization known as the Christian Association of Nigeria is one recent attempt to do this.[45] Due to its nature and history, Islam is much more able to speak with one voice than are the fragmented branches of Christianity. But the easy identification of traditional religion in the middle belt with a colonialistic Muslim administration is past. Christian churches in these areas are young and dynamic and feel that they are not being taken seriously.

With no census available, claims by either side to majority status cannot be documented. This may be a time when the *spirit* of a religion, whether Islam or Christian, will be put to the test for the sake of a nation. It is certain that the transitional people of central Nigeria will not allow their new Christianity to be ignored. Tomorrow is here. In a relatively short period traditional religion has become the sub-soil of both Islam and Christianity. The way in which this dynamic interaction will affect the entire nation will be decided by the year 2000.

◊

---

[45]The much older Christian Council of Nigeria would not be able to effectively unite *all* churches because of its denominational and southern image.

GLOSSARY

BIBLIOGRAPHY

INDEX

GLOSSARY

Adamawa   colonial province in northeast Nigeria
addini   religion
adiko   woman's headdress
Aku Uka   king among the Jukun
al'ada   custom, tradition
albarka   blessing
alhaji   one who has gone to Mecca on *hajj*
aljanu   evil spirits, devils (Ar. *jinn*)
alkali   judge (Ar. *qazi*)
Allah   Muslim name for God
amgbakpariga   Jukun with Muslim ancestry
anguwa   section of a village or town
Aondo   high god of the Tiv people
Ashama   ancestor masquerader among Jukun Muslims

babban dodo   great ancestor
Bagoda   leader of invaders of ancient Kano
bakauye   unsophisticated village person
bakin arna   pagan people who are strangers
bakon tsafi   alien pagan ritual
Barbushe   leader-priest of ancient Dalla people
Basali   traditional cult of the Kulung people
Bori   possession cult of the Hausa
bororo   migrant Fulani cattle herders
burkutu   strong alcoholic drink

cazba   Muslim prayer beads
Chidon   high god of the Jukun
cultus   religious myths and rites of a people

Dalla   pre-Hausa people residing around Kano
dan kasa   son of the land, native
detribalized   people who have lost their tribal identity
Dirki   early Hausa syncretism, Qur'an as a fetish
dodo   masquerader symbolizing the ancestors

duhun kai   darkness of head, i.e., ignorance

emir   highest Muslim ruler, sultan

Fare   area for celebrations of old Bachema religion
Fatiha   first chapter of the Qur'an, primary Muslim prayer
FESTAC   Festival of African Culture
feticheur   diviner, maker of charms (Fr.)
folk Islam   Islam mixed with indigenous belief and practice

Gabra   a former arm-slashing cult among the Wurkum
gunnu   Nupe cultic system

Ha'be   Fulbe name for non-Islamized people
hajj   pilgrimage to Mecca
Hausa   ethnic group having language by the same name
Hyel   high god among the Kilba and Bura

Id il fitr   ceremony marking the end of Ramadan (fast)
ikon kasa   having authority based on traditional rights
imam   Muslim cleric similar to a priest (Ar.)
iska na gida   familiar spirits
iska na waje   spirits from another place
iskoki   spirits
Islam   name for the Muslim religion meaning "submission"
Islamization   to become Muslim or Islamic
Izala   fundamentalist Muslim sect in Nigeria

jami, jama'a   the people, the community, usually Muslims
jihad   Islamic holy war
jinn   Muslim spirits

221

ka komo   to be a "returnee"
Ka'aba   Islam's most holy shrine at Mecca
kadara   predestination
kafir, kafirai   non-Muslim infidels
Kano Chronicle   a document accounting Islam's history in Kano
kasawanci   marketing
Kukwe   personage among the Kutep symbolizing the tribe
kwandalowa   pots containing medicine among the Longuda
Kwororafa   ancient people in Jukun history

lahira   the place of departed spirits
laya   amulets as small packets worn on the body
layar jebu   counterfeit *laya*
liman   Muslim cleric similar to a priest (Hausa)
luguji   prophetic divining ordeal among the Kilba

Ma   high god among the Jen people
magani   medicine, also used in magic and divining
maguzanci   the "pagan way" according to Muslims
Maguzawa   a large Hausa clan that did not accept Islam
mai boka   the traditional diviner, magician
mai unguwa   the head of an *anguwa*
Maitatsini   a radical right-wing Muslim who caused riots
malam   teacher, originally "literate person"
malamai   plural of *malam*
Mambila   ritual honoring the dead among the Pabir
mandyeng   rites associated with harvest among the Birom
marabout   Muslim teacher, cleric (Fr.)
masalaci   place where Muslim prayers are performed
mbatsav   "idols" or traditional gods among the Tiv
Middle Belt   central area, east to west, in Nigeria

Mshelia   clan of the Bura people
mugun iska   bad wind or spirit
Muhammed Bello   son of Uthman dan Fodio
Muridiyya   a Muslim sect (Murids) in Senegal
musulunci   the Muslim way, Muslim belief

NCNC   National Council of Nigerian Citizens
NPC   Northern Peoples' Congress
NPN   National Party of Nigeria
Nzeanzo   high god of the Bachema

okombo   Tiv cultic gods

pelma   traditional charms among the Kilba

Qadariyya   important West African Sufi brotherhood
qadi   judge

Ramadan   holy month of the Muslim fast
rashin wayewa   lack of education, unenlightened
riga   long folding gown of the Hausa
ruwan albarka   water that brings blessing

sadaka   Muslim alms
salat   Muslim prayer
salla   Muslim prayer (Hausa)
sarkin aljanu   chief of the evil spirits
sarkin bori   chief of the Bori
sarkin tsafi   chief of the traditional rites
shari'a   Muslim law
shirk   sin of identifying anything as/with God
Soko   high god among the Nupe
supra-tribal   beyond or above the tribe, universal
sujada   worship

tarika   "path" way of worship, used by Sufi orders
Tchakuwa   animistic practice in early Hausa Islam

Tchibiri   animistic practice in early
   Hausa Islam
Tijaniyya   important West African
   Sufi brotherhood
tsafi   Hausa term for animistic
   religious practice
turari   perfumed smoke
tuwo   pounded corn, rice, etc. eaten
   in small lumps

umma   the Islamic community of
   believers
Uthman (Usman) dan Fodio
   established Islam in Northern
   Nigeria

Vabo   active mediating god among
   the Mumuye
Vodusu   secret society associated
   with a god (Mumuye)

Wangarawa   African Muslims who
   brought Islam to Nigeria from
   Mali
watan gani   ancient cult among the
   Jukun
wayewa   dawn, i.e., experiencing
   understanding, enlightenment
wonkan birni   becoming a Muslim
   because of living in the city

Yaki da Jahilci   war on ignorance,
   adult education
yaku   diviner among the Kilba
Yemta-ra Wala   Pabir ancestor
   associated with early Islam

zamani   the present age, a certain era
zunubi   sin, wrongdoing

BIBLIOGRAPHY

Abun-Nasr, J. M.
1965   *The Tijaniyya*. London: Oxford University Press.

Adamu, Adamu
1986   "Sardauna: The Power of a Ghost," *New Nigerian*, January 19.

Ajayi, J. F. and Ian Espie, eds.
1965   *A Thousand Years of West African History*. Ibadan: Ibadan
        University Press.

Allen, J.
1943   *Native Policy in Nigeria*. Lagos: Twentieth Century Press.

Anene, J. C. and G. N. Brown, eds.
1965   *Africa in the Nineteenth and Twentieth Centuries*. Ibadan: University
        Press.

Arnold, Thomas W.
1955   "The Spread of Islam in Africa." *Al-Islam*, III. Nos. 12-14, 59-67.

Atterbury, Anson P.
1899   *Islam in Africa*. New York and London: G. P. Putnam's Sons.

Bascom, W. R. and M. Herskovits.
1959   *Continuity and Change in African Culture*. Chicago: University of
        Chicago Press.

Battuta, Ibn
1929   *Travels in Asia and Africa, 1325-1354*. Trans. by H. A. R. Gibb.
        New York: Robert McBride and Co.

Baulin, Jacques
1962   *The Arab Role in Africa*. Hammondsworth: Penguin Books.

Baum, Edward
1975   *A Comprehensive Periodical Bibliography of Nigeria*. Athens, OH:
        Ohio University Press.

Beattie, John and John Middleton
1969   *Spirit Mediumship and Society in Africa*. London: Routledge and
        Kegan Paul.

Bello, Ahmadu
1962   *My Life*. Cambridge: Cambridge University Press.

Binji, M. Haliru
1957   *Littafin Addini II*. Zaria: The Gaskiya Corp.

Blackwell, Basil
1954   *The Institutions of Primitive Society*. Oxford: Oxford University
        Press.

Blyden, Edward
    1967   *Christianity, Islam and the Negro Race.* African Heritage Books,
            Vol. I. Edinburgh: Edinburgh University Press.

Bohannen, P. and G. Dalton, eds.
    1965   *Markets in Africa.* Garden City, NY: Doubleday & Co.

Bohannen, Paul and Laura
    1955   *The Tiv of Central Nigeria.* London: International African Institute.

Bowen, Elenore S.
    1964   *Return to Laughter.* Garden City, NY: Doubleday & Co.

Bretton, Henry L.
    1962   *Power and Stability in Nigeria.* New York: Frederick A. Praeger.

Cherbonneau, M. A.
    1855   "Histoire de la litterature arabe au Soudan." *Journal Asistique,*
            Series 5, 6.

Coleman, James S.
    1963   *Nigeria: Background to Nationalism.* Berkeley: University of
            California Press.

Conant, Francis P.
    1963   "The Manipulation of Ritual Among Plateau Nigerians." *Africa,*
            XXXIII, No. 3, July, 227-36.

Crowder, Michael
    1962   *The Story of Nigeria.* London: Faber & Faber.

Davidson, Basil
    1959   *The Lost Cities of Africa.* Boston and Toronto: Little, Brown & Co.

    1966   *A History of West Africa.* Anchor Books. Garden City, NY:
            Doubleday & Co.   Davidson, Basil and A. Ademola, eds.

    1953   *The New West Africa.* London: George Allen & Unwin.

Dieterlen, Germaine
    1951   *Essai sur la Religion Bambara.* Paris: Universitaries de France.

Durkheim, Emile
    1915   *The Elementary Forms of the Religious Life.* London: George Allen
            & Unwin, Ltd.

Edgar, Frank
    1924   *Litafi na Tatsuniyoyi na Hausa.* 2 vols. Lagos: C.M.S. Bookshop.

Eliade, Mircea
    1958   *Patterns in Comparative Religion.* Cleveland and New York: The
            World Publishing Co.

    1959   *The Sacred and the Profane.* New York: Harcourt Brace.

    1963   *Myth and Reality.* Trans. by Willard R. Trask. New York and
            Evanston: Harper and Row.

    1965   *The Myth of the Eternal Return.* Trans. by Willard R. Trask. New
            York: Pantheon Books.

Elias, T. O. and Taslin Alawala
1956   *The Nature of African Customary Law.* Manchester: Manchester University Press.

Epstein, A. L.
1958   *Politics in an Urban African Community.* Manchester: Manchester University Press.

Forde, Daryll, ed.
1954   *African Worlds.* London: Oxford University Press.

Fortes, Meyer
1959   *Oedipus and Job in West African Religion.* Cambridge: The University Press.

Fortes, Meyer and G. Dieterlen, eds.
1965   *African Systems of Thought.* London: Oxford University Press.

Frankfort, H. A. and H., J. A. Wilson, and T. Jacobsen
1964   *Before Philosophy.* Baltimore: Penguin Books.

Frazer, Sir James G.
1933   *The Fear of the Dead in Primitive Religion.* 2 vols. London: Macmillan & Co.

Frobenius, Leo
1913   *The Voice of Africa.* 2 vols. London: Hutchison & Co.

Froelich, J. C.
1964   *Les Musulmans d'Afrique Noire.* Paris: Editions de l'Orante.

Gargan, Edward A.
1986   "A Burst of Moslem Fervor in Nigeria," *New York Times*, February 21.

Gibb, H. A. R.
1954   *Modern Trends in Islam.* Chicago: University of Chicago Press.

Gouilly, Alphonse
1952   *Islam dans l'Afrique Occidentale Francaise.* Paris: Loire.

Greenberg, Joseph H.
1941   "Some Aspects of Negro-Mohammedan Culture Among the Hausa." *American Anthropologist*, XLIII, 51-61.

1946   *The Influence of Islam on a Sudanese Religion.* Seattle: University of Washington Press.

1947   "Arabic Loan-Words in Hausa." *Word*, 87-97.

1955   *Studies in African Linguistic Classification.* New Haven: Compass Publishing Co.

1963   "The Languages of Africa." *International Journal of American Linguistics*, 29, Part II, No. 1, January, 45-50.

Greschat, H. J.
1968   "Understanding African Religions." *Orita*, II, No. 2, December, 59-68.

Grimebaum, Gustave E. von
   1955   *Unity and Variety in Muslim Civilization.* Chicago: University of
         Chicago Press.

Gunn, Harold
   1953   *Peoples of the Plateau Area of Northern Nigeria.* Ethnographic
         Surveys of Africa, D. Forde, ed. London: International African
         Institute.

   1956   *Pagan Peoples of the Central Area of Northern Nigeria.*
         Ethnographic Surveys of Africa, D. Forde, ed. London: International
         African Institute.

Gunn, Harold and F. P. Conant
   1953   *Peoples of the Middle Niger Region, Northern Nigeria.* Ethnographic
         Surveys of Africa, D. Forde, ed. London: International African
         Institute.

Herskovitz, Melville J.
   1938a *Dahomey, An Ancient West African Kingdom.* 2 vols. New York:
         A. A. Knopf.

       b *The Human Factor in Changing Africa.* New York: A. A. Knopf.

Hiskett, Mervyn
   1984   *The Development of Islam in West Africa.* New York: Longmans.

Hodgkin, Thomas J.
   1957   "Muslims South of the Sahara." *Current History,* 23, No. 109,
         June, 345-50.

Hogben, S. J. and A. H. M. Kirk-Greene
   1966   *The Emirates of Northern Nigeria.* London: Oxford University
         Press.

Horton, Robin
   1962   "The Kalabari World View: An Outline and Interpretation." *Africa,*
         XXXII, No. 3, July, 197-219.

   1967   "African Traditional Thought and Western Science." *Africa,* Pt. 1,
         XXXVII, No. 1, January, 50-71; Pt. 2, XXXVII, No. 2, April, 155-
         87.

Howells, William
   1962   *The Heathens.* Garden City, NY: Doubleday & Co.

Hudson, R. S.
   1957   *Provincial Authorities, Report by the Commissioner.* Kaduna,
         Nigeria: Government Printer.

Hunter, Guy
   1962   *The New Society of Tropical Africa.* London: Oxford University
         Press.

Idowu, E. Bolaji
   1967   "The Study of Religion, with Special Reference to African Traditional
         Religion." *Orita,* I, No. 1, June.

Ikimi, Obaro
1977   *The Fall of Nigeria*. London: Holmes and Meir, Inc.

Isichei, Elizabeth
1982   *Studies in the History of Plateau State*. London: Macmillan & Co.

James, E. O.
1961   *Comparative Religion*. London: Methuen & Co.

Jensen, Adolf E.
1963   *Myth and Cult Among Primitive Peoples*. Trans. by Marianna
       Chaldin and W. Weissleder. Chicago: University of Chicago Press.

Johnston, H. A. S.
1966   *A Selection of Hausa Stories*. Oxford: Oxford University Press.

Kerekes, Tibor, ed.
1961   *The Arab Middle East and Africa*. London: Thomas & Healdson.

King, Noel O.
1986   *African Cosmos*. Belmont, CA: Wadsworth Publishing Co.

King, Winston L.
1954   *Introduction to Religion, A Phenomenological Approach*. New York:
       Harper and Row.

Kirk-Greene, A. H. M.
1971   *Crisis and Conflict in Nigeria*. Vol. II. London: Oxford University
       Press.

1981   *Nigeria Since 1970*. New York: Africana Publishing Co.

Kritzeck, James and Wm. H. Lewis, eds.
1969   *Islam in Africa*. New York: Van Nostrand-Reinhold Co.

Krusius, Paul
1915   "Die Maguzawa." *Archiv fur Anthropologie*, Vol. 42, 288-315.

Lammens, Henri
1929   *Islam, Belief and Institutions*. Trans. by E. D. Ross. London:
       Methuen and Co.

Last, D. M. and A. M. Al-Hajj
1965   "Attempts at Defining a Muslim in 19th Century Hausaland and
       Bornu." *Journal of the Historical Society of Nigeria*, III, No. 2,
       December, 231-35.

Last, Murray
1967   *The Sokoto Caliphate*. London: Longmans, Green & Co.

Latif, Syed Abdul
1962   *The Mind Al-Quran Builds*. Agapura, Hyderabad: The Academy of
       Islamic Studies.

Le Chantelier, L.
1899   *L'Islam dans l'Afrique Occidentale*. Paris: G. Stendhell.

Leeuw, G. van der
1963 *Religion in Essence and Manifestation.* 2 vols. Harper Torchbooks. New York: Harper and Row.

Lessa, W. A. and E. Z. Vogt, eds.
1965 *Reader in Comparative Religion.* 2nd ed. New York: Harper and Row.

Levy-Bruhl, Lucien
1928 *The Soul of the Primitive.* London: George Allen & Unwin.

Levitzon, Nehemia
1979 *Conversion to Islam.* New York: Holmes and Meier Publisher.

Lewis, I. M., ed.
1966 *Islam in Tropical Africa.* Oxford: International African Institute.

Lloyd, Peter C.
1953 "Kings, Chiefs and Local Governments." *West African Review*, January-February, 79, 103.

1967 *Africa in Social Change.* Harmondsworth: Penguin Books.

Mabogunje, Akin L.
1968 *Urbanization in Nigeria.* London: University of London Press.

McCall, E. F., ed.
1971 Aspects of West African Islam. Boston: Bennett.

Mair, L. P.
1958 "African Chiefs Today." *Africa*, XXVIII, No. 3, July, 257-69.

Malinowski, Branislaw
1945 *The Dynamics of Culture Change.* New Haven: Yale University Press.

Marty, Paul
1917 *Etudie sur l'Islam au Senegal.* Vols. II & IV. Paris: Ernest Leroux.

Mbiti, John
1969 *African Religions and Philosophy.* London: Heinemann.

1970 *Concepts of God in Africa.* London: S.P.C.K.

Meek, C. K.
1925 *The Northern Tribes of Nigeria.* 2 vols. Oxford: Oxford University Press.

1931a *A Sudanese Kingdom.* London: Kegan Paul, Trench, Trubner & Co., Ltd.

   b *Tribal Studies in Northern Nigeria.* 2 vols. London: Kegan Paul, Trench, Trubner & Co., Ltd.

1934 "The Kulu in Northern Nigeria." *Africa*, VII, No. 3, July, 257-69.

1943 "The Religions of Nigeria." *Africa*, XIII, No. 1, January, 106-17.

Middleton, John
1967 *Gods and Rituals.* Garden City, NY: The Natural History Press.

Miner, Horace
1965   *The Primitive City of Timbuctoo*. Revised ed. New York:
        Doubleday & Co.

Mitchison, Lois
1960   *Nigeria, Newest Nation*. New York: Frederick A. Praeger.

Na'abi, M. Shuaibu and Alhaji Hassan
1942   *A Black Byzantium, The Kingdom of Nupe in Nigeria*. London:
        Oxford University Press.

1969   *Gwari, Gade and Koro Tribes*. Ibadan: Ibadan University Press.

Nadel, S. F.
1954   *Nupe Religion*. London: Routledge & Kegan Paul, Ltd.

Nelson, Harold, ed.
1982   *Nigeria, A Country Study*. Washington, D. C.: American University
        Press.

Niven, Rex
1970   *The War of Nigerian Unity*. Ibadan: Evans Brothers (Nigeria
        Publishers), Ltd.

Obi, John
1986   "No Shari'a Court, Please," *New Nigerian*, January 16.

Ohonbamu, Obarogie
1968   *The Psychology of the Nigerian Revolution*. Devon: Arthur H.
        Stockwell.

Otto, Rudolf
1936   *The Bornu Sahara and Sudan*. London: His Majesty's Stationery
        Office.

1958   *The Idea of the Holy*. Galaxy Books. New York: Oxford University
        Press.

Palmer, H. R.
1908   "The Kano Chronicle." A translation of the history of Hausa kings
        from 1000-1892. *Journal of the Royal Anthropological Institute of
        Great Britain and Ireland*, XXXVIII, 58-98.

1910   "Notes on Traces of Totemism and Some Other Customs in
        Hausaland." *Man*, No. 40, 72-76.

1928   *Sudanese Memoirs*, a translation of various documents covering 19th
        Century Hausaland and Bornu. 3 vols. Lagos: Government Printing
        Office.

Panikkar, K. Mahdu
1963   *The Serpent and the Crescent*. Calcutta: Asia Publishing House.

Parrinder, E. G.
1962   *African Traditional Religion*. London: S.P.C.K.

Pilkington, Frederich
1957   "Islam in Nigeria." *The Contemporary Review*, CLXXXII, No.
        1099, July, 41-45.

Plotnicou, Leonard
1967   *Strangers to the City, Urban Man in Jos, Nigeria.* Pittsburgh: University of Pittsburgh Press.

Powers, Charles, T.
1986   "Nigeria Divided Over Closer Islamic Ties," *Los Angeles Times,* February 15.

Radin, Paul
1957   *Primitive Religion.* New York: Dover Publications.

Rattray, R. S.
1913   *Hausa Folklore, Customs and Proverbs.* 2 vols. London: Oxford University Press.

Retif, R. P.
1958   "L'Expansion de l'Islam in Afrique Noire." *Etudes,* juillet-aout, 48-58.

Smith, M. G.
1959   "The Hausa System of Social Status." *Africa,* XXIX, No. 3, July.

1960   *Government in Zazzau.* London: Oxford University Press.

Smith, Mary F.
1954   *Baba of Karo.* London: Faber & Faber, Ltd.

Tahir, Ibrahim
1986   "A Veritable Phoenix," *New Nigerian,* January 20.

Taylor, John
1963   *The Primal Vision.* Philadelphia: The Fortune Press.

Temple, Charles L., ed.
1922   *Notes on the Tribes, Provinces, Emirates and States of the Northern Provinces of Nigeria.* 2nd ed. Lagos: C.M.S. Bookshop.

Temple, O.
1915   "Bori Beliefs and Ceremonies." *Journal of the Anthropological Institute of Great Britain and Ireland,* Vol. 45, 23-68.

Tremearne, A. J. N.
1913   *Hausa Superstitions and Customs.* London: John Bale Sons & Danielson, Ltd.

n.d.   *The Ban of the Bori.* London: Heath, Cranton & Ouseley, Ltd.

Trimingham, J. Spencer
1959   *Islam in West Africa.* Oxford: Oxford University Press.

1962   *A History of Islam in West Africa.* London: Oxford University Press.

1968   *The Influence of Islam Upon Africa.* New York: Frederick A. Praeger.

Wach, Joachim
1944   *Sociology of Religion.* Chicago: University of Chicago Press.

Wallace, Anthony F.
1966 *Religion, An Anthropological View.* New York: Random House.

Watt, W. Montgomery
1948 *Free Will and Predestination in Early Islam.* London: Luzao & Co., Ltd.

1961 *Islam and the Integration of Society.* London: Routledge & Kegan Paul.

Westermann, Diedrich
1939 *The African Today and Tomorrow.* Revised ed. London: Oxford University Press.

Westermarck, E. A.
1933 *Pagan Survivals in Mohammedan Civilization.* London:

Wilson Haffenden, J. P.
1930 *The Red Men of Nigeria.* Philadelphia: J. B. Lippincott Co.

Young, Michael
1966 "The Divine Kingship of the Jukun: A Re-evaluation of Some Theories." *Africa*, XXXVI, No. 2, April, 135-53.

Zwemer, Samuel M.
1920 *The Influence of Animism on Islam.* London: S.P.C.K.

INDEX

235

236

238

About the Author

Dean Stewart Gilliland arrived in Nigeria as a United Methodist missionary in January, 1956. He lived there with his family until September, 1976. During those significant years Nigeria saw the end of colonial administration, the rise and fall of the First Republic, the Civil War and three military regimes. The author has kept in close touch with Nigeria since 1976 through frequent visits and by teaching graduate students from Nigeria.

Dr. Gilliland mastered the Hausa language while residing in Gongola State. He worked with both local and State governments in the administration of educational institutions. He taught at all levels, both in English and Hausa and was Principal of the Theological College of Northern Nigeria from 1971 to 1976.

Dean Gilliland holds the B.A. degree from Houghton College (NY), the B.D. from Evangelical Theological Seminary (Ill.) and the Th.M. from Princeton Seminary (NJ). His Ph.D. is in the History of Religions from Hartford Seminary Foundation (Conn.) in the field of African Islam. Gilliland is the author of *Pauline Theology and Mission Practice* (Baker: 1983). He is currently Associate Professor of Contextual Theology and African Studies at Fuller Theological Seminary, Pasadena, California.